Financing Your Small Business

Jeffrey L. Seglin

McGraw-Hill, Inc.

New York   St. Louis   San Francisco   Auckland   Bogotá
Caracas   Hamburg   Lisbon   London   Madrid
Mexico   Milan   Montreal   New Delhi   Paris
San Juan   São Paulo   Singapore
Sydney   Tokyo   Toronto

Library of Congress Cataloging-in-Publication Data

Seglin, Jeffrey L., date.
    Financing your small business / Jeffrey L. Seglin.
        p.   cm.
    Includes bibliographical references.
    ISBN 0-07-056064-1
    1. Small business—Finance.   I. Title.
HG4027.7.S44   1990   90-30383
658.15'92—dc20   CIP

1 2 3 4 5 6 7 8 9 0   DOC/DOC   9 5 4 3 2 1 0

ISBN 0-07-056064-1

*The sponsoring editor for this book was Barbara B. Toniolo, the editing
supervisor was Georgia Kornbluth, the designer was Naomi Auerbach, and the
production supervisor was Dianne L. Walber. It was set in Baskerville by the
McGraw-Hill's Professional & Reference Division composition unit.*

Printed and bound by R. R. Donnelley & Sons Company.

The author is not engaged in rendering legal, tax, accounting, or
similar professional services. While legal, tax, and accounting issues
covered in this book have been checked with sources believed to be
reliable, some material may be affected by changes in the laws or in
the interpretation of such laws since the manuscript for this book
was completed. For that reason the accuracy and completeness of
such information and the opinions based thereon are not guaranteed. In addition, state or local tax laws or procedural rules may
have a material impact on the general recommendations made by
the author, and the strategies outlined in this book may not be
suitable for every individual. If legal, accounting, tax, investment,
or other expert advice is required, obtain the services of a compe-
tent practitioner.

*For more information about other McGraw-Hill materials,
call 1-800-2-MCGRAW in the United States. In other
countries, call your nearest McGraw-Hill office.*

To Eddie and Bethany

May you keep your vision clear
as you fulfill your hopes and dreams.

Contents

v

Part 2. Sources of Money

Part 4. Pulling It All Together

Understanding the Business Proposal, Loan Package, and Financial Ratios

About the Author

Jeffrey L. Seglin is senior editor for *Inc.* magazine. A graduate of Harvard University and Bethany College, he has written an extensive array of guidebooks and articles on banking, marketing, and small business issues. He was consulting editor for WGBH-TV's 13-week personal finance series, "On the Money." His articles on financial matters have appeared in *Inc., Venture, Adweek's Marketing Week, Boston* magazine, and *USA Today.* Seglin has done marketing projects for organizations including Shawmut Bank, Digital Computer, and The New England. He is the author of *The McGraw-Hill 36-Hour Marketing Course* and other books.

Preface

Financing Your Small Business is a book about finding money. Perhaps you're looking for a small amount of money to keep a small enterprise running, or maybe you're looking for hundreds of thousands to start up a new operation. Whatever your reason, the basics of securing financing are laid out in the pages that follow.

The book has a simple structure. Part 1 examines what it takes to start a small business. Should you even own your own business? Should you start a new business or buy one that already exists? How can you tell whether or not you'll succeed? Is franchising the way to go? Should you set up as a sole proprietor, partnership, or corporation? How much money will you need to start and operate your business?

Part 2 examines basic sources of money that almost any small business owner will want to consider when looking for money to start and operate a business. It looks at the difference between equity and debt financing. There is a frank discussion of banks as sources of money and the types of loans they offer. I also look at commercial finance companies, venture capital funds, and other sources of funds, including life insurance companies, your home, lease financing, trade credit foundations, pension funds, commercial paper houses, credit unions, credit cards, the Export-Import Bank of the United States, and equity financing.

Part 3 provides a thorough look at borrowing through the Small Business Administration (SBA), including such topics as regular business loans from the SBA, special loan programs of the SBA, the process of filling out an SBA loan application, and nonfinancial SBA assistance. Part 4 includes information that will show you how to pull everything together to make an application for financing. There's a whole chapter on putting together an effective business plan. Chapter 14 walks you through the process of preparing a loan package. Finally, you'll get a quick course on financial ratios that will help you get a handle on what financing sources might be looking for from your business's performance. You'll also get a good handle on how to measure your business's performance in relation to that of other businesses in your industry.

The Bibliography lists books and publications that you can use to dig deeper into issues affecting your small business. The Glossary will help you understand some words and concepts that may be new to you. There are also five appendixes to help you get more information when and where you need it. These include directories of SBA field offices, Small Business Investment Companies (SBICs) and Minority Enterprise Small Business Investment Companies (MESBICs), SBA business publications, and trade associations that provide ratio analyses.

This book is designed to get you started on the road to finding money for your small business. It will arm you with the basics and guide you to future sources of information. By the time you finish reading the book, you should be secure in your knowledge of whether you have a good idea for a business, how much money you'll need to finance it, and what options you have for financing sources. At the time of publication, the book is as up-to-date as possible. Whenever relevant, I have cited sources of the most recent figures and information available, so that you will be able to update your knowledge on an ongoing basis.

To keep abreast of current developments in small business issues, I suggest that you refer to *The Wall Street Journal* and *Inc.* magazine, both of which do a wonderful job of covering issues of relevance to small business owners. They also feature information specifically related to financing small businesses.

Financing Your Small Business would not have been possible without the support of many people. McGraw-Hill once again provided me with a steady supply of professionals who shared their talent, patience, and enthusiasm for the project. In the early stages, Martha Jewett and Elisa Adams helped keep the book focused and on target. Barbara Toniolo saw the book through to the end, never swerving from her goal of making it as good as it could be. On more than one occasion, Jane Palmieri, who has been involved in this and two other projects I've worked on for McGraw-Hill, has helped keep me on deadline. I have worked with Georgia Kornbluth on two books now and would find every project much easier if I always had such a sharp and creative editor working with me. Of course, Bill Sabin has made the whole process much easier by helping me to keep in perspective what the book was and what it wasn't. It is always a joy to write a book for his list.

My family and friends were tolerant of my absences and encouraging of my progress. Larry Grimes was of particular help in getting me over the hurdle of putting the finishing touches on the project, and Evan Marshall's insightful critiques always help to strengthen my books.

Nancy Seglin, my wife, was by far the best sounding board and consistent source of editorial feedback I had. I am in constant wonder at her endless supply of wisdom and love.

Jeffrey L. Seglin

PART 1

What It Takes to Start a Small Business

1
Do You Really Want to Own a Small Business?

The Dangers and Rewards of Business Ownership

In a working-class neighborhood of Boston, Massachusetts, a sign on a garage lists the owner's name, followed by his telephone number and the words "Dream Builder." Here, on Hartland Street of all places, a businessman has hung out his shingle to tell the world what he does for a living. He builds dreams. How American.

This Boston dream builder is not alone in his desire to flourish in his own business. From 1981 to 1988, there were more than 6.15 million business incorporations and starts in the United States.[1] In 1988 alone more than 624,000 businesses were begun in this country.

Businesses were started at this brisk pace even though more than a half a million bankruptcies and more than 360,000 failures were reported during the same period.[2] According to the Small Business Administration (SBA), 23.7 percent of all businesses will have failed by the end of the first 2 years of operation.[3] After 4 years, 51.7 percent have failed. And after 6 years, 62.7 percent have failed. Many of the businesses that make up these numbers do not fail in the sense of going

---

[1] *The State of Small Business: A Report of the President*. Washington: U.S. Government Printing Office, 1989, p. 23.
[2] Ibid., p. 24.
[3] Ibid., p. 25.

3

bankrupt. Some business owners, particularly those who are sole proprietors, choose to close up shop or to work for someone else if a more attractive offer comes along. Even so, after 6 years in operation, only 37.3 percent of businesses will still be around. If these numbers hold true, then more than 598,000 of the more than 954,000 businesses started in 1986 will be out of business by 1992.

The spirit of the prospective small business owner is hard to break, even in the face of such figures.

One chief problem of keeping a business going is securing adequate financing—making sure that you have enough money to run your business once it is started. The greatest-in-the-world idea for a product or service cannot survive unless the business owner has enough capital to develop the product, run the business, produce the product, and afford the costs of running the business.

The chief function of this book is to guide you toward basic sources of financing and instruct you about how to get your hands on cash when you need it to start a business and keep it running. Before you begin to worry about where to find the money, however, you must have a solid idea of the business you want to start. Refer to Figure 1-1 for a checklist of 10 major things you should consider before you go into business.

Choosing a Profitable Business

In 1987, there were 683,686 business incorporations and 232,948 business starts.[4] That's more than 915,000 new businesses in 1 year alone. How could you possibly expect to compete not only with these hundreds of thousands of new businesses in the marketplace but also with the countless others that already exist?

Often the competition is treacherous. In the mid-1970s, Hillel Stavis decided to open WordsWorth, a general trade bookstore, in Harvard Square, an area in Cambridge, Massachusetts, that was already dominated by many flourishing, specialized independent bookstores. Stavis rented 4000 square feet of a new building on Brattle Street, secured a $90,000 loan through the Small Business Administration, and decided to offer 10 percent discounts on all paperback titles and 15 percent discounts on all hardback titles. Publishers traditionally give booksellers discounts of 40 to 50 percent off cover prices. The bookseller uses the difference to cover the costs of doing business. Since Stavis was passing

[4]Ibid., p. 23.

✔1. Does this business meet a customer need? Can it do so profitably?

✔2. Are your skills matched to your business?

✔3. Are there others who are in the same business? If so, how are they doing?

✔4. Is the market saturated with this type of business, or can you add something new that the market needs? Is the market so big that another business of this type stands a good chance of attracting its own niche?

✔5. If there are no businesses like this in the market, is there a reason for their absence?

✔6. If there are only a few competitors, how are they doing? Are they failing because there is no demand for their product or service in your prospective market?

✔7. You must ask yourself what chances your business has against factors outside your control (e.g., the economy).

✔8. You should choose a geographical area in which you and your family could live comfortably and which you could enjoy.

✔9. If you are starting a wholesaling or manufacturing business, is it located in an area that provides you with all the shipping facilities you need? Are you close enough to customers to keep costs affordable?

✔10. If you are a retailer, have you considered the 15 basic issues listed below?
- Area industry
- Population trends
- Competition
- Public transportation
- Banking service availability
- Parking
- Neighboring businesses
- Traffic patterns
- The pool of potential employees
- Wages of employees in the area
- Functional utilities
- Tax base for the area
- City or town services such as fire, police, and emergency care
- Attractiveness of lease (cost and provisions)
- Room for growth if necessary

Figure 1-1. A checklist of 10 major things to consider when you go into business.

on 10 and 15 percent of his discounts to the customer, he would need to sell more books to make money.

Two hard tasks faced Stavis: competing in an already crowded market and succeeding at a level high enough to make up for the discounts he gave on his books. Today, WordsWorth sells more general trade books than any of the more than two dozen other bookstores in Harvard Square.[5]

Clearly there is room for new businesses to succeed in the marketplace. Stavis found a niche in an already crowded market and succeeded by providing customers with a product and service they desired. This attention to the customer lies at the heart of most successful businesses. This customer orientation is part of what is called the *marketing concept*. Three principles at the heart of the marketing concept are:

Customer orientation

Profitable sales volume

Organizational coordination[6]

The marketing concept is one key to running a successful business, but it also can be used to determine what business to get into. Far too often, prospective business owners choose a business simply because it seems like fun or would be "neat," without giving any thought to whether or not the particular business will meet customer demand. Without customer demand, there are no sales. Without sales, no business can succeed.

Two fundamental questions the prospective business owner must ask when deciding which business to start are:

1. Does this business meet a customer need?
2. Can it meet that need profitably?

Coming Up with a Business Idea

Once the above questions have been answered positively, the prospective business owner can go forward with an idea for a business. Successful business ideas are generated from countless numbers of sources.

---

[5]Michael Melford, "Best Sellers," *The Boston Globe Magazine,* May 7, 1989, pp. 22–38.
[6]Jeffrey L. Seglin, *The McGraw-Hill 36-Hour Marketing Course.* New York: McGraw-Hill, 1990, p. 9.

Hobbies, recognizable market gaps, and technological advances are all possible sources of business ideas.

Hillel Stavis's idea of putting a bookstore in Harvard Square was hardly unique. It was positioning the bookstore to offer different products and services at discount prices that made WordsWorth unique.

Often product ideas are inherently unique. Wayne Lackey started Dentec Corp. in Boca Raton, Florida, to market what he calls "The Dentec 4000 Toothbrush Sanitizer." Lackey based his product development on a report issued by the University of Oklahoma College of Dentistry that said toothbrush bristles are a haven for bacteria. By recognizing a need in the marketplace and developing a product to meet that need, in the first year of operation Lackey was able to sell around 25,000 sanitizers, retailing for $60 apiece.[7]

There are many ways to find ideas for profitable businesses. If you have not been blessed with an enlightening epiphany experience that shows you the best of all possible businesses for you, there are a number of publications that regularly publish stories about new business ideas. *Inc.* magazine publishes stories of new business ideas throughout the magazine and especially in its "Insider" section. *Success* magazine does the same in its "Inside Track" section.

Matching Your Skills to Your Business

If you do decide to start a business, make sure to ask yourself whether it's a business that's right for you. Do you have the necessary skills to run a business like this? The more background you have in a business similar to the one you're thinking of starting, the more likely you are to succeed. While some people have an innate ability to succeed in whatever business they try, most of us find it wiser to stick to a business we know something about. Starting or running your own business is a difficult, time-consuming undertaking. You lessen the risk of failure if you bring some experience to the table.

Gauging the Outlook for Success

There is no way to tell for sure whether the business you choose to go into will succeed. But you can get a reading of how well it might do by looking at a few things:

[7]Judith Newman, "Debugging Toothbrushes," *Venture,* May 1989, p. 8.

- First, are there other companies in the same business?

  If so, how are they doing?

  Is the market saturated with this type of business, or can you add something new that the market needs?

  Is the market so big that another business of this type stands a good chance of finding its own niche?

- Second, if there are few or no already-established businesses like the one you are considering, is there a reason for their absence?

  If there are only a few competitors, how are they doing?

  If they are failing, is it because there is no demand for their product or service in your prospective market?

Businesses succeed or fail for a variety of reasons. A major reason is undercapitalization, not having enough money to run your business. Even if sales are going well, undercapitalization can bury a business, since it may cause problems like not having the money to buy inventory with which to meet sales demand. This book seeks to guide you toward getting enough money to adequately start and run a successful business.

Aside from undercapitalization, other reasons for business failures abound. Economic conditions, technological advances, fashion and trend shifts, new regulations, a new shopping mall, changing traffic patterns, and countless other factors might cause the demise of an initially successful business. For every business that is hurt by one of these factors, however, other businesses may flourish because of that same factor. It's a difficult question, but you must ask yourself what chances your business has against factors outside your control.

If you can afford a sophisticated market analysis of the area in which you plan to do business, a variety of marketing research approaches, such as test marketing, focus groups, and demographic analysis, may shed some light on the likelihood of your business's success. Any number of marketing research firms are capable of using the latest techniques to give you ideas of what to expect in your market.

For many start-up operations, hiring a marketing research firm is cost-prohibitive. If that's the case for you, you can get similar results by doing your own informal marketing research. (You can also read George Breen and A. B. Blankenship's *Do-It-Yourself Marketing Research,*[8] which gives advice on how to use the same marketing research techniques as the experts do.) Some potential competitors may be willing to discuss the business with you to give you an idea of the lay of the land. You can also talk to customers, venture capitalists, bankers,

[8]New York: McGraw-Hill, 1989.

and professional trade groups (see the partial list in Appendix E), and you can keep a look out for information on businesses like yours in the business press.

While your gut instinct may tell you that your business will succeed, you should not rely on it alone to convince you. You must do the necessary legwork to discover the potential strength of your prospective business in your market; this is essential to convince not only yourself but also the individuals or institutions from whom you may want to secure financing.

Selecting a Viable Location

There are almost as many theories about successful locations for businesses as there are new businesses every year. But for each theory, there is surely an exception that proves the rule.

Remember Hillel Stavis of WordsWorth? When he started his bookstore in 1976, the store space available to him was on the less traveled side of Harvard Square: experiential research had shown that 30 percent fewer shoppers passed by the prospective storefront than on the other side of the street. Stavis took the 4000 square feet anyway, and has managed to dominate the area with his sales.[9] The results of his experiential research did not keep his business from succeeding.

Other prospective business owners have decided to move to areas that are growing rapidly in the United States, such as the Sunbelt in the Southwest. But just as one such entrepreneur was about to decide to take the plunge and open shop in Phoenix, she read a headline in *The Wall Street Journal*: "Arizona's Boom Fades to a Mirage as Several Sectors Hit a Severe Slump." This headline indicates that the bloom is off the rose in the economic growth of at least one popular Sunbelt locale.[10]

All this just goes to prove that there are no sure things when it comes to setting up shop. But there *are* some factors about choosing a location that, if you take them to heart, greatly heighten the chances of your survival.

Though personal preference should not be your sole reason for opening a business in a particular location, you should choose an area which you and your family would enjoy living in and could live in comfortably. Consider all the factors you'd normally look at in choosing a place to live, whether or not you were planning to open a business—

[9]Melford, op. cit., p. 24.
[10]Pauline Yoshihashi, "Arizona's Boom Fades to a Mirage as Several Sectors Hit a Severe Slump," *The Wall Street Journal*, May 9, 1989, p. A2.

factors such as educational facilities, housing, cultural events, and community activities.

There are plenty of sources of information about cities and towns throughout the United States. Chambers of commerce (or their equivalents) can give you information on the types of businesses in a community. City or county agencies can give you information on traffic, zoning laws, and other regulatory issues. You can also find out about the cost and availability of various prospective locations from talking with real estate agents.

Wholesaling and manufacturing businesses are usually limited in their choice of location to areas that are zoned for appropriate use. These businesses should be located in an area that provides them with all the shipping facilities they need and are in close enough proximity to customers to keep costs affordable.

While commercial zoning affects retailing industries as well, it is important for prospective retailers to consider a variety of factors before settling on a location. Among these are:

- *Area industry.* For any business to succeed, there must be customers with money to buy its products. Areas that have healthy industries or a growing industry base provide a market that can afford what you have to offer. Obviously, different types of retail establishments will attract different types of customers. Locating your retail business in an area where there is a ready base of prospects, however, is usually a good move.

- *Population trends.* As in Phoenix, growing population trends are not always an assurance that a market will grow forever. It's still important, however, to try to get a handle on whether the population of an area will be large enough or appropriate for what you have to offer. The areas of the country that are dwindling in population do not bode particularly well for a massive influx of new businesses. It's also important to make sure that your business is appropriate for the population. Selling outdoor house paint in a floor-level shop of a downtown Manhattan apartment building, for example, may not be the wisest market-product match.

- *Competition.* A little competition never hurt anyone. But if the market is saturated with efficient firms, tread carefully. The best way to compete in a crowded market is to look for a market that is expanding and is full of businesses that do not efficiently serve its needs.

- *Public transportation.* Ask yourself whether public transportation is an issue for your business. A downtown location may require it; small-town locations may not.

- *Banking service availability.*   Are there banks in the area with which you can establish a relationship? You may not need to rely on local banks for borrowing needs, but the depository and checking services that are important for all businesses should be readily available.

- *Parking.*   Can customers park near your prospective business site? While heavily pedestrian-trafficked downtown locations may succeed on the basis of drop-in customers, convenient parking and access to your business may be important in areas where customers will be driving to your store.

- *Neighboring businesses.*   Will your business fit well with other businesses in the vicinity? Are the customers of nearby businesses good potential customers for your business?

- *Traffic patterns.*   Consider both automobile and pedestrian traffic when you are choosing a site for a business. While you can get this information from various organizations, you can also observe the prospective site yourself and see just how well frequented the area is. Ultimately, pedestrian traffic is a key to success since you want to get the people out of their cars and into your establishment.

Other issues that you'll want to consider in choosing a location for your business include:

The pool of potential employees

Wages of employees in the area

Functional utilities

The tax base of the area

Availability of city or town services such as fire, police, and emergency care

The attractiveness of the lease (cost and provisions)

Room for growth

When you are setting up your business, it's crucial that you do not simply rent the first space available. Give careful consideration to your business's location. Location can spell the difference between success and failure. Furthermore, a poorly chosen location can hinder your chances of finding money to finance your business, if a prospective financing source deems it to be inappropriate.

Advantages and Disadvantages of Buying an Existing Business

A decision that plagues many prospective business owners is whether to start from scratch or to buy an existing business. Sometimes, buying an existing business is out of the question, particularly when your idea for a new business involves new technology or centers on your unique talents. But often there are opportunities to purchase an existing business. Along with those opportunities come a fair number of advantages and disadvantages. Some of them are described below.

Advantages

Among the advantages are:

1. *The owner may be eager to sell.* Sometimes you can find a good buy on a business because the owner is eager to sell. The reason for this eagerness may be, for example, the owner's pending retirement, illness, or desire to cash in on what he or she has built or to change occupations.

2. *You can inherit inventory, suppliers, equipment, and a facility.* You can save money and time if you don't have to accumulate these things yourself.

3. *You might inherit good employees.* Training new employees can be time-consuming and expensive. Inheriting a good staff when you buy a business may cut down this time and expense and enable you to keep the business operating smoothly.

4. *You may inherit an existing customer base.* One of the most difficult things to find for a new business is loyal clientele. If you can buy an established business that has a good following, your chances of success may increase.

5. *You may be the beneficiary of goodwill, positive recognition, and a solid reputation.* If the previous owner was a pillar of the community and known as a sound businessperson who sold quality products or services, you may acquire the benefit of those assets along with the business.

6. *There may be less risk.* If the business is already successful and profitable, the risks associated with start-up are diminished. You

may be buying a business that has already hurdled many of the obstacles to success and profitability.

7. *You may realize profits more quickly.* The costs of opening a new business may be great. If you buy an existing business that has everything in place, including a healthy clientele, you may begin realizing profits on sales more quickly than had you started from scratch.

8. *You may find it easier to do financial and marketing planning.* If you do your homework before you buy an existing business, you will know the market it attracts and you will know roughly what operating capital you will need to keep the business going smoothly.

9. *Buying an existing business involves one transaction.* When you start a business from scratch, you must make dozens of transactions to get the business up and running. When you buy a going concern, you buy the whole works in running order.

10. *A good track record can increase chances of success.* If the previous business owner did well in the business, your own chances of success are better than if you were to invest in less of a sure thing.

11. *You may inherit a good, established location.* "Location, location, location," goes the old saw. It's difficult to get just the right location for a business. You may be able to buy a good location as part of the business deal.

Disadvantages

The disadvantages of buying an existing business include:

1. *The business may be overpriced.* If you buy an overpriced business, making a profit will be difficult. Overpricing may spell failure for the survival of the operation.

2. *The owner may have a bad reputation.* Just as a previous owner's good reputation can translate into continued sales for the new owner, a bad reputation can have a devastating effect on sales.

3. *You may inherit bad employees.* If you buy a business that includes a large staff, you may inherit some bad apples in the crew. When two brothers bought a restaurant south of the Boston area, they inherited a staff that included dishwashers who showed up late for work, if at all, and waitresses who did not add drink prices to the bills they gave customers. Unfortunately, it took the brothers weeks

to find out what was going on. In the meantime they had a business to run, which was difficult under those conditions. Eventually, it was necessary to bring in new employees and train them, in order to make the restaurant succeed.

4. *The business may be in a bad location or building.*   Nothing is worse than a bad location or building. If a previous owner had problems with zoning laws that prevented expansion, or with the lack of nearby parking, the new owner is sure to face the same problems. Ask the previous owner why he or she is selling. Observe and talk to local business owners about potential problems in the area.

5. *You may inherit antiquated equipment and fixtures.*   You gain little advantage if you buy a business but then have to replace all equipment and fixtures. Before you agree to purchase an existing business, make sure to discount the cost of any unusable equipment from the asking price. Find out how old the equipment is and whether you can still get parts for it. Also keep in mind that antiquated equipment sometimes presents safety hazards. When the brothers mentioned above first took over their restaurant, the old, greasy stoves in the kitchen started fires. The result? A hefty price tag on new stainless steel stoves.

6. *There may be bad inventory.*   If you are buying an existing inventory as part of the purchase, make sure it is usable. Have it appraised rather than accepting the seller's assessment of its value. If the inventory is worthless or of little value, you don't want to pay for it and then have to replace it.

7. *The existing procedures may be cumbersome and ineffective.*   When you buy a new business, you may inherit bad procedures put into effect by the previous owner. Not only will such an inheritance cut into efficient operation of the business, but also it is often difficult to convince employees who are used to doing business in an established way that there is a better way of doing business.

8. *You may inherit inappropriate customers.*   Find out whether the existing customers are the type of customers you want to attract. The owner may cater to an entirely different clientele than those you would like to attract.

9. *You may be burdened with a surly landlord.*   If you are considering buying a business but will have to lease the building in which it is located, make sure that the landlord is flexible enough to allow you to run your business efficiently. Difficult, stubborn landlords can sound the death knell for businesses.

10. *The owner may take the customer base to a new business.* Ask about the owner's future plans. If he or she plans to open a new, similar business, the existing clientele may transfer their loyalty to the new business.

11. *The owner may have run up exorbitant debts.* If the current owner has many liabilities, you might face difficulties if you bought the business. Are suppliers still making good on deliveries? Are bankers at their wit's end trying to collect payments?

Weighing the Advantages and Disadvantages of Buying versus Starting

Consideration of some specific issues, discussed below, may help you make the decision to buy or not to buy.

Figure out what you think the business's future earning potential will be. To determine whether or not the business may be profitable in the future, analyze all the financial statements and projections the current owner has given you. Keep in mind that the current owner's projections are likely to be overly optimistic. Look at past sales records to determine whether they are in line. If it's a retail business that you are considering, ask the current owner to allow you to spend some time in the store, observing the business and monitoring the cash receipts at the end of the business day. This will help you to evaluate the current owner's sales projections.

Ask the owner to give you balance sheets and operating statements for the last 5 years. These will tell you whether or not the business has been profitable. If not, study the operation to determine whether you could cut out excessive costs or make other changes that would affect the future profitability of the business. All the information that you develop will help you to estimate how much the business can make in the future.

Become familiar with competing businesses in the area. Talk to competitors. Observe their businesses. How are they doing, compared to the seller? Are there things they are doing that you could do to improve profits in the future? Or is the area so saturated with similar, efficiently run businesses that there is little room for the one you are considering buying to become successful?

If the business has been profitable, has it been so every year out of the past 5 years? Have the profits risen every year? Or have they gone up and down? In 1989, I looked at the financial statements of a wholesale business in North Dakota. These statements showed increased sales of 2 percent from one year to the next and increased profits of 50 percent. If you encounter such statements, find out what accounts for the drastic rise in profits when sales were not that much higher. Look for any aberrations, and ask the current owner about them.

Based on the information you have about the business's past sales and profits, make an estimate of the following year's profit and loss statement. You should also ask the current owner to make a projection for the same period—keeping in mind that he or she is trying to sell the business and will likely make an overly optimistic projection. Compare the two projections, and talk with the current owner about any drastic differences.

You should also figure out what you think it will cost to run the business, which will enable you to calculate how much capital you will need for each month of operations. You can also approximate what the assets and liabilities may be by the end of your first year of ownership.

When you are looking over the books, pay particular attention to any accounts receivable (the amount owed to the business) that the owner figures as part of the business' assets. Are they so old that they will likely become bad debt that is never collected?

For your own information, calculate how much more money you would make if you bought this existing business than if you started a similar one on your own. Also take goodwill into account. Are there enough goodwill and other intangible assets (such as patents or trademarks) in the existing business to make buying it more attractive than starting your own? Talk to customers, lenders, suppliers, and competitors to get an idea of just how much goodwill the current owner has built up in the community.

In calculating the value of a company, make sure to subtract any liabilities (e.g., outstanding loans and mortgages, money due to suppliers) from the assets to come up with a fair value for the business.

Once you have all these projections and calculations in hand, you can calculate what you think your *return on investment* will be by using the following equation:

$$\frac{\text{Projected net profit } \infty \text{revenues minus expenses} \times}{\text{Price of business } \infty \text{plus additional investment necessary} \times}$$

$$= \text{return on investment}$$

If the estimated return on investment meets your needs, then the asking price is probably reasonable. If it does not, then the asking price is too high. Don't pay more than you think is reasonable. If the return on investment isn't attractive, this is most likely not the investment for you.

Should You Consider a Franchise?

In 1987 alone, $591 billion worth of business was conducted through the more than 499,000 franchise outlets that were in operation.[11] This is up from 396,000 units accounting for $120 billion in sales in 1970, and 442,000 units accounting for $336 billion in 1980. Franchising— obtaining a license to sell a franchisor's products or services using that franchisor's name—has grown dramatically.

For many prospective business owners, franchising is a good way of buying into a business. A franchised business has the backing of a big organization that provides a known product or service, management and operations guidance, marketing support (often including national advertising), and name recognition. But the advantages don't come cheaply.

The Costs of Franchising

The cost of starting a franchise can range from as low as $2000 to as high as $900,000. Franchisees pay the franchisor a franchise fee, spend money on start-up costs, and typically pay an annual royalty on sales. For example, if you decided to open a Create-A-Book franchise—a company that sells personalized children's books—you'd pay around $3000 for the franchise fee; in return, you'd receive lifetime rights to an exclusive territory. Another $1500 to $2000 would cover start-up costs, including buying a computer, printer, and supplies from the franchisor. You'd have the comfort of knowing that there are between 125 and 250 Create-A-Book outlets in the United States, which presumably would help to establish the credibility and recognizability of your new company.

If, on the other hand, you decided you wanted to open a Rax Restaurant, it would cost you a franchise fee of $25,000 for 20-year rights to an exclusive territory, land costs of between $200,000 and $300,000, building and site preparation costs of between $300,000 and $310,000, employee training costs of around $50,000, and a 4 percent royalty on gross sales to pay for advertising. Furthermore, to qualify for buying a

---

[11]U.S. Bureau of the Census, *Statistical Abstract of the United States: 1988,* (108th ed.), Washington: U.S. Government Printing Office, 1987, p. 742.

franchise for a Rax Restaurant, you have to have had at least 3 years of restaurant experience.

Weighing the Risks of Franchising

Franchising may be growing rapidly, but it is not without failures. In 1986 more than 5500 outlets (representing 78 franchises) failed financially and more than 5000 outlets (representing 105 franchises) closed up shop. Altogether, these outlets accounted for more than $2.8 billion in sales of goods and services. Franchising is also not growing rapidly in all industries. While children's-product franchisers grow at an average of more than 30 outlets a year, clothing-store franchises only grow at about 2 stores a year. You will want to make sure that the franchise you are considering has been around for a while. Look for operations that have a proven track record over at least a 5-year period.

While franchising does give you the advantages of management advice, central purchasing capabilities, and strength in numbers, it is not without drawbacks. For example:

- The most obvious drawback is that you give up the autonomy of the independent business owner. You are instead required to follow the operating and marketing instructions of the franchisor.

- Not all franchises offer central purchasing, which means that product inconsistency could be a problem. What's more, when central purchasing is provided, the goods may be more costly than if the franchisee bought them independently.

- The franchise fee and royalty may be a good deal for franchisees who purchase a quality franchise, but they can be a real drain on those who unknowingly buy into a franchise that has little marketing or management support.

The Federal Trade Commission provides protection to prospective franchisees. At least 10 days before you sign a franchise agreement, the franchisor must provide you with a disclosure statement that gives you information about the franchise, including (1) the names, addresses, and telephone numbers of other franchisees; (2) an audited financial statement for the franchisor's business; (3) the background of the franchise executives; (4) an estimate of the costs of starting and operating a franchise unit; (5) your responsibilities as a franchisee; (6) the franchisor's responsibilities as a franchisor.

When you are considering a franchise, it is critical that you do your homework and investigate the legitimacy of the franchisor. Look at the terms of the agreement. Look at the competition in your territory. Examine every aspect of the business plan and the risks that might be involved in buying into a franchise outlet.

There are scads of books available on franchising that include information on everything—from general information on how much it costs to get started to lists of specific franchises that are available and how much they cost to run. Before you get too deeply into your exploration of any specific franchise, send for an excellent publication available from the Federal Trade Commission called "Advice for Persons Who Are Considering an Investment in a Franchise Business."[12]

After you get an idea of what it takes to start a small business, you will face a slew of other issues. What form should your business take? Where can you find the money to finance it? Where can you turn for help? Whereas Chapter 1 laid the groundwork for helping you think through your decision to own and run a small business, the remainder of the book will tackle these other issues.

---

[12]Consumer Bulletin No. 4, available from the Federal Trade Commission, 6th Street and Pennsylvania Avenue, N.W., Washington, DC 20580.

2
What Form Should Your Business Take?

**Deciding How
Things Will
Take Shape**

Once you know what type of business you want and where you'd like it to be located, you should consider what form you want it to take. There are basically three options: sole proprietorship, partnership, and corporation. Each has its advantages and disadvantages. At given stages in the life of a business, one form usually stands out as more appropriate than others.

A broad look at each of the three forms of business will be included in this chapter. Table 2-1 gives a brief rundown of the advantages and disadvantages of each form of business. If you decide to form a partnership or corporation, you should consult with an accountant or attorney to work out the fine points.

Sole Proprietorship

By far the easiest type of business to set up is a sole proprietorship. This is also the least expensive business form to start, partly because you do not need to hire a lawyer to prepare papers to file with state agencies. A

Table 2-1. Advantages and Disadvantages of Different Forms of Business

	Advantages	Disadvantages
Sole pro- prietorship	Easy to set up. Autonomy in decision making. Owner keeps all profits. Few regulatory restrictions. Closing up shop is easy. Possible tax advantages. Low initial capital require- ments.	Possible inexperience of one and only owner. Raising capital hard. Exposure to liability. Business does not live beyond owner.
Partnership	Easy to set up. Pool of experience. More capital available. Business becomes legal entity. Possible tax advantages. Possible low initial capital re- quirements. Few regulatory restrictions.	Exposure to liability. More than one boss. Partners may not see eye to eye on decisions. Business may not live beyond partners. Finding good partners is tough.
Corporation	Limited exposure to liability. Business can survive owners. Ownership is easily transferred. Expansion is simpler. Useful for different-size firms. Business is legal entity. Possible tax advantages. Raising capital is easier.	Costly to organize. Must follow corporate charter. Record keeping can be extensive. Double taxation is possi- ble.

sole proprietorship is a business that is owned and operated by one in-dividual. As such, business decisions can be made quickly and carried out just as fast as the sole proprietor deems appropriate. The only time it may be necessary to file legal papers is if you decide to do business using a name other than your own. Many municipalities will require you to file the name you've chosen to use for your business with a licensing office. Regulations differ from municipality to municipality, so you should check with your local licensing board or town council if you de-cide to use a name other than your own.

The sole proprietor reports income and expenses on schedule C of the IRS personal income tax return. Net income (gross total income mi-nus expenses) is added to any other wages earned, and taxed at the tax-payer's personal rate. The sole proprietor also must pay self-em-ployment tax on all net income reported on schedule C. This tax is designed to cover Social Security payments.

A drawback to this form of business is that as a sole proprietor you are liable for all business expenses and your personal assets may be exposed to cover any debts, lawsuits, or other costs associated with doing business. While this liability is widely known as one of the most common drawbacks associated with sole proprietorship, what is less well known is that lending institutions often require owners of small business corporations to provide personal guaranties, effectively pledging their personal assets as collateral on a loan, which results in similar personal exposure.

Partnership

When two or more people decide to operate a business as co-owners, they form a partnership. While having a partnership agreement drawn up by an attorney is not a legal requirement, it is wise to spend the money to have an attorney put in writing the duties and obligations of each partner in the partnership.

The Uniform Partnership Act was developed by the National Commissioners on Uniform State Laws as a model to prescribe the behavior of partners in a partnership. The act has been adopted as law in many states. It also provides a useful template on which to base a partnership relationship.

The Uniform Partnership Act sets out specific rights and obligations of each partner in the partnership. Among the rights are:

- To share in the management and profits of the business
- To receive repayment of original investment and interest on advances made to the business
- To have access to partnership records and formal accountings of partnership affairs

Among the obligations are:

- To contribute toward reimbursement of any losses the partnership experiences
- To work for a share of profits instead of customary pay
- To follow the majority vote (or the findings of an outside arbitrator) if differences occur
- To inform partners of information about partnership affairs

Partners are taxed individually. The business is not taxed as a partnership. Partnerships do not file income tax returns (unlike corporations, which do; see the discussion below), but one of the partners must sign and file form 1065, an IRS information return which reports on the partnership's gross income and deductions, and lists the names of the partners and the percentage of the business owned by each. Partners pay individual taxes in proportion to how much of the business they own. Each partner must pay self-employment tax.

Partnerships are dissolved automatically if any partner leaves the partnership, dies, is expelled, sells his or her percentage of the partnership, or declares bankruptcy. Dissolution is not the same as termination of the partnership. If the partnership operations continue, the partnership is not terminated.

Buy-sell provisions, allowing surviving partners to buy dead partners' interests, are often established in partnership agreements. A buy-sell agreement should be funded, typically with an insurance policy on each partner. If a partner dies, the insurance proceeds are used to buy out the dead partner's share of the business. To set up a buy-sell agreement, partners should consult a reputable insurance salesperson or a firm that specializes in setting up insurance benefits for businesses.

Termination of a partnership signals that it is ceasing operations. Because there are tax ramifications involved in terminating a business, partners should consult with an accountant before settling on the terms of a termination.

Corporation

Each state in the United States has laws governing the establishment of a corporation. Usually a business will file for incorporation in the state in which it does business. If it does business in a state other than that in which it is based, it is considered a foreign corporation. (Corporations from another country doing business in this country are called "alien corporations.") It is generally advisable for a small business to incorporate in the state in which it does business.

Advantages of Incorporation

The main advantages of incorporation are that it limits your liability and gives you the ability to attract outside capital by selling shares of the corporation. Some experts argue that the limited liability provided by corporation status makes it the only way to go when choosing what form your business should take, and that the $250 to $300 you might spend to incorporate is the best investment you will ever make. But there are many people who go into business appropriately as sole proprietors, for example, free-lance writers, designers, and others who have relatively small operations. Once a business grows larger, it may then be appropriate to shift to a different business status.

Once you decide to incorporate, you should hire an attorney to file all the papers necessary to set up your corporation. The attorney should also advise you on the rules of doing corporate business, which includes electing officers, setting up a board of directors, adopting corporate by-laws, and issuing stock. An attorney may also help you do a search to determine whether the name you choose for your business has already been taken. If you file using a name that has already been taken, the state may delay your incorporation until you come up with a new name.

If you are the principal shareholder of a corporation which is a small business, the limited liability provided by this form of business may effectively be an empty blessing. You may already have put up most of your assets to start the business, and a lender may require you (and principal shareholders) to file a personal guaranty to give them additional assurances that you will make every effort to make the business work and pay back your loans.

An advantage of choosing the corporation form of business is that it is relatively easy to transfer the ownership of the business by selling stock. Shareholders can also sell out their stock when they want to. To protect the other shareholders' interest in the corporation, it is possible in a private corporation to restrict sales of stock to people who are already within the corporation, or to those approved by the other shareholders. Shareholders can sign an agreement to this effect.

Unlike partnerships, corporations are treated like individuals when it comes to paying federal income tax. Corporation are treated as taxable entities separate from the owners.

S or C Corporation?

Businesspeople can choose to set up corporations as either C corporations or S corporations. A C corporation reports its taxable income and pays income tax on it. The individuals within the corporation pay individual taxes on any salary, dividends, or interest received from the corporation.

Reasonable salaries, interest, and similar expenses are deductible on a corporate tax return, and the remaining amount is subject to a corporate tax. A shareholder who receives a dividend from the corporation pays a tax on it, filing an individual return.

An S corporation avoids this double taxation by allowing the stockholders to pay tax directly on the corporate income. In the S corporation, the income or loss of the corporation is passed directly to the shareholders. The S corporation is often used to reduce taxes, but it is a highly complex form of business that is subject to many rules and restrictions. Since S corporations are so complex, shareholders should opt to file for S corporation status only after consulting with their attorney.

To qualify for S corporation status, a corporation must meet many requirements, including the ones listed below.

- The S corporation must be incorporated in the United States and must not be a financial institution, an insurance company, or a domestic international sales corporation (DISC). (A *DISC* is a company the assets and gross receipts of which are 95 percent related to the export business.)

- Shareholders must consist of individuals, estates, or trusts.

- Shareholders cannot be partnerships or corporations.

- Nonresident aliens cannot be shareholders.

- There must be only one class of common stock.

- There must not be more than 35 shareholders. (Husbands and wives count as one shareholder even if their stock is owned individually.)

A company that meets the requirements above (along with some others that might exist in some cases) can become an S corporation by having all shareholders sign and file Internal Revenue Service form 2553 within the first 75 days of the corporation's first tax year as an S corporation.

The S corporation can be terminated by having shareholders who own more than half the stock sign and file a revocation form. If the revocation is filed within the first 2½ months of that tax year, it is effective for the tax year in which it is filed. Otherwise, it won't become effective until the following year. Once a company decides to terminate as an S corporation, it cannot choose to become one again for another 5 years without special dispensation from the Internal Revenue Service.

Corporations choose to become S corporations for a variety of reasons. This form of corporation is especially attractive to companies that expect to take a loss in the first few years of business. These losses are passed on to shareholders, who may use the losses to offset other income. Once the corporation starts to make substantial profits, it is wise to shift to C corporation status, so as to use the profits to help the corporation grow. Once the company stops sustaining losses, there is little or no tax benefit to be gained from passing the corporate earnings on through to the shareholders.

If you are just starting out in business on your own, it is wise to consider beginning as a sole proprietor and later growing into a partnership or corporation. It is far more cost-effective to pay the cost of setting up a partnership agreement and then a corporation only after you are sure it is advantageous to do so. The cost and hassle of dissolving a corporation that was inappropriate for your business can be cumbersome. Incorporation is best avoided if unnecessary.

3
How Much Money Will You Need?
Determining that Magic Figure

In later chapters, you'll discover how to use various financial ratios that can help you put together a crackerjack business plan and a proposal package that you can present to prospective lenders. (See especially the discussion of financial ratios in Chapter 15.) But before you step into the preparation of a more formal business proposal, it's a good idea to get a handle on just how much cash you're talking about when you decide you want to go into business.

Too often, a prospective business owner hits upon an ace idea for a business, only to be waylaid by the recognition that he or she has absolutely no idea what it would cost financially to lift the company off the ground and set it flying. This chapter will help you to get a grip on the realities of what it might realistically cost to get things going. Having a sense of what you need will give you a good idea of the type of money you need to seek for start-up and operations. In some cases, it may surprise you to find out that your capital needs are small enough that you can fund the business out of your own savings and with a little help from your friends.

Let's address the obvious first. Different businesses require different amounts of money to get going. The total amount of capital you'll need will depend on many factors, including:

- The type of business you are planning to go into
- What kind of inventory you might need to stock
- How much demand you expect from customers

- Whether or not you know suppliers who will offer you generous payment discounts and schedules
- How expensive your employees are
- How strong the economy is in your area

Table 3-1 will help you to figure out how much money you need. To find the estimated figures to plug into the table, you can make use of financial ratios. These ratios can help you to understand a variety of information about businesses like yours, including the relationship between expense items and net sales. Many companies publish lists of typical financial ratios for specific types of businesses. Among the better known are:

- *Dun & Bradstreet, Inc.* (99 Church Street, NY 10007). *Key Business Ratios* lists operating ratios for 125 lines of business activity.
- *Robert Morris Associates* (Philadelphia National Bank Building, Philadelphia, PA 19107). *Statement Studies* lists business ratios for around 300 different lines of business.
- *Accounting Corporation of America* (1929 First Avenue, San Diego, CA 92101). *Barometer of Small Business* gives operating ratios for many types of small businesses.
- *National Cash Register Company* (Marketing Services Department, Dayton, OH 45409). *Expenses in Retail Businesses* gives operating ratios for many retail businesses.
- *Federal Trade Commission—Securities and Exchange Commission* (U.S. Government Printing Office, Washington, DC 20402). *Quarterly Report for Manufacturing Corporations* gives raw data on manufacturing corporations in the United States that you can use to calculate your own financial ratios for various types of expenses.

Appendix E also lists trade associations which have researched industry-related ratios.

If you can find a typical financial ratio for your business, you won't need to pull costs for expenses out of the air. You can multiply your estimated sales by the ratio of expenses to sales and use the result as an estimated expense in Table 3-1. For example, if you find that the industry standard ratio of expenses to sales is 1 to 2, and you estimate that sales for your business will be $1 million, then you can estimate expenses of $500,000. (For every $1 spent on expenses, you'll get $2 in sales, if the ratio holds true.) Of course, if there are special circumstances that will involve higher expenses, you can add those to your ex-

Table 3-1. How Much Money Do I Need?

A. Estimated Monthly Expenses

Item	Estimate of monthly expenses based on annual sales of $_____ 1	Estimate of cash needed to start your business (use figures from col. 3) 2	Figures to use in col. 2 3
Owner's salary	$	$	2 × column 1
All other salaries			3 × column 1
Rent or mortgage payment			3 × column 1
Advertising and publicity			3 × column 1
Distribution expenses			3 × column 1
Supplies			3 × column 1
Telephone and Fax			3 × column 1
Utilities (gas, electricity, etc.)			3 × column 1
Insurance			Estimate from insurance company
Taxes (federal, state, local, social security)			Accountant's estimate of monthly amount × 4
Interest			3 × column 1
Maintenance			3 × column 1
Professional fees (lawyer, accountant, etc.)			3 × column 1
Miscellaneous			3 × column 1
		Total (col. 2) $_____	

Table 3-1. How Much Money Do I Need? (*Continued*)

B. Estimated Furniture and Equipment

Item	If paying fully in cash, enter full amount below and in last column on right.	If paying in installments, list below. In last column on right, enter down payment plus one installment payment.			Total cash needed for furniture and equipment.
		Price	Down payment	Each installment	
Tables and chairs	$	$	$	$	$
Counters					
Awning, signage					
Displays					
Lighting					
Hand trucks, dollies, other delivery equipment					
Computer					
Time clock					
Cash register					
Other costs relevant to your business					
Total furniture and equipment costs (add all figures in last column)					$

C. One-Time Start-Up Costs

Furniture and equipment (Use final figure from part B, above.)

Remodeling (Get estimates from general contractors.)

Installation costs for furniture and equipment (Get estimates from suppliers.)

Starting inventory (Get estimates from suppliers or use a traditional ratio of inventory to sales, if available for your industry.)

Utilities deposits (Talk to the utilities companies: telephone, electric, gas, oil, water, and other utilities.)

Professional fees

Licenses (Check with local municipal offices to see what types of licenses you might need to conduct your type of business in that town or city.)

Publicity—advertising, public relations, promotions, etc. (Plan what you want to do, and check with local media and professionals to see what it will cost you.)

Accounts receivable (Cash you'll need until you begin receiving money from customers who owe you.)

Cash (Estimate what you should have available for emergencies or unforeseen purchases.)

Table 3-1. How Much Money Do I Need? *(Continued)*

C. One-Time Start-Up Costs

Other (Rack your brain for any other
start-up costs you might have, and
enter the costs here.)

Total
Total from column 2 in part A

$ _____
+ $ _____   = Estimated cash needed to start business

SOURCE: Adapted from Richard Rubin and Philip Goldberg, *The Small Business Guide to Borrowing Money*. New York: McGraw-Hill, 1980, pp. 39–40.

pense estimates. You should also adjust the ratio to reflect unique market characteristics or other information you may have at your disposal. (Financial ratios are discussed in greater detail in Chapter 15.)

Estimating Sales Volume

Estimating sales volume for your business will require some homework. If you are buying an existing business, check old sales figures and determine how much better you think you'll be able to do. Evaluate the competition in your marketplace. Talk to area businesspeople and business groups about what you might expect to take in. Realize that it may take you time to build up a reputation in the market. Don't expect to achieve immediate sales higher than anyone else has ever achieved in your type of business in the same market. Maybe a few years down the road, but not right away.

There are exceptions, of course; optimistic projections do occasionally come true. A young businessman who bought a restaurant in Hingham, Massachusetts, is a case in point. He had previously managed a restaurant in a nearby, less affluent community. He knew what the restaurant he was buying had done in sales volume under previous ownership. From his previous experience in managing a restaurant, he also knew ways in which he could improve the restaurant. The previous owner had taken in a weekly average of $7000 in gross sales. By making several improvements in the restaurant, the new owner optimistically figured that he could slightly more than double that figure. He redecorated, increased hours of business, offered a more extensive menu, and stressed quality service. Five months into operations, the restaurant was averaging $19,000 in gross sales a week.

Sometimes new business owners will calculate what they have to do in gross sales by figuring what they want to make for themselves from the business every year. Say a small manufacturer wanted $75,000 for himself at the end of the year, and he knew that the average net profit (revenues minus expenses) for his type of firm was 11 percent of gross sales (total sales before discounts, returns, or other adjustments are taken into account). To take home the $75,000, the business owner would have to do more than $680,000 in gross sales. The danger of estimating gross sales this way is that it doesn't take into account market conditions or other factors that are more realistic determinations of sales. For sales-volume estimates to be useful, they must be in the ballpark; they must be based on a realistic assessment of what a business can actually expect to make in its particular market.

Estimating Expenses

To calculate ongoing monthly expenses, you can use industry operating ratios or market estimates. Because operating ratios are often figured in terms of a yearly amount, you may have to calculate the monthly amount.

You'll have to make additions to and deletions from Table 3-1 to get an accurate picture of how much cash you'll need to get started. Inventory costs vary from business to business, but most industry suppliers will be glad to provide you with costs. After all, they're going to want a piece of your business. If you open a manufacturing firm, you'll have to calculate market demand for your product and estimate sales of your product. You'll have to calculate how many people you'll need on the line and what you'll have to pay them. Harbor Sweets, a candy company in Salem, Massachusetts, had the benefit of being located near Salem State College, which gave it a ready pool of college students who were willing to adapt to the ebb and flow of seasonal employment at untraditional work hours.

You'll also need to do some research to find out equipment costs for a business like yours. But Table 3-1 is adaptable to most business situations. Tailor it to your own needs.

Making Accurate Predictions

The finished package you present to a prospective source of money will be much more polished than the calculations you make in Table 3-1, but the numbers you come up with here are important. Your prospective sources of financing will want to know how you arrived at the figure you are looking for to run your business. Take the time to make accurate estimates. Do your homework and check into industry standards. Prospective lenders want to know they're lending to someone who knows the business. If you can back up your estimates and intelligently explain how you arrived at your numbers, you'll, at the very least, convince your prospective lender that you are serious about your business, that you understand what you've gotten yourself into, and that you know what you need to keep going.

Try to come as close as you can to an accurate prediction of sales. Falling short of your projection could spell cash-flow disaster. And surpassing your own predictions, which could be a pleasant testament to your strength in the market, could also result in real problems if you can't meet demand. At the height of their popularity, Cabbage Patch Dolls and Trivial Pursuit were able to keep customers waiting, but more often than not, if a business can't meet demand, it will lose many prospective customers.

After you make your calculations, it may be wise to seek more money than your needs analysis shows. Try to get enough cash on hand for a couple of extra months of operating expenses, plus enough to take care of any emergencies that may arise. Emergencies vary from business to business (e.g., in the restaurant business, a stove may catch fire and need replacing; in a sheet metal factory, a computer used to design a project may need to be replaced), but they do occur in almost any business. If you don't have enough money to meet your initial operating expenses, you may find yourself cutting corners that ultimately hurt your business. Don't cut yourself short. Find the amount of money you need to run your business right.

Once you have worked your way through Table 3-1, you will have a rough idea of how much money you'll need to run your business. Then it will be time to move on to Chapter 4, where we'll begin to look at sources of money.

PART 2
Sources of Money

4

Equity versus Debt Financing:

What's the Difference?

In the best of all possible worlds, the prospective small business owner would be able to finance the start-up of a business out of savings or other personal resources. Then it would be possible, in this utopia of entrepreneurship, to make the business grow by using cash flow to fund the growth. Loans? Who needs them? Selling off equity in the company to friends, relatives, and venture capitalists? Who needs the hassle of giving up total control?

Can You Bootstrap?

But this is not the best of all possible worlds. Oh sure, there are examples of young companies that have been bootstrapped, using only personal savings and profits to grow, but examples are few and far between. When Allen Turnbull and four partners incorporated Bike Virginia (which now is named Four Seasons Cycling), a bicycle touring company based in Williamsburg, Virginia, they made a conscious decision to fund the growth of the company out of sales. In 1981 the partners put up the money to get the business going. During the first 4 years of operation, they put about $15,000 of profits back into the company. By 1991 Turnbull hopes to hit $1 million in sales.[1]

[1] Jeffrey L. Seglin, "Growing by Their Bootstraps," *Venture,* July 1985, p. 48.

Clearly, Four Seasons Cycling is a textbook example of bootstrap financing: a low initial investment boosted by current revenues to produce slow but steady growth. In fact, Paul D. Reynolds, professor of sociology at the University of Minnesota, and his research associate Steven West found that the average firm started with only $71,000 in financing, with personal savings as the largest single source.[2]

It's not just smaller companies like Four Seasons Cycling that bootstrap their way to growth. Robert L. Daniels had built PSDI, a project management software manufacturer based in Cambridge, Massachusetts, to more than $20 million in sales 20 years after he began the company in 1968. Daniels admits, "in the beginning I was living off savings and paying off one employee with fumes,"[3] However, he was able to begin his company with no initial investment—simply an idea based on some public-domain research he had done while at Massachusetts Institute of Technology. To fuel his company's growth, Daniels leased his software, thus creating a regular cash flow on which he could draw to operate his business.

Bootstrapping successfully for growth most often requires that you let the company's sales dictate the growth. But a problem may arise when a small business owner finds that orders come in faster than expected, and does not have the capital necessary to manufacture the products to fill the orders. When no cash reserves have been built from sales or stock sold and no line of credit is available, a small business on the verge of making it big can fail. Needless to say, a lack of funds can also spell doom for a small business undercapitalized to the point of not even being able to get a product to market, or a product or service advertised.

Relying on Outside Sources of Money

No matter how self-reliant they are or wish to be, most small business owners find themselves in the position of having to find outside sources of money to ensure success. When your personal savings are tapped out, it might be time to turn to family and friends for loans or investments. Rest assured, you're in good company. Even companies that envision themselves as bootstrappers turn to outside cash.

When C. B. Vaughn founded CB Sports, Inc., a ski apparel manufac-

---

[2]"1984 Minnesota New Firm Study." Minneapolis: University of Minnesota at Minneapolis St. Paul, 1984.
[3]Seglin, op. *cit.*, p. 48.

turer based in Bennington, Vermont, he immediately tried to leverage his company's assets. "We're cross-collateralized upside down, sideways, and inside out," says Vaughn.[4] Vaughn invested $5000 of his own money in 1969 and began making ski apparel. He shopped around a business plan, looking for a $50,000 dollar loan later that year. Every year since, Vaughn has borrowed more money, basing each year's loan on sales during the preceding year. Its first year in business, CB Sports did $67,000 in sales; the next year Vaughn borrowed $100,000. The following year he borrowed $250,000. By 1985, sales had hit around $40 million and Vaughn had a $25 million revolving credit line, a $7 million letter of credit, and $6 to $7 million in long-term loans. Vaughn estimates that the borrowing needs of CB Sports are normally 50 to 60 percent of the next year's projected sales. (See Chapter 5 for a discussion of the types of loans banks offer.)

Frequently, small business owners must rely on both debt (money they borrow and are obligated to pay back) and equity (selling off ownership interest in a corporation) to fund their businesses. In 1969, when Paul Merriman started TSI, inc., a jewelry-making supplies mail-order business in Seattle, Washington, he did so with $10,000 and one product. The company that sold him the product was going under because it had been undercapitalized. Merriman saw an opportunity to market one of this company's products, which had been being used in the dental field to mold wax, in a new field. To get the seed money he needed, Merriman, who is now president of a family of market-timed mutual funds, made a small public offering of stock to friends; he raised $100,000. First-year sales were around $175,000. A few years later he was granted a Small Business Administration loan (see Chapters 9 to 12) for around $90,000. By 1976, sales were up to around $1.2 million. Seeing a need for more working capital, Merriman obtained a $250,000 line of credit, again through the SBA. By 1982, when Joanne Merriman had taken over running the company, TSI, inc., had paid off all its loans. In 1989, it had 22 employees, close to $2 million in sales, and healthy profits.

At some point in the life of many businesses, outside sources of income in the form of debt or equity become necessary for the survival of the company. Undercapitalization is one of the chief causes of failure of start-up businesses. When a company is not succeeding in moving its products or services to market and does not have enough capital to give the business the overhaul it needs, undercapitalization is fatal; but when a company fails because it doesn't have the capital to meet and keep up with demand, undercapitalization is not only fatal but heartbreaking.

[4]Ibid., p. 52.

How Can You Balance Debt and Equity?

How do you know how much equity to sell and how much debt to take on? First, in today's financial climate, clearly delineating the two isn't always a cut-and-dried matter. There are, of course, still basics that hold: e.g., common stock is equity and a bank loan is debt. But today there are options, preferred stock, warrants, and many other vehicles that can be used to finance a company—vehicles that are neither solely equity nor solely debt. To decide on the appropriate method of financing, small business owners must look at current financing trends in their line of business; they must consult their accountants or tax attorneys about the various tax ramifications; and they must sift through the maze of available options to find the blend of financing that fits their needs.

Many small business owners are reluctant to opt for equity financing because they fear they may be giving up too much control. But a bank also can potentially place a lot of restrictions on its borrowers—restrictions that ultimately could result in the bank's declaring the business in default on a loan. Debt can be used to great advantage, as in the case of CB Sports, as leverage to build a bigger and bigger company when sales are soaring. It can also be the kiss of death when business takes a downturn.

Seeking outside financing can, under the right circumstances be very beneficial to a company. For example, after a failed attempt to use an oil company's sales force to market his sophisticated oil separation equipment (designed to recycle used oil), George Sanborn needed capital to get his product to market. He found that Bain Capital Fund, a Boston venture capital fund, was willing to lend him expertise and capital in exchange for part of his company. "Ultimately one of their guys fell in love with what we were doing and is now vice-president of marketing," says Sanborn. Giving up a piece of the pie can sometimes result in a good business relationship.[5]

When a company declares bankruptcy and sells off its assets, the first people to get paid are the secured creditors. After they have all been paid off, unsecured creditors get their share of the spoils. Stockholders are last in line for repayment. If the company goes out of business, their investment stands a good chance of going down the tubes. So it is often in their best interest to do everything in their power to help the business stay afloat.

When a business begins to show signs of failure, a creditor may decide to call a loan or threaten to take over the business. A less-than-sympathetic banker, for instance, may be tempted to get the bank's money

---

[5]Jeffrey L. Seglin, "Bain Practices Its Teamwork," *Venture*, May 1986, p. 136.

out of a business when it shows signs of failing, in order to recover most of the outstanding principal on the loan. If the bank waits too long, the reasoning might go, the business may reach a point where the possibility of retrieving any of the money owed to the bank is remote.

People with money who are looking to finance a start-up or growing company may take a great risk, but the rewards of buying stock in a fledgling company as opposed to lending money to the company can be large, if the company succeeds. Long before he became President, George Bush learned just such a lesson. In 1970 a friend suggested that Bush invest $26,000 in stock of Fidelity Printing Company, a Houston-based printer of financial legal documents. His reward? $496,000 in 1973, a return of 1900 percent.[6]

There are no set rules about how much debt capital a business should have versus its equity capital. If there are not a lot of assets to use as collateral, some bankers want small business owners to be able to match the bank dollar for dollar in financing the company. More often than not, a banker will also require a small business borrower to sign a personal guaranty on a loan. Many small business owners, of course, would prefer not to risk their personal assets, but bankers may insist; personal guaranties show that small business owners are willing to back the company with their own money should tough times prevail.

Some small business owners may decide to go in search of equity capital by selling stock to raise the capital needed to make their companies grow. This tactic may enable them to raise the money they need without placing their homes and other personal assets in jeopardy. The investors take the risk. But like George Bush, they also have a chance at a big return on investment.

There are advantages and disadvantages to both equity financing and debt financing. Among the drawbacks to debt financing are the stringent repayment schedule. Among the most commonly stated drawbacks to equity financing is that you do indeed give up some of your 100 percent ownership.

Equity capital needn't be raised from venture capital firms or other similar sources. Small business owners can opt to take the route Paul Merriman took when he was starting TSI, inc., namely, selling stock to a small circle of friends. Friends are more likely to stick by a company when it is facing a tough time than are venture capital firms. Of course the friendship may suffer, but friends are more likely to be understanding than strangers.

This is not to suggest that bank loans are inappropriate for small business owners who are seeking to finance the start-up and growth of their

[6]Greg Anrig, Jr., "The President and His Money," *Money*, June 1989, p. 89.

companies. Nothing could be further from the truth. In fact, since one of the reasons many business owners open up shop in the first place is to be able to call their own shots, it is often best to acquire as much nonequity capital as possible when starting out. The small business owner can pull together as much seed money as possible from personal savings and, with business plan in hand, approach a bank about a loan. Small business owners should entertain a variety of financing options before deciding on the one that best suits their needs.

Fortunately for the small business owner, financing for a start-up most often involves fairly traditional sources of financing. The chapters that follow will explore these sources, most of which—such as commercial banks, commercial finance companies, and life insurance companies—involve debt financing but also include equity financing like venture capital.

5

To Bank or Not to Bank:

Using Banks as Sources of Money

Though 83 percent of respondents to a survey of banks conducted by the Bank Administration Institute, a trade group based in Rolling Meadows, Illinois, said that they "aggressively pursue the small business segment of the market," few young companies will tell you that bankers are begging them to take loans.[1] In fact, the old cliché that banks are willing to lend you money when you least need it is often all too true. That said—short of being able to bankroll your business out of the cash flow provided from sales, which is becoming increasingly difficult for companies with any growth potential—banks are nevertheless perhaps one of the most common sources of funds that small businesses turn to when they need cash.

Establish a Banking Relationship Early

A simple trick may be to borrow before you need the cash. Joan Schneider, president of Schneider & Associates, Inc., a public relations firm in Brighton, Massachusetts, decided to take out a $50,000 line of

[1]Deborah L. Colletti, Marjolijn van der Velde, and Jeffrey L. Seglin, *Small Business Banking: A Guide to Marketing and Profits*. Rolling Meadows, Ill.: Bank Administration Institute, 1987, p. 1.

credit (a recurring source of loans up to an agreed-upon amount and at a set interest rate) in 1987 from the Boston Trade Bank, even though her company, with revenues of $1.5 million, was profitable and had no immediate need for the loan. "Everyone always told me that it's better to get a line of credit when things look good than when they look bad," she reasoned.[2]

Schneider, like many other small business owners, approached the bank sensibly. Perhaps the best way to ensure that a bank will be there for you when you need it is to establish a solid working relationship long before you need a bundle of cash. The business owner should approach the bank well-prepared to show that he or she is really capable of making the business sing and that repaying a loan will be no problem. The approach is simple:

- Secure a small loan before you really need it, to familiarize the banker with your business and to build a credit history.

- Approach the banker equipped with balance sheets, year-end statements, cash-flow projections, and a business plan (which are discussed in Chapter 14).

- For added credibility, consider hiring a well-known accounting firm to do your financials.

- Try to build a business relationship with a loan officer at the bank.

Schneider drew $30,000 as a short-term loan to cover cash flow after she purchased some computer equipment for her company. "I think that once you establish the line of credit you should take it for a drive around the block to see how it's going to work," says Schneider, "so if you need it at a critical time, there are no surprises."[3] Schneider paid the loan back in 30 days. "My loan officer was happy I paid it back, and I was happy he had given it to me."

Courting a Banker

Simply having your company accounts at a bank will not ensure that the bank will award you a loan. The bank wants to know that the prospective borrower is a good risk, particularly if it is a borrower who is just starting a new business.

John Marston, cofounder of Boston Trade Bank, which specializes in

---

[2]Jeffrey L. Seglin, "Court a Banker Now, Borrow Money Later," *Venture*, August 1988, pp. 65–67.

[3]Colletti, van der Velde, and Seglin, op. cit., pp. 9, 1.

lending to small and midsize companies, spends time "scoping out" a prospective borrower's situation even before the two parties sit down to talk. The prospective borrower is asked to send in financial statements and projections, product or service information, and résumés and personal net-worth statements for its principals. If, on the basis of these materials, the business doesn't measure up, Marston or one of the bank's lending officers will suggest what it can do to increase its chances of becoming a good loan candidate. If such prospects later reapproach the bank, the loan officer is in a position to judge whether or not they followed the advice. "Their ability to change and become serious about being successful is one of the criteria we use," says Marston.[4]

If you are going to approach a bank for a loan, keep in mind that you may have to do some courting before you achieve your goal. Particularly when interest rates are high, the economy is not strong, or there is not much competition among banks in your market, loans can become harder to get. But just how far you should go in courting a banker is open to question. It's important to keep a prospective lender abreast of your financial situation, but sending reams of financial statements to a prospective banker is not necessarily a good idea. "Monthly financial statements [from prospective borrowers] would drive me a little bit nuts," says Marston.[5] Probably the best tactic is to seek your prospective lender's advice, pay heed to that advice, and then approach the bank again if your first attempts at borrowing were unsuccessful.

The Five C's of Credit

Traditionally banks use "the *five C's of credit* when they evaluate loan applications. The five C's are the five criteria banks look for in a borrower, as follows:

1. *Character.* While character is difficult to quantify, bankers want to deal with people whom they consider to have integrity and honesty. Lenders look at prospective borrowers' credit histories and check their references to get a read on their characters. They may also do a credit check on borrowers.

2. *Capacity.* After evaluating assets and liabilities, lenders measure the prospective borrower's capacity to repay a loan. With small businesses, lenders look at financial statements—income (profit and loss) statements and balance sheets—and historical trends in similar

[4]Seglin, op. cit., p. 68.
[5]Ibid., p. 66.

businesses in an attempt to judge the borrower's ability to repay the loan. They also study the borrower's personal financial statement. (Figure 5-1 shows a typical personal financial statement.)

PERSONAL FINANCIAL STATEMENT
(CONFIDENTIAL)

NAME_____   EMPLOYMENT_____

RESIDENCE
ADDRESS_____   POSITION_____

                                          BUSINESS
CITY, STATE, & ZIP_____   ADDRESS_____

The following is submitted for the purpose of procuring, establishing and maintaining credit with you in behalf of the undersigned or persons, firms or corporations in whose behalf the undersigned may either severally or jointly with others execute a guaranty in your favor. The undersigned warrants that this financial statement is true and correct and that you may

OF_____   consider this statement as continuing to be true and correct until a written notice of a change is given to you by the undersigned.

Date:_____   Signed:_____

ASSETS		LIABILITIES & NET WORTH	
1. Cash (on hand and in banks) (see schedule 1)		13. Notes Payable, Banks, Unsecured (see schedule 1)	
2. U. S. Government and Agency Securities (see schedule 2)		14. Notes Payable, Banks, Secured (see schedule 1)	
3. Marketable Securities (see schedule 2)		15. Notes Payable, Others (see schedule 1)	
4. Non-Marketable Securities (see schedule 3)		16. Loans Against Life Insurance (see schedule 4)	
5. Notes Receivable—Itemize		17. Accounts and Bills Payable (see schedule 7)	
6. Cash Value—Life Insurance (do not deduct loan) (see schedule 4)		18. Real Estate Mortgages Payable (see schedule 5)	
7. Real Estate in Own Name (see schedule 5)		19. Income Taxes Due	
8. Partial Interests in Real Estate—Net Equity Values (see schedule 6)		20. Other Liabilities—Itemize	
9. Automobiles			
10. Furniture and Personal Property			
11. Other Assets—Itemize			
		21. Total Liabilities	
		22. Net Worth (Total Assets Less Total Liabilities)	
12. TOTAL ASSETS		23. Total Liabilities and Net Worth	

SOURCES OF ANNUAL INCOME				
INCOME FROM ALIMONY, SEPARATE MAINTENANCE OR CHILD SUPPORT NEED NOT BE REVEALED IF YOU DO NOT CHOOSE TO RELY ON IT IN CONNECTION WITH THIS FINANCIAL STATEMENT.		GENERAL INFORMATION		
Salary		Are you a partner, stockholder, or officer in any other business venture?		
Commissions and Bonuses		If so, what		
Dividends				
Real Estate Income				
Other Income—Itemize		Do you have a will?		
TOTAL ANNUAL INCOME		Name of Executor		
CONTINGENT LIABILITIES		CASUALTY INSURANCE COVERAGE		
As Endorser, Guarantor or Co-Maker		Homeowners	Company	Amount
On Leases or Contracts		Automobile		
Legal Claims		Professional Liability		
Income Tax Claims		Are you, or have you ever been defendant in any legal actions, suits, or bankruptcy?		
Other—Itemize		Explain		

FORM L158— 11/77   (Complete Schedules on Reverse Side)

Figure 5-1. Sample personal financial statement. *(Source: Loren Gary, Commercial Loan Forms Handbook. Rolling Meadows, Ill.: Bank Administration Institute, Andover Parris Publishing Group, 1989.)*

SUPPLEMENTARY SCHEDULES

SCHEDULE 1 — BANKING RELATIONSHIPS

Name of Bank	Location	Checking Balances	Savings Balances	Loan Balance	Terms or Maturity	Collateral	High Credit

SCHEDULE 2 — SECURITIES (GOV'T. AND MARKETABLE)

No. Shares or Face Value	DESCRIPTION	Cost	Market Value	Source of Valuation	Registered in Name of	Is Stock Pledged?

SCHEDULE 3 — NON-MARKETABLE SECURITIES

DESCRIPTION	No. Shares Owned	No. Shares Outstanding	Book Value Per Share	Financial Statement Date	Total Value	Registered in Name of

SCHEDULE 4 — LIFE INSURANCE COVERAGE

Face Value	Insurance Co.	Owner of Policy	Name of Beneficiary	Total C.S.V.	Policy Loans	Yearly Premium	Is Policy Assigned?

SCHEDULE 5 — REAL ESTATE IN OWN NAME

Description Including Location or Address	Dimensions or # Acres	Improvements	Cost	Date Acquired	Market Value	Mortgage Balance	Terms or Maturity	Mortgage Holder

SCHEDULE 6 — PARTIAL INTERESTS IN REAL ESTATE — NET EQUITY VALUES

Description Including Location or Address	Improvements	% of Ownership	Total Cost	Date Acquired	Market Value	Mortgage Balance	Terms or Maturity	Value of Equity

SCHEDULE 7 — FINANCE COMPANIES, SAVINGS & LOAN ASSOCIATIONS, STORES, AND INDIVIDUALS FROM WHOM CREDIT HAS BEEN OBTAINED.

NAME	ADDRESS	High Credit	Current Balance	Monthly Payments	Collateral

Figure 5-1. (Continued)

3. *Collateral.* The collateral, or security put up for a loan, is usually something that could be sold to pay off the loan if necessary. When a borrower secures a loan, the collateral is assigned to the lender in the event of a default. An unsecured loan does not require any collateral

and usually has a higher interest rate, since the lender takes a bigger risk of not recouping any money in the event of a default.

4. *Capital.*   In a borrowing situation, capital is typically reflected by the net worth of the borrower—the amount by which his or her assets exceeds liabilities. This gives the lender an indication of how much cash the borrower has access to for repayment of the loan. This information is garnered from the financial statements the borrower provides the bank.

5. *Conditions.*   The "conditions" criterion is the current economic climate. Lenders judge the effect current economic conditions will have on the borrowers' ability to repay the loan.

Find the Right Bank

When you begin shopping for a bank, you will likely see quickly which banks are prone to do business with start-up operations and small businesses, and which are not. Waste no time being intimidated by a banker who condescends to you. You have a lot at stake in starting or owning your own business. If a banker, or for that matter any other professional who provides a service, belittles your efforts and abilities, think long and hard about whether you want to be giving him or her your business. Your company is not General Motors, but your fees and loan payments do earn you the right to be treated with respect. For years, a sole proprietor of a small business in the Northeast allowed his accountant to taunt him, to put down his efforts, and to suggest that the accountant was much more qualified to run the business than the sole proprietor. Finally, after much aggravation, the sole proprietor found a new accountant who was totally supportive of his business and never condescended.

The banking relationship is far too important to the survival of your business to make it worth your while to waste time wooing an uncooperative banker. Get recommendations from the professionals with whom you do business—accountants, lawyers, vendors—about good bank prospects. Some banks cater to start-ups or young businesses. Seek them out.

Find the Right Loan Officer

Ultimately, your relationship with your loan officer will be far more important than your relationship with the bank itself. A loan officer who knows your company and will go to bat for it can be one of your business's biggest assets. Doug Pearson, president of NSS Corp., a company based in Bedford, New Hampshire, that sells hardware and software to banks, found out how important an ally his loan officer had been when the loan officer was transferred and Pearson had to face a new one. In 1984, Pearson had established a $30,000 line of credit. His company had earned $80,000 on $500,000 in sales that year. After he established his line of credit, Pearson continued to provide the banker with financial statements and 1-year operating plans. Pearson needed to increase the line and he thought he had a commitment from the bank to do so, but the bank "kind of reneged," he says, when the NSS account was given to a different loan officer.[6] Pearson switched banks based on a recommendation of his financial adviser.

Sometimes the switching of a loan officer can be even less pleasant. Such was the case with Mercury Business Services Inc., a Boston-based package delivery company that serves as a middleman between upscale business clients and overnight shipping agencies. Peter Salisbury, president of Mercury Business Services, got the company's first line of credit in 1985. "Our initial contract with the bank was phenomenal," he says. "It all rests with the loan officer you get. We got a loan officer who came into our office and was able to size us up."[7] Mercury had sales of $231,000 in 1984 and established the 1985 line of credit for $15,000. Salisbury had set up the loan not because he was in need of cash, but because he thought it was important to develop a good borrowing relationship with a bank. But then the loan officer left the bank.

The account was given to a loan officer whom Salisbury describes as "arrogant." When Salisbury wanted to increase the line in 1986, he says, "they wanted all sorts of additional documentation that they didn't require before. And the new loan officer was pretty tacky. We got a knock on our door from a friend of his who was a financial planner. We told the bank to go scratch."[8] Mercury Business Services found a new bank.

Large banks are likely to move their loan officers around quite a bit, which means that the loan officer with whom you build a relationship may not be at the same branch or in the same position at the bank when you need him or her the most. "What the small business needs is a relationship with a bank," Marston says. "The turnover at many of the large banks flies in the face of that."

One of the key things you want to investigate when you're scoping out a good loan officer is how much power he or she has to make loan approvals. John Marston suggests that in some large banks loan officers

[6]Ibid., p. 68.
[7]Ibid., p. 66.
[8]Ibid.

may not have the authority to extend credit when the small business owner needs it.

Marston further suggests that prospective borrowers use a subtle approach to finding out how a loan officer fits into the bank's hierarchy. Ask simple questions about how the loan process will work when the time comes. "You can't go up and say, 'Listen, if you don't have the authority, then I want to talk to someone who does,'" he says. "But you can express an interest in meeting the person who makes decisions. It's very delicate to find out the structure, but it's in the entrepreneur's best interest."[9]

At the Small Business Banking Conference sponsored by the Bank Administration Institute (BAI) in the fall of 1986, small business owners expressed their concerns about dealing with bankers.[10] Among these were:

- Since small business owners are busy running their businesses, they need bankers who are responsive to their needs and will help them function in their roles as business owners. They need advice in the financial area as well as tips on how to make better, quicker financial decisions.

- Banks should educate small business owners about the products and services a bank offers and how the small business owner might be able to use them in his or her own situation.

- Small businesses need money to run their companies. They need the banks to provide them with a source of capital.

- Small business owners want banks to try to understand their business—what their goals are and how they want to achieve them. Bankers should use that understanding to help the small business owner function more efficiently.

While the above is obviously a wish list for small business owners, you should try to find a banker who will at least attempt to work with you to provide you with these types of service.

Ask questions. Get to know the loan officer and judge whether or not he or she is the type of person who is going to help you make your business succeed. Shopping around may enable you to save an eighth of a percentage point on a loan, but this saving will mean very little if you do not have a loan officer who is willing to go to bat for you. You need to

[9]Ibid., p. 68.
[10]Colletti, van der Velde, and Seglin, op. cit., pp. 8–9.

look for the bank that gives you the best rates on financing *and* the best people with whom to do business.

If Possible, Shop Around

Bankers are indeed increasingly in the market to lend to small businesses. According to the BAI survey mentioned at the beginning of this chapter, bankers see lending to small businesses as a method to increase deposit growth, expand relationships and cross-sell products and services, increase loan growth, improve bank profitability, and increase fee income.[11] Find the right banker and you could find a real ally.

Shop around. Check out the rates banks offer. Find out which banks cater to your type of business. Find out how good they are at giving advice to small businesses. And pay particular attention to the rapport you have with each bank's loan officer. Is he or she someone you want on your team?

Interest rates can vary from borrower to borrower. Banks may offer more attractive interest rates to low-risk borrowers who have collateral to secure a loan. But be aware that secured loans will often have a higher interest rate than unsecured loans (those for which collateral is not pledged). The reasons for this are that unsecured loans take up less administration and personnel time and that unsecured loans are usually extended for shorter periods of time than secured loans. Obviously, unsecured loans will be appealing to small business borrowers if these borrowers can get attractive interest rates.

Sometimes you'll have fewer bank offerings to choose from than other times. As mentioned earlier, when there is little competition among banks, and when interest rates are high and the economy is not strong, the chances of banks lining up to woo you for your business are unlikely. In such times, your relationship with a loan officer is of particularly crucial importance. When the funds the bank doles out are tight, you want someone on your side who will fight for you and who has the power to get you the capital you need.

On the other hand, when interest rates are low, the economy is strong, and there are a lot of competitive banks in your market, you may find a wide variety of banks which will be glad to do business with you. Try to make sure that the bank giving you the best financial offer really plans on backing it up with advice and consistent support. There's no way to tell for sure what your future will hold, but you can check out

[11]Ibid., p. 1.

a bank by talking with other business owners or financial professionals (e.g., accountants, insurance agents, lawyers) who have worked with the bank in the past. Banks get a reputation for both the positive and the negative ways they treat customers.

Advantages and Disadvantages of Bank Loans

Borrowing from a bank has advantages, and it also has disadvantages. Obviously, being beholden to another party for money when you are trying to run a business always presents something of a disadvantage. But realistically, there are times when you are simply in the position of needing to have ready access to cash, to make your business work. When you are choosing a bank to approach for a loan, consider the advantages and disadvantages described below.

Advantages

Among the advantages of borrowing from a bank are the following:

1. Banks are usually the cheapest sources of private funds available. Banks are the only sources of funds that can borrow at discount rate from the Federal Reserve Bank. Other sources of funds must sell bonds, stocks, or limited partnerships to raise money to invest or loan. None have the advantage of Federal Reserve rates.

2. By borrowing money from a bank and paying it back, you are building one of the best credit histories you can have. Vendors and future lenders will look favorably upon this. A good credit history can present you as a creditworthy customer, giving prospective business associates the sense that you meet your financial obligations.

3. With a bank, you can pick and choose from more types of loans (and only get them with the bank's approval, of course) than with any other source of funds.

4. You can take advantage of the many services that banks often offer to small businesses, including:

   Financial and managerial advice
   Lockboxes (for remittance collection)
   Check clearance
   Customer credit reference checks

Payroll accounting services
Personal investment advice
Trust and estate services

5. Once a bank lends you money, you can count on it to do everything possible to make sure you don't lose your shirt.

6. There are lots of sources of information on which banks lend to which types of business, which banks are most solvent, and which banks have the best rates in town.

7. Banks have the capability of matching your needs with innovative loan offerings.

Disadvantages

Among the disadvantages of banks are the following:

1. They will require you to fill out more paperwork that most other sources of funds. They might want projected cash flows, annual budgets, projected budgets, monthly financial statements, and a slew of additional information that other sources might not request in such volume.

2. Banks are traditionally conservative (although many banks in recent times have made questionable loans, resulting in shaky or defaulted banks) and will not take risks on unproven track records.

3. Banks may lend you the money, but perhaps only with very restrictive terms. You might, for example, find yourself in technical default on your loan if you did not maintain very clearly defined financial ratios.

4. Banks will try to influence your business decisions if they believe their money is at risk.

5. You might find your loan officers passing through a revolving door, particularly if the bank is large and has many branches. This makes it difficult to build up a solid, long-lasting relationship with a banker you trust and with whom you enjoy working.

6. Because your bank will not want you to lose your shirt, its officers will watch you very closely. The bank will have a record of every check you write, plus you will be asked to show annual, semiannual, quarterly, or monthly income (profit and loss) statements. When you borrow from a bank, you'll typically have someone looking over your shoulder as you are trying to do business.

Types of Bank Loans

Before you approach a bank for money, it's a good idea to have an idea of the types of loans a loan officer might offer you. Going to a bank to talk about a loan has nothing in common with going to an Italian bakery in the North End of Boston and choosing a delectable treat. In the bakery, it's fine to let spontaneity be your guide. In the bank, you want to know ahead of time what you're looking for or at least what your options may be.

Many of the different types of bank loans available are described below. Some are classified by the length of time for which they are offered; others by the type of collateral you might have to put up. The list is not exhaustive. An innovative loan officer can come up with different types of financing to serve a business's needs. For example, loan officers can arrange staggered payment schedules to allow a business to pay off more of a loan in peak sales months and less in the off-season when it is trying to use capital to build inventory. But this list should give you an idea of what's on the menu of most banks offering commercial (business) financing.

Term Loans

There are three basic types of *term loans,* as follows.

1. *Short-term loans.* The term for a short-term loan typically runs from 30 to 180 days, and certainly no longer than 1 year. This is the easiest type of term loan to get, one reason being that banks often figure it is unlikely a borrower would go under in less than 30 days. The loans are typically made to cover temporary or seasonal needs. Interest is paid on the outstanding principal balance, while you are using the loan proceeds. The repayment takes the form of one lump sum, due when the term is reached. The repayment includes principal. Most short-term notes (loans) can be renewed. If the note is renewed, the borrower may pay only interest on the due date, deferring payment of any principal until the new due date arrives.

It would be unwise to use a short-term loan to cover long-term needs, since it might be difficult to generate the cash necessary to pay off the loan when it is due. There are, however, relatively few restrictions on what short-term funds can be used for and, as long as the business owner is scrupulous about providing requested financial statements, the bank will generally not look over the business's shoulder to make sure everything is going according to plan after a short-term loan is made.

Short-term loans are usually unsecured loans that do not require collateral. The bank may require that you, as principal of the business, provide a personal guaranty that covers the bank in case of default. (See Figure 5-2.) You will also need to provide a business financial statement and perhaps a personal financial statement. (See Figure 5-1.)

Many business owners will take out a short-term loan for the same reason that Joan Schneider of Schneider & Associates did, as described above in this chapter. Taking out a short-term loan is an excellent and fairly easy way to establish a relationship with a bank and, just as important, a good credit rating.

2. *Intermediate-term loans.* Intermediate-term loans typically run from 3 to 5 years. These loans are a little harder to get since the bank must take a bigger risk that you'll be around in 3 to 5 years to pay off the loan. You will have to prepare a complete loan package for an intermediate-term loan. (See Chapter 14 for information on preparation of a loan package.)

While banks would like to see intermediate-term loans used to purchase long-term assets that could be used as collateral, they will sometimes, if necessary, provide these loans for other needs as well, including acquisitions, debt retirement (paying off other loans or obligations), and working capital.

Depending on the relationship you have with the bank and the credit standing you've developed, intermediate-term loans may be secured or unsecured. Banks can add restrictive clauses to the loan agreement which give them the right to approve or disapprove major business decisions you make.

3. *Long-term loans.* The term for a long-term loan is typically 5 years or longer. Banks are not crazy about giving long-term loans to a small business, unless they are secured by real estate or building construction.

Typically, a bank making a long-term loan for real estate will want to hold the first mortgage on the property. It might also want other collateral offered to secure the loan, such as accounts receivable (money your business is owed for goods or services) or personal assets. Often the value of the collateral you put up for the long-term loan will have to be greater than the loan you receive. Long-term loans usually have monthly repayment schedules, calling for you to pay interest plus a portion of the principal.

When you get a long-term loan, you will usually be assigned a loan officer who will follow your business, making sure things are running smoothly. You will be required to provide this loan officer with regular

Guaranty

TO: METROPOLITAN NATIONAL BANK

Date _____, 19___

Gentlemen:

To induce you to purchase or otherwise acquire from _____ (hereinafter called "Debtor") accounts receivable, conditional sale or lease agreements, chattel mortgages, drafts, notes, bills, acceptances, trust receipts, contracts or other obligations or choses-in-action (herein collectively called "receivables"), or to advance moneys or extend credit to the Debtor thereon, or to factor the sales or finance the accounts of the Debtor (either according to any present or future existing agreement or according to any changes in any such agreement or on any other terms and arrangements from time to time agreed upon with the Debtor, hereby consenting to and waiving notice of any and all such agreements, terms and arrangements and changes thereof) or to otherwise directly or indirectly advance money to or give or extend faith and credit to the Debtor, or otherwise assist the Debtor in financing its business or sales, (without obligating you to do any of the foregoing, we, the undersigned, for value received, do hereby jointly and severally unconditionally guarantee to you and your assigns the prompt payment in full at maturity and all times thereafter (waiving notice of non-payment) of any and all indebtedness, obligations and liabilities of every kind or nature (both principal and interest) now or at any time hereafter owing to you by the Debtor, and of any and all receivables heretofore and hereafter acquired by you from said Debtor or in respect of which the Debtor has or may become in any way liable, and the prompt, full and faithful performance and discharge by the Debtor of each and every the terms, conditions, agreements, representations, warranties, guaranties and provisions on the part of the Debtor contained in any such agreement or arrangement or in any modification or addenda thereto or substitution thereof, or contained in any schedule or other instrument heretofore or hereafter given by or on behalf of said Debtor in connection with the sale or assignment of any such receivables to you, or contained in any other agreements, undertakings or obligations of the Debtor with or to you, of any kind or nature, and we also hereby jointly and severally agree on demand to reimburse you and your assigns for all expenses, collection charges, court costs and attorney's fees incurred in endeavoring to collect or enforce any of the foregoing against the Debtor and/or undersigned or any other person or concern liable thereon; for all of which, with interest at the highest lawful contract rate after due until paid, we hereby jointly and severally agree to be directly, unconditionally and primarily liable jointly and severally with the Debtor, and agree that the same may be recovered in the same or separate actions brought to recover the principal indebtedness.

Notice of acceptance of this guaranty, the giving or extension of credit to the Debtor, the purchase or acquisition of receivables, or the advancement of money or credit thereon, and presentment, demand, notices of default, non-payment or partial payments and protest, notice of protest and all other notices or formalities to which the Debtor might otherwise be entitled, prosecution of collection or remedies against the Debtor or against the makers, endorsers, or other person liable on any such receivables or against any security or collateral thereto appertaining, are hereby waived. The undersigned also waive notice of and consents to the granting of indulgence or extension of time payment, the taking and releasing of security in respect of any said receivables, agreements, obligations, indebtedness or liabilities so guaranteed hereunder, or your accepting partial payments thereon or your settling, compromising or compounding any of the same in such manner and at such times as you may deem advisable, without in any way impairing or affecting our liability for the full amount thereof; and you shall not be required to prosecute collection, enforcement or other remedies against the Debtor or against any person liable on any said receivables, agreements, obligations, indebtedness or liabilities so guaranteed, or to enforce or resort to any security, liens, collateral or other rights or remedies thereto appertaining, before calling on us for payment; nor shall our liability in any way be released or affected by reason of any failure or delay on your part so to do.

This guaranty is absolute, unconditional and continuing and payment of the sums for which the undersigned become liable shall be made to you at your office from time to time on demand as the same become or are declared due, notwithstanding that you hold reserves, credits, collateral or security against which you may be entitled to resort for payment, and one or more and successive or concurrent actions may be brought hereon against the undersigned jointly and severally, either in the same action in which the Debtor is sued or in separate actions, as often as deemed advisable. We expressly waive and bar ourselves from any right to set-off, recoup or counterclaim any claim or demand against said Debtor, or against any other person or concern liable on said receivables, and, as further security to you, any and all debts or liabilities now or hereafter owing to us by the Debtor or by such other person or concern are hereby subordinated to your claims and are hereby assigned to you.

Each guarantor shall continue liable hereunder until you actually receive written notice from him by registered mail terminating the same as to him; but the giving of such notice shall not terminate this guaranty as to any other guarantor, nor relieve the one giving such notice from liability as to any debt, undertaking or liability incurred or undertaken prior to such time. The death of any of the guarantors shall not terminate this guaranty as to his estate or as to the surviving guarantors, but the same shall continue in full force and effect until notice of termination of this guaranty is given and received as hereinbefore provided and all of said indebtedness, liabilities or obligations created or assumed are fully paid.

In case bankruptcy or insolvency proceedings, or proceedings for reorganization, or for the appointment of a receiver, trustee or custodian for the Debtor or over its property or any substantial portion thereof, be instituted by or against the Debtor, or if the Debtor becomes insolvent or makes an assignment for the benefit of creditors or attempts to effect a composition with creditors, or encumber or dispose of all or a substantial portion of its property, or if the Debtor defaults in the payment or repurchase of any of such receivables or indebtedness as the same falls due, or fails promptly to make good any default in respect of any undertaking, then the liability of the undersigned hereunder shall at your option and without notice become immediately fixed and be enforceable for the full amount thereof, whether then due or not, the same as though all said receivables, debts and liabilities had become past due.

This guaranty shall inure to the benefit of yourself, your successors and assigns. It shall be binding jointly and severally on the undersigned, their heirs, representatives and assigns, regardless of the number of persons signing as guarantors or the turn or order of their signing.

This instrument shall be governed as to validity, interpretation, effect and in all other respects by the laws and decisions of the States of _____, unless this instrument is delivered to your office in the City of _____ , _____, in which event the laws and decisions of the State of _____ shall govern.

_____ (SEAL)

_____ (SEAL)

Figure 5-2. Sample personal guaranty. *(Source: Loren Gary, Commercial Loan Forms Handbook. Rolling Meadows, Ill.: Bank Administration Institute, Andover Parris Publishing Group, 1989.)*

financial statements, as stipulated in the loan agreement. The loan agreement will contain whatever restrictions the bank deems necessary to enable it to loan the money to you. If the restrictions are particularly complex, you will want to have an attorney with you at the closing. Certainly you will want to read the entire loan agreement and consult with your attorney before signing it. Failure to live up to any of the provisions of the loan agreement may result in the bank finding you in default on your loan, in which case it may have the legal right to take possession of any assets you pledged as collateral.

Before granting a term loan, a bank will examine a business's financial statements to determine its financial position. Payments must be stipulated and agreed upon; usually, they will be on a monthly, quarterly, semiannually, or annual payment basis.

Unsecured Loans

When a bank makes an *unsecured loan,* it doesn't require you to put up any collateral. The bank has determined that your creditworthiness is good. This testament to your creditworthiness is usually a boon to businesses that work with a number of vendors. It is a statement by the bank that your business can be trusted.

Banks will usually require that the borrower present a personal guaranty for an unsecured loan (see Figure 5-2). In effect, such a guaranty states that should your business default, the guarantor's personal assets will be used to pay the loan off. The amount of the loan and the interest rates will generally reflect the borrower's business performance and the net worth of the guarantor. If the amount offered is too low to suit the business's needs, it may have to opt for a secured loan instead. Banks most typically make unsecured loans for short-term needs, up to a year in duration. They will generally not offer unsecured loans for large amounts.

Some common types of unsecured loans are:

- *Simple commercial loans.* These are usually short-term loans offered for terms of 30 to 180 days. The business applying for a simple commercial loan usually provides the bank with a financial statement. The loan is paid off out of cash flow and may be used for a variety of short-term needs, including short-term personal, inventory, or seasonal uses.

- *Installment loans.* Large banks generally make installment loans to businesses for a variety of needs. Payments are usually monthly, and provision is usually made for refinancing.

■ *Lines of credit.*   A line of credit is set up between a bank and a business to provide the business with a recurring source of loans up to an
agreed-upon amount. Lines of credit are usually unsecured and are
in force for an agreed-upon amount of time, usually a year.

Lines of credit are used by businesses that have seasonal needs for
cash. NSS Corp., the computer and software company discussed
above in this chapter, has $1.9 million in lines of credit available to it.
One reason for this amount is that IBM required NSS to have at least
a $1 million line of credit when NSS began remarketing IBM equip-
ment in 1985. NSS's case is a great example of why it's good to have a
solid relationship with a loan officer. When the company overdrew its
line by $450,000 in early 1988, the loan officer called and worked it
out with the company. "That just tells you what kind of relationship
we have with these guys. They're close enough to know we're not per-
fect," says company president Doug Pearson.[12] (*A little tip:* No matter
how close you are to your loan officer, it's never wise to overdraw
your line of credit.)

■ *Character loans.*   Banks usually offer character loans as unsecured
loans for personal needs, not for business needs.

Secured Loans

Borrowers must pledge assets as collateral for a *secured loan.* Often, to
ensure that they are repaid, banks will require a business to put up collateral that is worth more than the loan being granted. Borrowers can
often negotiate with banks about the exact amount of collateral they
must put up for a loan. It is obviously in the borrower's best interest to
put up as few personal assets as possible.

In some cases you might be able to find a vendor from whom you
plan to buy a significant asset who will agree to sign as a guarantor on a
loan. The vendor might initially be hesitant, but if your credit history is
solid, if the vendor really wants to make the sale, and if the bank won't
offer the loan without a guarantor, the vendor may become convinced
that signing as guarantor is a good way to close the sale.

Cosigner Loans.   A *cosigner* (or "comaker") who signs a loan along
with the borrower becomes equally responsible in the event of default
on the loan. Banks look favorably upon cosigners who are creditworthy.
Borrowers who are not able to secure a loan on their own sometimes
find cosigner loans a viable route. Many banks are not thrilled about the

---

[12]Seglin, op cit., p. 68.

idea of having to chase down a cosigner should the loan be defaulted on, but nevertheless cosigner loans can be an option for the starting business owner.

Equipment and Other Fixed-Asset Loans. A small business owner can use *equipment as security* (collateral) for a loan. Another possibility is to buy equipment on an installment basis, financed either through a bank or directly by the company that is selling the equipment.

Large items like buildings, equipment, and improvements in existing structures are often financed by fixed-asset loans. The fixed assets are used as collateral on the loans. The term of such a loan is usually for more than 1 year.

Accounts Receivable Financing. *Accounts receivable financing* is secured financing in which the business puts up its accounts receivable as collateral on a loan. The bank evaluates the accounts receivables, judges which current receivables are most likely to come in (receivables over 90 days old are not considered likely to be collected), and will usually agree to lend the business 70 to 80 percent of the value of those accounts.

One obvious advantage of accounts receivable financing is that it enables you to get your hands on money owed to you by customers, and to put it to use in running your business. You do not have to borrow against all your receivables, but can simply borrow as much as you need.

There are two methods of accounts receivable financing, as follows.

- *Notification.* The customer is notified that the bank is financing the receivables and he or she should pay the bank directly.

- *Nonnotification.* The customer pays the business, and the business pays the bank the pledged accounts receivable.

Because some businesses do not like their customers to know they have financed accounts receivables, they prefer to use the non-notification method. However, certain states require that you notify customers that you have financed their accounts receivable.

If the receivables you have pledged are not paid on time, the bank will require that your business pay the amount pledged. Obviously, you will then have to make an extra effort to collect the accounts receivable, in order to get your money.

Banks charge interest on accounts receivable for the time between the date of the loan and the date of collection of the accounts receivable. There is also usually a service fee, based on a percentage of the accounts receivable you sell the bank.

Factoring. In a variation on accounts receivable lending, the bank buys the accounts receivable, usually on a discounted basis for cash. It becomes the bank's responsibility to collect the receivables. This practice is called *factoring*. If the receivables do not come in, collecting them is the bank's responsibility, not yours. The amount of the accounts receivable is taken off your books when the factoring arrangement is made. Banks will not accept all accounts receivable for factoring, only those which they believe they have the best possibility of collecting.

As with any form of accounts receivable financing, banks charge interest on the accounts receivable for the time between the granting of the loan and the collection of the accounts receivable. And again, there is also usually a service fee, based on a percentage of the accounts receivable you sell the bank.

Inventory Financing. When *inventory loans* (sometimes called "warehouse loans" or "field warehouse loans") are made, the lender takes legal possession of the merchandise being used as security. The bank lends capital based upon warehouse receipts given to it by the borrower. The merchandise must be easy to sell, in case the bank has to recoup its loan. These loans are particularly useful in a seasonal business in which there may be a cash crunch just at the time you need money to build up inventory. Inventory financing can loosen up some cash to keep your business going strong and to enable you to take advantage of good off-season buying opportunities.

Inventory financing is used when a business has a great deal of inventory on hand but needs cash to make the business run. Banks do not take possession of the inventory being financed through the inventory loan, but rather have a third party control the collateral. The bank usually holds title to the inventory, which may be warehoused in a public warehouse or at the borrower's warehouse in a segregated area.

When *floor financing* is used, the borrower retains possession of the collateralized goods but gives a note to the bank giving it title to the goods. (Banks are not the only lenders to provide inventory financing. Commercial finance companies also provide it. See Chapter 6 for a discussion of commercial finance companies.) When the borrower sells a piece of the collateralized goods, he or she pays the lender that amount toward the outstanding loan. Inventory loan agreements usually contain a variety of provisions that are designed to protect the lender in the case of default. In floor financing, *trust receipts* are signed by the business owner, who agrees to keep the collateralized goods in trust for the lender and to pay the lender what is due as the products are sold.

For a bank, the drawback to inventory financing is that it must rely on the integrity of the borrower since it will not have possession of the inventory being used as collateral. For a borrower, the drawback is that inventory financing adds to the expense of maintaining an inventory and may slow down inventory turnover. For this reason, inventory financing should not be used for fast-moving items or goods in production. Rather, its use is more practical with slower-moving goods such as cars or automated teller machines.

6
Commercial
Finance Companies

When the Bank Says No,
Where Do You Go?

You've probably seen advertisements in the classified section of *The Wall Street Journal* or your daily newspaper under the "Capital Available" heading, or even in your telephone yellow pages under "Financing"—ads that promise "Immediate cash for accounts receivable," "Convert accounts receivable into cash," "We purchase your accounts receivable," or similar offers. Chances are these ads have been placed by *commercial finance companies*, or "commercial credit companies" as they are sometimes called.

Commercial finance companies make loans to businesses just as banks do, but they generally charge higher interest rates. In the past, commercial finance companies would often charge 3 to 4 percentage points higher than a bank would on loans, but in recent years that spread has narrowed quite a bit.

These companies make only secured loans to businesses. The loans are usually secured by inventory, equipment, or accounts receivable. Commercial finance companies also offer equipment-leasing services. Besides their policy of making only secured loans, commercial finance companies also generally require that borrowers provide them with personal guaranties.

While these companies make the same variety of secured loans as commercial bankers, accounts receivable lending is the staple of the industry. Whenever you see an ad claiming "We can turn your accounts receivable into cash," chances are it was placed by a commercial finance company.

Who Uses Commercial Finance Companies?

Most commercial finance company loans are short-term, for periods ranging from 90 days to 1 year. Companies that do a great deal of seasonal business will sometimes find commercial finance company loans an ideal source of cash with which to run their business while they build up stock. Though most loans are short-term, commercial finance companies will make longer-term loans if the purpose of the loan warrants it. A company like CB Sports, the ski apparel manufacturer mentioned in Chapter 4, might borrow money in late summer to build up clothing inventory and then repay the loan in the winter, after its major sales have occurred. If C. B. Vaughn wanted to borrow money to purchase a warehouse or equipment to manufacture the garments, he could probably get a loan that matured in up to 5 or 10 years.

Small businesses with little or no credit history may find it easier to get long-term financing from commercial finance companies than from banks. This ease may be a mixed blessing: Because you may be able to get a longer-term loan from a commercial finance company, your monthly payments may be lower than if you took out a short-term bank loan—but your interest rates will probably be higher. A company strapped for cash from month to month when it is just starting out may find such long-term financing attractive, even though the loan will end up costing more in the long run.

Manufacturers like CB Sports, as well as wholesalers, are likely to get a better deal on a loan from a commercial finance company than a retailer would get. Because the goods used to secure the loan are more easily tracked in a manufacturing or warehousing operation than they would be in a retailing operation, there is less risk for the lender.

Understanding the Loan Agreement

Whenever you take out a loan from any source, whether a bank, a commercial finance company, or some other source, read the loan agreement carefully and make sure you understand the terms. Commercial finance companies may be flexible, but sometimes their flexibility results in a complex lending arrangement. For example, they may offer a loan rate that is pegged to the prime rate (the rate banks charge their best customers on loans) or to the London Interbank Offered Rate (LIBOR—the rate that creditworthy international banks charge each other for loans), but it may go up at a slightly higher pace than those rates do.

A quarter of a percentage point here and a quarter of a percentage point there can add up if you're borrowing a lot of money. You should make sure that you are clear on your deal. You don't want to find yourself surprised at the outcomes.

You will also want to make sure that there are no prepayment penalties for paying off a longer-term loan early. If there are prepayment penalties, at least be aware of them, so that you will not end up paying off the loan early only to be socked with the same interest payments you would have had to make if you had let the loan run its course.

Some finance companies use the *rule of 78s* (also called the "sum-of-the-years-digits method") to calculate interest payments. Such a loan is based on a sum-of-the-years-digits method, used by some companies to figure out monthly payments. In this method, the months of the year are added up, and then a percentage of the total is used to calculate each month's interest.

It works like this. Say you have a 1-year loan. The sum of the numbers between 1 and 12 (used because there are 12 months of loan payments) is 78. When the rule of 78s is used, first the total interest for the year is calculated; then you pay 12/78 the first month, 11/78 the second, 10/78 the third, and so on. As a result, you end up paying most of the year's interest in the first month.

You should always find out whether a commercial finance company is using a prepayment penalty or the rule of 78s. The simplest way to do this is to ask, "Do you have a prepayment penalty or apply the rule of 78s?" Sometimes the simplest questions can save you the biggest headaches down the road.

When the Bank Is Not an Option

If commercial finance companies offer loans similar to banks but at higher rates, why would any business owner decide to turn to one for a secured loan? Chiefly because commercial finance companies, which are traditionally less conservative and more flexible than banks, will make loans that are considered more risky. They also will often consider collateral items that banks would not.

Commercial finance companies specialize in making accounts receivable, factoring, and inventory loans, so they are often more readily able to meet the needs of a business that could not qualify for other kinds of loans. (See Chapter 5 for a discussion of these other types of loans. There is no difference in basic structure between these bank loans and the ones of the same name offered by commercial finance companies.) A higher-risk loan often involves more administrative work for the commercial finance company because it must audit the borrower; this extra work is one reason for the higher interest rates charged.

Commercial finance companies are often used by businesses that are seeking capital and cannot get it from a bank. The traditional approach has been to try the banks first, and if none are forthcoming with a loan, to turn to other private lenders, such as commercial finance companies. In fact, sometimes bank loan officers will refer a business to commercial finance companies, if they cannot meet the needs of the prospective borrower.

While commercial finance companies will lend money to higher-risk businesses than banks will, they too place restrictions on the types of borrowers with whom they do business. Often, they will require a minimum net worth or receivables volume. But here too, many commercial finance companies are more likely to negotiate these requirements than a bank would be.

Besides higher interest rates, another disadvantage of working with commercial finance companies is that they have traditionally been less likely to champion the success of a business than to make sure that the collateral used to secure a loan is of high enough caliber in case of default. In other words, commercial finance companies want to be sure that, if you can't make your loan payments, your collateral can be liquidated (easily sold and converted to cash) so that they get the money they are owed. Banks see collateral as a security measure in case the business fails, but they are more likely to want to help a business succeed and pay back its loans.

An advantage of commercial finance companies, however, is that they have often been in the accounts receivable lending and factoring business for years. Thus, they are sometimes able to give expert advice to specific industries that are more likely to use their services than others. Businesses in the textile industry, for example, might gain much insight from a commercial finance company that had expertise in factoring arrangements in that business.

Types of Loans Available

The menu of loans available through commercial finance companies is almost identical to that offered by banks. A quick overview and review of the major options is given below.

Accounts Receivable Lending

Commercial finance companies specialize in accounts receivable loans. In fact, commercial finance companies evolved as a result of an accounts receivable deal that was set up in the early 1900s between an encyclopedia salesman who sold on the installment plan and a financer who agreed to loan the salesman the money due on the encyclopedias he sold. The financer got paid when the encyclopedia buyers paid their installments.

Pleased with the success of their idea, the two decided to carry the concept to other businesses, and set up a commercial finance company that would pay cash for accounts receivable that were due to businesses. A similar concept had been used earlier, in the form of factoring in the textile industry, but it was this encyclopedia arrangement in the early 1900s that resulted in the broader commercial financial companies being set up. Because many businesses found that their customers would assume their business was failing or in trouble if an outside source began collecting accounts receivable directly (as they do in a factoring arrangement where they buy the accounts receivable outright), the two loaned the cash to their business customers, who paid them after they received their accounts receivable. The result was accounts receivable financing on a nonnotification basis (discussed in Chapter 5). Of course, accounts receivable lending can also be done on a notification basis, but it was the concept of nonnotification that broadened the appeal of this type of financing.

Basically, accounts receivable financing is a method of secured financing in which a business puts up its accounts receivable as collateral on a loan. The commercial finance company evaluates the accounts receivables, judges which current receivables are most likely to come in, and will usually agree to lend the business 70 to 80 percent of the value of those accounts. The loan can, as described above, be set up on a notification or a nonnotification basis. If the receivables pledged are not paid on time, the commercial finance company will require your business to pay the amount pledged. The business will then have to act aggressively to collect the accounts receivable, in order to get its money.

Accounts receivable financing is inappropriate for companies that already have excess capital on hand with which to run their business. It is effective, however, for companies that have a lot of accounts receivables and need to generate cash to keep the business going, or for businesses that simply cannot get loans from other sources.

An advantage to doing accounts receivable financing with a commercial finance company instead of a bank is that banks will sometimes levy service charges and require compensating balances to be held at the bank. Of course, not all banks have the same requirements, but you should scope out the total picture before making a decision.

Commercial finance companies certainly charge for their services on accounts receivable loans. Typically, they calculate the debt outstanding every month and apply a daily decimal percentage of the interest rate they're charging against the outstanding debt on that day. If a commercial finance company charges 15 percent, the daily rate is 0.0411 percent (15 percent divided by 365). The commercial finance company charges the borrower 0.0411 percent on all outstanding accounts on a particular day of a month, because the amount of outstanding accounts receivable borrowed against can vary from day to day, depending on which receivables are paid off. As a result, the daily collection method is more accurate than a weekly or monthly interest calculation would be.

Factoring

Factoring is a variation on accounts receivable lending in which the commercial finance company acts as a *factor* and buys the accounts receivable, usually on a discounted basis for cash. It becomes the factor's responsibility to collect this receivable. The amount of the accounts receivable is taken off the business's books when the factoring arrangement is made.

Factors charge (1) an interest charge on the cash given for accounts receivable, (2) a percentage commission charge on the total value of the accounts receivable being factored, or (3) both.

A typical arrangement would be for the factor to give the business 70 percent of the total cash value of the accounts receivable being factored. When the total accounts receivable being factored was collected, the factor would give the business another 25 percent and keep 5 percent of the total for its services. Since factoring arrangements are usually done on a short-term basis—maybe 60 to 90 days—to free up cash, this 5 percent can add up to a substantial interest rate when figured on a yearly basis.

A business that has a good credit rating would be well-advised to attempt to get traditional bank financing or an accounts receivable loan before getting into an expensive factoring deal. In fact, many reputable companies specializing in factoring will advise a prospect that factoring may not be the most cost-efficient way to seek cash for a business. One well-known Manhattan factor told me that, since the factors buy the accounts receivable for cash, the transaction is not really a loan, and usury laws do not apply. As a result, the amount of money you pay on a factoring deal is not regulated, as it would be in other, more traditional, loans.

When a company enters into a factoring arrangement, the factor marks the company's bills to indicate that the factor owns the payment being made. (This puts the deal on a notification basis, as discussed above. Most accounts receivable financing, on the other hand, is done on a nonnotification basis, unless state law requires otherwise.) The factor is traditionally paid directly by the customer. An obvious advantage to this arrangement is that it eliminates billing costs for the accounts receivable being factored.

Say, for example, that Bethany Book Company, which manufactures and sells $1.5 million worth of college notebooks to retail outlets each year, needs money to buy new equipment so that it will be able to produce enough notebooks to meet the fall semester demand. Bethany allows its customers 60 days to pay their bills and usually has accounts receivable of about $200,000. But the company really needs cash so that it can buy the necessary equipment. Bethany agrees to set up a factoring deal with Grimes Factors, and to allow Grimes to send out Bethany bills with the Grimes mark on them.

Grimes Factors looks over the accounts receivables to determine Bethany's creditworthiness, and agrees to factor $180,000 out of the $200,000 outstanding. Grimes doesn't pay the total $180,000 of the receivables, but rather gives Bethany an agreed-upon percentage on consummation of the deal—say 70 percent, or $126,000. Now the players have two options. Grimes Factors can charge on a daily interest basis, as described above. Or it can pay the remainder of the receivables to Bethany Books upon receipt, less a set percentage (say 5 percent, or $10,000) as its fee. In either event, Grimes Factors will take over all billing and collection matters.

As you can see, factoring can be a complex and expensive financing option. It is, however, a legitimate option for a manufacturing or wholesaling company that has plenty of accounts receivable but needs cash to keep the company running.

As mentioned above, factoring is not technically a loan, since the factor buys the accounts receivable from the business. In the example of Bethany Books, no debt has been created; rather, accounts receivable have been converted to cash. The balance sheet of the Bethany Books factoring transaction would result in the scenario shown in Table 6-1.

Bethany has more cash and has improved its current ratio, making

Table 6-1. Bethany Book Company Balance Sheet

Current assets		Current liabilities	
Before Factoring			
Cash	16,000	Accounts payable	230,000
Accounts receivable	200,000		
Accrued taxes	65,000		
Inventory	300,000	Bank loan	35,000
Total	516,000	Total	330,000
Current ratio of assets to liabilities: 1.57 to 1.*			
After Factoring			
Cash	27,000	Accounts payable	115,000
Accounts receivable	74,000	Accrued taxes	65,000
Inventory	300,000	Bank loan	35,000
Total	401,000	Total	215,000
Current ratio of assets to liabilities: 1.86 to 1.†			

*See Chapter 15 for a complete discussion of current ratio.
†The sum of $126,000 (70 percent) came from Grimes Factors. Bethany used $115,000 to pay down some of its payables and added $11,000 to its cash account. This balance sheet doesn't take into account fees or interest charges for the factoring arrangement.

itself a more attractive credit risk for other prospective lenders. The factor might also improve the collection process for Bethany Books.

If you have a short payment-due period or sell on a cash basis, factoring would be inappropriate for your business. But factoring, like accounts receivable financing, can present a financing alternative for warehousing or manufacturing concerns that have fairly long payment terms and need cash to keep the business running.

Equipment financing

Commercial finance companies do make equipment loans, but they often charge much higher interest rates than banks do on similar loans. It is generally a good idea to approach banks first if you need to borrow money for equipment, but if you can't get a bank loan, commercial finance companies can be a good alternative.

Some companies that sell equipment have established arrangements with commercial finance companies to help customers finance their purchases. Some companies even have their own financing companies. While these financing arrangements might make the purchase seem easy, you should always do your homework and make sure that what you're getting is the best deal available to you. Check with banks or government sources or even other commercial finance companies to see whether you can get a better deal. With equipment financing in particular, be careful that you do not enter into an unattractive financing deal rather than a better one that may be available if you just look for it.

Besides being available to finance the purchase of new equipment, commercial finance companies will sometimes grant 1- to 5-year loans, usually at high interest rates, for the purchase of new equipment, and allow you to use the equipment you currently own as collateral.

Commercial companies may also arrange for a *sales–leaseback* deal in which a business sells its equipment to a commercial finance company and then leases it back by paying a monthly leasing fee. This sort of deal gives a company cash it may need to run the business.

Inventory Loans

Accounts receivable and factoring borrowers at commercial finance companies can also use inventory loans to get access to cash. Inventory loans are useful when a business needs to build up its inventory in anticipation of its busiest selling season but does not have the necessary cash. A commercial finance company with which the business already has a relationship can arrange for an inventory loan.

Again, take Bethany Book Company as an example. Say the company has $300,000 in inventory, but wants to purchase $150,000 more in inventory. The commercial finance company loans Bethany $150,000 and places a lien (a claim in case of default) on the existing inventory. Commercial finance companies are conservative in evaluating inventory as collateral, and they may require that the borrower use warehouse receipts. (See Chapter 5 for a discussion of warehouse receipts.)

For an inventory loan, the commercial finance company will usually charge interest rates similar to those it would charge for accounts receivable lending. Inventory loans are most often short-term loans.

Wholesale Sales Financing (Floor Financing)

Businesses that sell large goods, such as household appliances and automobiles, that they need to have on hand to show customers can approach a commercial finance company for floor financing. The commercial finance company advances the money to enable the business to buy the inventory, and holds a lien on the items. In essence, the finance company maintains ownership of the goods. The finance company charges a monthly interest payment based on how much outstanding debt the business has with it. When the business sells the product, it pays the commercial finance company back. The business can then decide whether or not it wants to buy more goods through the finance company, financed in a similar fashion.

Industrial Time-Sales Financing

An industrial time-sales financing arrangement is similar to a retail sales financing arrangement in that the seller of goods sells the merchandise on a credit basis to a buyer and then sells the debt to a commercial finance company. The buyer pays down the debt to the commercial finance company. The commercial finance company charges the buyer interest. This type of financing is used by businesses to buy equipment and fixtures for their business.

Both commercial finance companies and banks are legitimate sources of debt financing. In Chapter 7, we'll look at a well-known source of equity financing—venture capital. While most small businesses are unlikely to seek or attract venture capital financing, this is an area that is commonly discussed as an alternative financing source. It has also been used to finance many small businesses that have grown into quite successful companies. As such, venture capital is worth taking a look at.

7
Venture Capital

**Who's in
Control Here?**

Any budding business owner is bound to have an opinion about venture capital. Unfortunately, the opinion does not always accurately depict the nature of the venture capital industry. Since venture capital companies will take 10 to 80 percent ownership of a business, depending on the company's stage of development, and usually require that at least one venture capital fund partner or associate sit on the business's management board, the most common perception of venture capital companies is that you give up control of your company in exchange for capital. Thus, many small business owners have even resorted to calling venture capital firms "vulture" capital firms—implying that they stalk companies that may be in trouble, in hopes of a big meal if a company fails.

Though venture capital firms do require equity in exchange for capital, it is not a fair assessment to say that all of them want to control your company. Ownership is not necessarily control and, particularly in the cases where less than 50 percent of the company's stock is owned by the venture capital firm, the role of the venture capital firm can sometimes be a positive one. A venture capital firm can give much-needed capital and management advice, which can make a company grow and succeed dramatically in the marketplace.

Venture capital, however, is certainly not for everyone. Not wanting to give up a goodly percentage of ownership of your business concept, which you dreamed up and want to bring to life, is certainly legitimate. Indeed, in cases in which an owner's management abilities do not measure up to his or her dreaming capacity, it is possible for a venture capital investor to have enough influence over the board of directors to force the original owner out and put their own people in. Yes, there is a real risk: If you don't make your company successful enough to satisfy your investors, you can lose control.

Even when a small business decides it wanted to seek venture capital, the chances of its doing so successfully are slim. While more than $12 billion in venture funds was raised for investment between 1984 and 1986,[1] only 1 to 2 percent of the businesses who applied for venture capital financing got it. Still, because some venture capital investments have paid off dramatically, because venture capital has received a great deal of press attention, and because your business may happen to end up as one of the 1 to 2 percent of businesses who succeed in securing venture capital financing, it is worthwhile to take a look at this source of financing and how it works.

How Venture Capital Funds Work and What They Are Looking For

Basically, venture capital companies raise private funds to invest in companies with high growth potential. Venture capital firms can structure financing for businesses in which they invest as equity, convertible securities, loans, or hybrid securities.

A Small Business Investment Company, (SBIC) is the only type of venture capital company that borrows money from the government to invest. Since that borrowed money must be paid back to the government with interest, SBICs structure deals that often involve loans. Other venture capital funds have more flexibility in providing capital since they do not have to worry about repaying the government. See the discussion of SBICs and Minority Enterprise Small Business Investment Companies (MESBICs) in Chapter 10.

Some businesses are turned down for venture capital financing because they are not high-growth prospects and because they have no in-

[1]G. Jackson Tankersley, Jr., "How to Choose and Approach a Venture Capitalist," in Stanley E. Pratt and Jane K. Morris (eds.), *Pratt's Guide to Venture Capital Sources*, 11th ed. Needham, Mass.: Venture Economics, 1987, p. 43.

tention of going public or being acquired. Venture capital investors would not have a way to make their investments liquid in the 7 to 10 years during which they would usually want the investments to mature.

If you're looking for a short-term loan to keep things going or a small investment to help you get off the ground, venture capital is not likely to be the best place for you to look. Most venture capital companies have minimum investment requirements that range from $250,000 to $500,000. And it would be foolish to puff up your numbers to suggest that you need more money than you actually do, since venture capitalists worth their salt would be able to see right through such a ruse. Wasting a financing source's time now would be a bad idea, since your reputation would follow you into the future, when you really might become a legitimate prospect for venture capital.

Venture capitalists make such large investments because of their investment goals; they want high growth that they can cash in on, in 7 to 10 years. As a result, venture capital is invested in companies that can do their marketing research, develop a prototype, and gain market acceptance quickly. Venture capital has traditionally been relegated to companies that focus on high technology, electronics, communications, medical products, or other areas in which high growth is a likely outcome.

In 1985, according to *Pratt's Guide to Venture Capital Sources*, the breakdown of all venture capital investments was as follows:[2]

Product or service	Percent	
Electronics-related companies:		
Computer hardware and systems	20	
Software and services	15	
Telephone and data communications	10	
Other electronics	13	
Total electronics-related companies	58	
Medical and health-care–related companies		11
Commercial communications		4
Genetic engineering		3
Energy-related companies		2
Industrial automation		4
Industrial products and machinery		4
Consumer-related products		8
Other products and services		6
Total		100

[2]Elwood D. Howse, Jr., "Investments of Interest to Venture Capitalists," in *Pratt's Guide to Venture Capital Sources*, op. cit., p. 38.

Clearly, most small businesses will not fall into the purview of venture capital companies. While expectations will vary from firm to firm, most venture capitalists look to earn 10 times what they invested in 3 to 5 years, and expectations of 25 to 35 percent annual compounded return on investment after 3 to 5 years into the initial investment are common. Most small businesses lack the growth potential that venture capitalists want. Bookstores, restaurants, stationery shops, public relations firms, and similar ventures simply do not usually have the growth potential through which venture capitalists can get the kind of returns they need to justify their initial investment. The exception, of course, may occur when a business of this type has great franchising or expansion possibilities; then some heads might turn in a venture capital office.

A good example of an unlikely candidate for venture capital is a stationery store done on a small scale. But expand the idea into a warehouse store for office supplies, and you just might be able to attract the interest of venture capitalists. Former supermarket executive Thomas Stemberg opened the first Staples Inc. store in Newton, Massachusetts, in 1986. By the spring of 1988, Staples had opened 16 stores. Sales from May 1987 to April 1988 were $40 million. The concept is simple, yet attractive enough to get quite a bit of venture capital money invested. It works like this: Staples customers are offered products in warehouse-size buildings for prices that are 50 percent or more off retail list prices. Staples members get an even larger discount off selected items. For example, a box of 10 computer floppy disks which retails for $29.99, sells for $9.49 at Staples. And when it is touted as a "featured product," members can buy the box of floppy disks for $6.95. Venture capitalists have poured $18.5 million into Staples.[3]

When Venture Capital Is Invested

Venture capital companies invest their money at various stages of a business's life. The hardest investors to find are those who invest seed money in start-up operations. At most 20 percent of venture capital firms specialize in financing companies that are just getting up and running. Ask around, and you'll find that successful business owners will tell you that they have had many prospective investors lined up for second- or third-stage financing, but that finding the lead investor was the toughest nut to crack. Some of the difficulty occurs simply because

[3]Reed Abelson, "They Can Get It for You Wholesale," *Venture*, August 1987, pp. 27–28.

some firms don't specialize in seed investing. But undoubtedly, in spite of their risk-prone reputation, many venture capital firms gain confidence in your venture, and become willing to invest in it, when they see that others have already made the commitment to get you off the ground. With venture capital companies, as with banks, it's most difficult to find money when you need it and much easier to find it when you are in relatively good shape.

Different venture capitalists, aside from those who invest seed money, may favor investments in first-stage businesses (which have been open for about a year and show promise), second-stage businesses (which are up and running but have not necessarily reached the break-even point), third-stage businesses (which have reached the break-even point or have begun to show a profit), and mezzanine businesses (which need financing just before they "go public"—i.e., offer stock in the corporation to the public.

Approaching a Venture Capital Firm

A major rule of thumb in seeking venture capital is not to shop your business idea around while you are looking for financing. Don't try to get various firms into a bidding war for your business. Instead, you should find a firm by asking one of your financial professionals (an accountant or lawyer) to suggest firms or to introduce you to people they know at venture capital firms that make investments in the type of business you are in.

Venture capital firms specialize by industry and size of investment. When you decide to go after venture capital financing, do some research (by asking your accountant or lawyer, or referring to a variety of published sources) to find the venture capital firms that might be appropriate for you to approach.

The best source of information about venture capital firms in the United States is *Pratt's Guide to Venture Capital Sources*.[4] *Pratt's Guide* is updated annually and costs $125 a year. You might want to check on whether the latest edition is available at your local library, or if you're located near a good graduate school of business, its library is likely to have a copy of the book. The book identifies venture capital companies and gives useful information about each: its officers, its project preferences (role in and type of financing), its minimum and preferred invest-

[4]Venture Economics, 75 Second Avenue, Suite 700, Needham, MA 02194, 617-449-2100.

ments, its geographical and industry preferences, how many investments it made in the previous year, and how much total money it invested during the previous year.

By no means should you send form letters to all the venture capital firms in *Pratt's Guide*. That's a sure way to strike out at securing financing. Do some research, talk to your financial advisers, and identify the venture capital firms most likely to be interested in you.

The best approach is then to arrange an introduction to one of the officers of the firm. Venture capital firms receive hundreds of business plans and proposals weekly. If you can arrange an introduction, your chances of standing out from the crowd are increased.

Once you find a venture capital firm willing to talk to you, you want to find out whether it is the kind of firm that will not only back you financially but also provide you with the kind of management and marketing expertise you'll need to make your business succeed.

- Ask the venture capitalist what kind of deals he or she has done in your industry, how much money was involved, and how the deals worked out. How have the firm's investments panned out? How about investments made during recessionary or slow economic times?

- Ask for a list of businesses the company has invested in. Talk to those companies' founders to get an idea of what the venture capital firm is like to work with.

- Just as you should find out how much authority a loan officer has at a bank, you should find out how much authority the person you're talking to at the venture capital firm has. Is he or she an associate with little decision-making capacity? Or a partner who pretty much can influence other partners to invest in your firm once a thorough background check on your business has been completed?

- Ask how the firm would plan to support your company's growth beyond the capital invested. Would someone from the venture capital firm sit on your board? Would the firm provide your company with a full-time consultant? Would the firm's officers hold regular meetings with you to make sure everything was going according to plan, or nearly so?

- Ask how long the venture capitalists plan to stick with your company. Are your goals and theirs synchronous? If the venture capital firm wants to take your business public or look for an acquirer in 7 to 10 years, will you be prepared?

As mentioned earlier, venture capitalists have a variety of options when it comes to deciding what type of securities they will use to finance your business. They might use one or more of the following options: senior debt (debt that has a claim on a company's assets before other debt or equity, in case the business has to liquidate) for long-term financing of more mature companies; subordinated debt (subordinated to banks and other financing) that can usually be converted to stock in the company; preferred stock; and common stock, the most risky alternative but also the one that may provide the biggest payoff should your company make it to the public offering stage. Most venture capital firms will use a combination of financing techniques when they invest in a company.

When you approach a venture capital firm, remember that there are some things that can improve your prospects. Most are obvious. You should have a marketable product and a professional management team to build the company. You should be willing to invest some of your own money in the business. You should have prepared a thorough business plan that points out your businesses' assets and liabilities, both in terms of money and in terms of abilities.

The Business Plan

The business plan you prepare for the venture capital company to review will be a key factor upon which a go/no-go decision will be made on investing in your company. (The preparation of the business plan is discussed in Chapter 13.) The venture capital firm will look to your business plan to get a clear idea of your business's management team and its capabilities for building the business. The business plan should be prepared by the business's principals, and should feature a history of the company to date plus future projections based on thorough research. The business plan will set the tone for what management believes the company can really do in the future. Not only should the business plan play up the uniqueness of a product or service; it should also identify the market demand and market segment the product or service will target. Great products are one thing; the potential for an audience pining for those products is quite another. The plan shouldn't be too hard-sell, nor should it sell the company's potential short. Rather, it should be a document that dissects the issues carefully and reaches a responsible conclusion about the prospects for the business.

Different venture capital firms will make different specific requests that they will want to see in your business plan. But they will all usually want to see a history of the business; a descriptive analysis of the products or services; a market analysis; sales projections; an analysis of the competition; a description of the technological aspects of the product; a distribution analysis; a pricing analysis, equipment specifications; a cash-flow analysis for 3 to 5 years; biographies of principals, including proposed salaries and ownership information; and, if the company has been in operation for 3 years or more, 3 years of balance sheets and profit and loss statements.

The Venture Capitalist's Decision

The process that a venture capitalist goes through in making a decision on an investment can take upward of 6 months from the time you first meet until the decision is actually made. This is just one reason why companies which need a quick fix to keep going are not good candidates for venture capital. You should talk to the venture capitalist early on to get an idea of how long he or she thinks the courting and investigation process may take.

A venture capital firm should be able to let you know in a couple of weeks whether or not it plans to make a serious investigation of your proposal. Once it decides to look into your company, the firm will investigate every aspect of your business, from the people involved to the product proposed.

If the investigation goes swimmingly and the venture capital firm decides to invest in your company, you will have to negotiate for financing terms that match both your needs and the venture capital firm's needs. Your chief executive officer (CEO) should be present at the negotiations with the venture capitalist, should be a key player, and should make the final decision. But your company's attorney should also be present—and preferably that attorney should be one who has participated in such negotiations before. The venture capitalist and the CEO will have to give and take to reach an agreeable plan. Both your business and the venture capital firm must feel that the plan agreed upon is a positive deal for both sides. Otherwise, the chances of success are minimal.

For most small business owners, venture capital will never be a viable option for financing. But for those who have a potentially high-growth product or service on their hands, it can be a legitimate solution. Should you go the route of venture capital, embark upon the journey with your eyes open. Know that the venture capitalist will want to play an active role in your business. Be aware that, if all does not go according to plan, and if the venture capitalist owns a substantial portion of your company and wields a good deal of influence with your board of directors, you could find yourself ousted from your own firm. This, obviously, is the least desirable option for both you and the venture capital firm. It is in both parties' best interest to make the business grow, and to have it become as profitable and successful as possible.

In addition to its list of sources, *Pratt's Guide to Venture Capital Sources* features some very good essays on venture capital and how to work with a venture capital firm. It is well worth reading. You also might want to look at *A Venture Capital Primer for Small Businesses,*[5] put out by the SBA.

---

[5]Washington: Small Business Administration.

8

Don't Give Up Yet

Other Sources of Loans

This book primarily focuses on how the prospective small business owner can find the money to get a business up and going. In most cases, small businesses are financed through personal assets or borrowed money. Banks, commercial finance companies, and venture capital companies are perhaps the most well-known sources of capital, but they are certainly not the only ones. In this chapter, we'll look at other possible sources of capital, ranging from the simple, yet expensive, credit cards to the more complex bankers' acceptances.

Life Insurance Companies

In *The Life Insurance Buyer's Guide,* William D. Brownlie clearly describes how life insurance companies work[1]: "They receive payments in the form of premiums from a large number of people, invest the premium payments to earn interest, and pay money to the beneficiaries of insureds who have died." Though the premium dollars that insurance companies take in every year tally up to billions, it is unusual for these companies to invest directly in small business companies as part of their

[1]William D. Brownlie with Jeffrey L. Seglin, *The Life Insurance Buyer's Guide.* New York: McGraw-Hill, 1989, p. 9.

investment portfolios. For the most part, small businesses are too risky and unproven to match insurance companies' requirements for sound investments. There are many other less risky investments open to life insurance companies.

Life insurance companies make long-term unsecured loans (at rates comparable to bank loan rates) to profitable businesses that have been around for some time and have good track records. A good deal of insurance company money is spread among investments related to larger businesses—e.g., loans for large commercial or residential real estate, common stocks, and corporate bonds. There are, however, a few ways that small business owners can use life insurance to finance their businesses.

Mortgage Financing

Life insurance companies sometimes lend money to businesses to build or purchase commercial real estate. As security on the loan, they hold the mortgages on the property being financed. The insurance companies want to make sure that the value and income potential of the property being financed is strong enough to indicate that the borrower will be able to pay back the loan.

Life Insurance Policy Loans

By far the most common type of loan that a small business owner will have access to through a life insurance company is a policy loan. Business owners who have had life insurance policies in force for several years will have policies with a cash surrender value that they can borrow against. (Term life is a death-benefit-only policy, so no cash surrender value is available to borrow against.) The rate of interest on loans depends on when the policy was issued. If you took out your policy about 20 years ago, you can expect to pay 3 to 4 percent interest on loans. Today, interest rates are in the area of 8 percent. Some companies also have variable rate options. If you want to take out a policy loan, you'll need to get a form from your agent. After you fill out the form and send it in, and if you qualify, you'll usually get the loan in a couple of weeks. All loan specifics are spelled out in the life insurance policy itself.

One of the advantages of taking out a life insurance policy loan is that you are merely required to pay the interest due on the loan. You are not really required to pay back the principal itself. But the drawback to not paying back the cash value borrowed is that your policy value will be decreased by the amount of loan and accrued interest outstanding. Your beneficiaries will receive that much less when you die. Most peo-

ple try to pay back the total amount borrowed, to protect their beneficiaries' proceeds.

Policy loans are excellent sources of capital if you cannot find the
money elsewhere. Often, the interest rates available are quite attractive
when compared with higher-rate bank loans. But you should keep in
mind that the primary reason people buy life insurance is to protect
their families or other beneficiaries. Obviously, you should not lose
sight of this objective when thinking of life insurance policies as a source
of capital.

Life Insurance as a Buy-Out Mechanism

Another interesting use of life insurance as a source of funds is as capital enabling one partner to buy out another, in the event of one partner's death. It's a simple arrangement. Say there are two partners in the
firm. Each takes out a life insurance policy with a face value equal to
half the business value. Each partner names the other partner as beneficiary. When one partner dies, the other partner receives the insurance
and uses it to buy out the partner's share of the business. The business
pays both partners' life insurance premiums as a business expense.

Owners can also use life insurance as a means to sell a business to a
valued employee. The owner and employee arrive at a fair price for the
business and take out a life insurance policy on the owner's life for that
amount, naming the employee as beneficiary. The employee pays the
premiums, since he or she will ultimately receive the death benefit.
When the owner dies, the employee uses the death benefit to buy the
owner's business from his or her estate. Obviously, this is a viable financing arrangement only for owners who do not want cash in hand
immediately and are willing to have the purchase price go to their heirs
instead of to themselves.

Life insurance can be used in a variety of creative ways to finance
businesses or business arrangements. I once collaborated on a book
project with another author who wanted to take a life insurance policy
out on me for an amount of money equal to my portion of the advance.
He would pay the premiums and be the beneficiary should I die. He
figured he could use the death benefit to find another collaborator, if
necessary.

Your Home

If you own a home, you can take out a second mortgage on the house to
free up some of the equity. You will have to pay the closing costs and

points on the mortgage, plus be subject to the prevailing interest rates of the day. Of course, all interest payments on primary home mortgages are tax-deductible.

You also can consider a home equity line of credit, which allows you to tap into the equity of your home. Typically, banks will appraise your home to find its value, then subtract whatever outstanding mortgage debt you have on the house to determine how much equity you have built up. Most banks have a limit on how large an equity line they will allow. After the amount has been sent, the bank will typically send you a book of checks that you can use to draw on the line of credit. Many banks even offer credit cards to their home equity customers. Under current law (which is subject to change at the whim of Congress), you can deduct the interest on up to $100,000 taken as a loan against your house, no matter what you use the money for.

Unless you opt for a fixed rate, most home equity loans work a lot like credit card loans. Each month you pay interest (usually pegged to the bank's prime rate or some other standard loan rate) on the outstanding balance, plus a portion of the balance. Home equity loans typically have a 10-year span. You can pay them off early if you wish. Make sure that there is no prepayment penalty for paying off the loan early.

The biggest problem with using a second mortgage or home equity loan to finance a business is that you put your house at risk. If your business begins to falter and you cannot pay the mortgage or home equity loan payment, the lender has the right to take possession of your home, which is collateral for the loan.

You should think long and hard about using either of these options to finance your business. It is usually not the best financing solution. (However, setting up a home equity line for personal use in case of emergencies may not be a bad idea. You don't have to draw on the line of credit, but should you or your family have a medical or home emergency, it may be a good source of short-term cash. On the nonbusiness side, it is also an excellent source of cash for remodeling or renovating your home. You can effectively tap into the equity to increase the value of your home.)

Lease Financing

Leasing is a method of financing whereby you essentially rent equipment, machinery, fixtures, or buildings by paying a set amount to a leasing company that holds title to goods. There are a variety of ways leasing can work, depending upon the goods being leased and upon the leasing company. You can lease goods over a variety of time periods—

e.g., monthly, quarterly, yearly, or longer. You can pay for a maintenance agreement which makes the leasing company responsible for regular maintainence of the goods being leased. You might be able to lease goods with an option to buy. You might also get the benefit of some tax advantages that are passed on to lessees.

Leasing may provide many benefits, including the following:

- You can have a maintenance contract, so that someone else worries about the upkeep of the leased goods.

- You can get out of a leasing agreement when the equipment no longer suits your needs or becomes antiquated, without having to continue payments on the equipment. If you had purchased the equipment and it became outdated, you would have been stuck with it.

- You don't have to make a large cash outlay all at once for the equipment; instead, you can allot your cash to another business purpose.

- You can plan for leasing expenses, since the leasing agreement spells out the amount of each payment.

- You can take advantage of whatever tax benefits pass through to you as the lessee.

Perhaps the biggest disadvantage to leasing is that it is a very expensive method of purchasing the equipment you are leasing, if that is what you ultimately decide to do. You will find that the total cost of buying the equipment from the leasing company at the end of the leasing agreement is much greater than if you had bought the equipment outright in the first place. You can end up paying a finance charge as much as prime plus 6 percentage points. Rates can vary from leasing company to leasing company, so you'll want to shop around.

Leasing is a particularly good option if you only need the equipment for a short period of time and have no intention of purchasing it, or if, because of a lack of enough capital, it is the only way to obtain the equipment you need to get or keep your business running.

Trade Credit

Small businesses often have access to trade credit, an arrangement in which suppliers of goods or services don't require immediate payment but instead offer credit terms for the payment due. Through trade credit a customer is given a discount for paying a bill within a specified period of time. This arrangement is also called *cash discount*.

Assume that a buyer of some product owes $550. On an invoice dated

January 18, the buyer is offered trade credit terms of 2/10 net 30 (sometimes written "2/10 n/30"). This means that if the buyer pays the bill within 10 days after the invoice date (January 28), he or she may deduct a discount of 2 percent ($11). If the buyer does not pay the bill by January 28, the entire bill must be paid within 30 days of the invoice date (February 17).

The buyer is effectively given a 20-day extension at 2 percent. That may free up cash for the short term, but if calculated on an annual basis, it adds up to a 36.5 percent annual rate, mighty steep indeed. Most wise businesspeople would take advantage of the 2 percent discount rather than pay that kind of annual rate. It's not unheard of, however, to negotiate for a more attractive payment schedule. If you could get the provider of goods to agree to a cash discount of 2/10 net 60, you would end up paying around 14.6 percent on an annual basis, which in some economic climates might be attractive enough to make you consider stretching the payment out to the full 60 days so that you could have use of the capital in the meantime.

There are three parts to a cash discount:

1. The percentage discount being offered
2. The time frame for which the discount is offered
3. An indication of the date after which the bill becomes overdue

Within industries there are traditional cash discount combinations.

Forward Dating

Forward dating is a combination of a cash discount and a seasonal discount pricing strategy. The buyer buys and is delivered goods during the off season, but doesn't have to pay for the goods until the season begins. A manufacturer of ski jackets might decide to fill wholesale and retail orders in summer months, but date the invoice October 1, with terms of 2/10 net 30, as of October 1. If the ski jacket manufacturer can keep the plant running during the summer months, production can be spread out over the year. The wholesalers and retailers do not have to pay their bills until after the season has started and they have begun to receive cash for sold merchandise.[2]

[2]Jeffrey L. Seglin, *The McGraw-Hill 36-Hour Marketing Course.* New York: McGraw-Hill, 1990, pp. 122–123.

Foundations

By 1985, there were more than 24,850 foundations in the United States, with assets of more than $74 billion dollars.[3] In spite of the large number of foundations and the asset strength of these organizations, small businesses tend to be beyond the purview of the foundations' investment criteria. Foundations have professional investors on board who are looking for relatively safe investments that typically are larger than small businesses need. The larger foundations will often make loans greater than $1 million to businesses. Like the insurance companies, the people doing the lending for the foundations will look long and hard at the experience of the prospective borrower's management team, as well as studying the validity of financial projections for the business.

There are, however, thousands of foundations in the United States— some small, some large. While foundations generally make only large investments or loans, each foundation has its own set of criteria. There are many good directories of foundations available in libraries. Browse through the directories and see if you can find a foundation that specializes in making loans to companies like yours. For small businesses it's a long shot, but when you're searching for capital, it's worth a try.

Pension Funds

If you thought the amount of assets that foundations hold was formidable, consider that by the end of 1986, the assets of public and private pension funds in the United States tallied up to $1.9674 trillion.[4] Collectively, pension funds have a tremendous potential to make loans and investments.

Unfortunately, the average small business owner is unlikely to be the beneficiary of a loan from a pension fund. The pension fund managers make investments (of the pension money invested in their particular fund) and loans to large borrowers who have a proven track record. Often these pension fund loans are in the millions of dollars. Since pension fund managers have a fiduciary responsibility to protect the people who are paying into the pension fund, they must make sound, relatively safe investments. Like the money of life insurance companies or foundations, pension fund money will typically be used to finance to an es-

---

[3]"Foundations—Number and Finances by Asset Size," U.S. Bureau of the Census, *Statistical Abstract of the United States: 1988*, 108th ed. Washington: U.S. Government Printing Office, 1987, p. 360.

[4]"Assets of Private and Public Pension Funds, by Type of Fund: 1970 to 1986," *Statistical Abstract of the United States: 1988,*, op. cit., p. 345.

tablished company with a track record of success and a solid management team, or at the very least, with an experienced management team
that shows strong probability of being a solid borrower.

Commercial Paper Houses

It is unlikely that a small business will be able to take advantage of a
commercial paper house's services, since commercial paper is typically a
borrowing mechanism restricted to large companies. In simple terms,
the way commercial paper works is that large companies issue unsecured promissory notes (written promises that the signer will pay a specified amount on demand, on a fixed date, with or without interest) with
a fixed, short-term maturity. The commercial paper houses sell these
promissory notes to other businesses or individuals. They are, in effect,
making a loan to the issuing company. The business issuing the commercial paper becomes the borrower.

Borrowing by way of commercial paper can become quite complex.
Commercial paper houses often issue new commercial paper to raise
money to pay off outstanding commercial paper obligations as they mature. Since bad economic conditions might make paying outstanding
obligations difficult, the commercial issuer will often back the commercial paper with a bank line of credit that guarantees the lender that the
outstanding obligation can be paid off. Banks often require commercial
paper issuers who use a line of credit as backup for their outstanding
obligations to place compensating balances (balances used by a business
to support a borrowing arrangement with a lending institution) or pay a
fee to the bank offering the line of credit.[5]

Credit Unions

Credit unions offer their members an array of financial services similar
to those offered by banks. Often, however, credit unions pay slightly
higher interest rates on deposits and offer loans at slightly lower interest rates. There are restrictions on how large a loan credit unions can
make, but for a small business owner seeking some working capital, a
credit union may be a possible solution. Credit union membership is
based on some common bond among its members; the nature of the

[5]Jeffrey L. Seglin, *Bank Administration Institute Dictionary of Banking*. Rolling Meadows, Ill.: BAI/Andover Parris, 1990, pp. 43–44.

bond, whether business, religious, ethnic, community, or something else, is dictated by the charter of the credit union.[6]

Credit Cards

A good friend of mine used to joke that his finances were so strapped he used his MasterCard to pay off his Visa bills. Well, in today's world of finances that may not be the most savvy maneuver, but for someone pressed for cash, it is indeed a possibility.

Credit cards offer small business owners and prospective small business owners quick access to cash. You can take a cash advance on your credit card for an amount up to your cash credit limit. If you have more than one bank credit card, you can borrow up to the cash credit limit on each card.

You can use the money you borrow for short-term cash needs or to build up the capital in your company in an attempt to make the company more attractive to a prospective bank lender. For business owners just starting out, with no track record and no other source of finances, credit card advances may be their only way to go forward rather than scratching the idea of starting their businesses.

Interest charges on credit cards vary depending on the bank issuing the card and the state in which that bank is located. Each state sets its own usury laws, and banks must work within the parameters of those laws. In recent years, there have been some good deals on bank credit card rates, but for the most part, interest rates are still very high. For that reason, it is best to use credit card advances only for emergency cash or short-term needs, and to pay off the debts as soon as possible, since the interest rates can be real killers.

As you probably know, you don't need to have a credit card issued by a bank in your home state. Often, if you shop around, you can find much more attractive rates elsewhere. A regularly updated list of banks with the lowest credit card interest rates is available for $1 from Bankcard Holders of America.[7] The association also publishes a list of banks with no annual fees on their credit cards for $1.95. A membership in the association costs $12, which includes these lists and a bimonthly newsletter. *The Credit Card Shopper* is a quarterly newsletter that regularly lists attractive credit card offerings.[8]

---

[6]Ibid., p. 48.
[7]460 Spring Park Place, Suite 1000, Herndon, VA, 703-481-1110.
[8]P.O. Box 55, Larkspur, CA 94939, 415-995-4700.

Export-Import Bank of the United States

The purpose of the Export-Import Bank (Eximbank), which is a U.S. government agency, is to help finance the export sales of U.S. goods and services. The Eximbank has several financial programs that are directed specifically at small business exporters, including:

- Preexport financial assistance to secure working capital from commercial banks that is to be used for export-related functions like inventory building or marketing efforts

- A new-to-export insurance policy that provides export coverage for companies just starting to export

- A Small Business Credit Program that enables banks to offer medium-term fixed rate export loans to be used to finance sales of small U.S. companies' products and services

The Eximbank has a toll-free small business advisory hot-line service. The number is 800-424-5201. Eximbank officers are available through this number to talk with small business exporters and give advice about their financing needs.

Equity Financing

In Chapter 4, we looked at how a business can reach a balance between equity and debt financing. In the real world of business, it is highly unusual for any business owner to be able to finance his or her business using just borrowed money. As the Paul Reynolds study cited in Chapter 4 suggests, the largest single source of financing for a new small business is personal savings.

But where do you go if your personal savings are tapped out and you've borrowed to your limit? One option is venture capital, which was explored in Chapter 7. But there are other options.

Steven J. Bennett, in his book *Playing Hard Ball with Soft Skills,* refers to some of these sources as "other people's excess cash" (OPEC).[9] Among some of the most traditional sources for funding a new business are friends and relatives. If you do borrow money from or get an investment from relatives or friends, make sure you set out the arrangement clearly in writing. If your aunt Beatrice and your best friend Sal

---

[9]Steven J. Bennett, *Playing Hard Ball with Soft Skills.* New York: Bantam, 1986, p. 116.

are making an equity investment, how much ownership will they get for their equity investment? Will they receive dividends? Do you have plans to go public with the company or to sell it? Lay your cards on the table if a friend or relative wants to make an equity investment and you want to accept it. Though aunt Beatrice and good buddy Sal may not foreclose on your house by virtue of their faith in you, these are people you do not want to offend or mislead. Unless they are giving you the money as a gift, do not assume that you don't have to be as businesslike in drawing up an investment agreement with friends or relatives as you would with other investors.

There are other sources of equity capital as well, which will scrutinize you and your business much more carefully than will friends and relatives, though they will not necessarily expect a stated guaranteed return-on-investment rate. They, like venture capital companies making an investment, will watch you closely to make sure you are not squandering their money. Small Business Investment Companies, which are discussed in Chapter 10, are one such source of investment money for small businesses. Others include pension funds, corporations, and wealthy individual investors. Before signing an agreement with any such source, you should consult your attorney to make sure you reach a fair agreement for the amount of investment you are receiving. You want to make sure that you don't give up so much equity that you wind up losing control of your business. Investment bankers, accountants, and other financial professionals should be able to steer you to potential sources of investors.

Going Public

Making an initial public offering (IPO) of stock is expensive and very risky. Unless your business has a product that is truly unique or promises great potential returns, the chances of attracting investors in your stock are minute. If you've developed a parallel-processing super database computer that promises to blow the competition away and you already have signed on some Fortune 100 clients, you might have some success with an IPO. For the average small business, however, going public is usually not a viable alternative.

Be forewarned, it is no easy task to raise equity capital. Potential investors will look long and hard while investigating your business before they make an investment decision. Few are willing to take a risk on a business that doesn't promise some solid financial returns in the future.

PART 3

Borrowing through the SBA

9
Small Business Channels

Regular Business Loans from the SBA

Within the federal government of the United States, there are many programs that cater to the needs of small business. In a foreword to a government publication entitled *Handbook for Small Business*[1] Senators Lowell Weicker and Dale Bumpers wrote: "Small business is an awesome, powerful force in the American economy and represents the heart and soul of the free enterprise system." The senators went on to laud the role of small businesses, which the Small Business Administration estimates account for 98 percent of all businesses in the United States, account for 55 percent of all private sector jobs, create more than 50 percent of all industrial innovations and inventions, and account for 43 percent of the gross national product.

Whether or not the U.S. government will continue to fund the agencies that provide financial, management, and general business assistance to small business owners has been a hotly debated subject. But clearly, the government recognizes the strength and economic contribution of the millions of small businesses in this country. *Handbook for Small Business* is an excellent source of information on programs that exist to aid small business owners. The book describes every agency from the Department of Agriculture to the Veterans Administration; it tells you

---

[1]Lowell Weicker, Jr., and Dale Bumpers, "Foreword," *Handbook for Small Business: A Survey of Small Business Programs of the Federal Government.* Washington: U.S. Government Printing Office, 1984, p. vii.

how you can get research or advice from these agencies as well as how you can sell services to these agencies. If you live in an area that has a government book store, it's worth the trip to get this $7 volume. If not, you can send for it.[2]

The Small Business Administration

If you're looking for financing sources within the federal government, the SBA is the one federal agency which has as its sole purpose championing the cause of small businesses in the United State. Congress created the SBA in 1953 to help people start and stay in business. There are four kinds of assistance available from the SBA:

- Financial
- Procurement
- Management
- Advocacy

In addition to helping privately owned small businesses get off the ground and running, the SBA in recent years has made special efforts and established special programs to help women, socially and economically disadvantaged people, the handicapped, veterans, and disaster victims start businesses.

There are SBA field offices in every state, as well as in the District of Columbia, Guam, Puerto Rico, and the Virgin Islands. Around 3700 employees staff these offices. (See Appendix A for a directory of SBA field offices.) You should be able to get most of your questions about SBA assistance answered by calling any SBA field office.

Eligibility for SBA Help

The SBA's eligibility requirements for obtaining loans and getting procurement assistance are based on business size and credit needs. Like most lenders, the SBA will make loans only "of such sound value or so

[2]Write to: Superintendent of Documents, U.S. Government Printing Office, Washington, DC 20402. Ask for Senate Document No. 98-33. Make a $7 check payable to U.S. Government Printing Office. While you're at it, ask for the free list of books focusing on small business—Bibliography No. 307.

secured as reasonably to assure repayment."[3] The SBA looks for applicants with "good character" (see the discussion of the five C's of credit in Chapter 5 of this book) and with enough capital already in their businesses to ensure that, with SBA assistance, the businesses can thrive. Business owners who get income from gambling activities or plan to use loan funds to speculate in real or personal property are not eligible for SBA loans.

The SBA assists virtually all types of small businesses, in manufacturing, wholesaling, retailing, general construction, farming, and other industries. The definition Congress uses for a *small business* is "one that is independently owned and operated and not dominant in its field."[4] The SBA can, however, establish more restrictive standards if it deems them appropriate.

Size Standards

Eligibility for SBA business loans based on size varies from industry to industry. Among the SBA's parameters for a "small" company are the following ("number of employees" refers to the prior year; "sales volume" is a 3-year average):

- *Manufacturing.* A manufacturing company is considered small if it has 500 or fewer employees, large if it has more than 1500 employees. Whether it is small or large when it has between 500 and 1500 employees depends on the industry.

- *Retail.* A retail business is considered small if it has annual sales of $3.5 million or less, large if annual sales total more than $13.5 million. Whether it is small or large when it has between $3.5 and $13.5 million in sales depends on the industry.

- *Wholesale.* A wholesale business is small if it has 500 or fewer employees, large if it has more than 500 employees.

- *Service.* A service business is small if annual sales are less than $3.5 million, large if annual sales are greater than $14.5 million. Whether it is small or large when it has between $3.5 and $14.5 million in sales depends on the industry.

- *Passenger transportation.* A passenger transportation business is considered small if annual sales are less than $3.5 million, except for air transportation companies, which are considered small if they have fewer than 1500 employees.

[3]*Handbook for Small Business,* op. cit., p. 155.
[4]Ibid, p. 154.

- *Trucking, warehousing, packing and crafting, and freight forwarding.* These businesses are considered small if their annual sales are less than $12.5 million.

- *General construction.* General construction businesses are considered small if they have annual sales of less than $17 million.

- *Special trade construction.* Special trade construction companies are considered small if they have average annual sales of less than $7 million.

- *Agriculture.* Agricultural businesses are considered small if annual sales are no greater than $0.5 to $3.5 million, depending on the type of industry the business is in.

The size standards described above are broadly stated, and the SBA can change them if it decides a change is appropriate. For the most up-to-date figures, you should get in touch with an SBA field office.

Other Eligibility Requirements

Through its various loan programs, the SBA funnels about $3 billion a year in loans to small businesses. Most are made as guaranty loans through banks. The name "guaranty loans" is used because these loans are guaranteed up to 90 percent by the SBA. However, the SBA is not trying to compete with private lenders in financing businesses. To be eligible for an SBA loan, a small business owner must have tried a bank or other lending sources before approaching the SBA. Once it is established that the prospective borrower cannot get financing elsewhere, he or she may become eligible for SBA loan programs.

Regular SBA Business Loans

The granddaddy of the SBA loan program is its regular business loan program, often referred to as "Section 7(a) loans" after the section of the Small Business Act of 1953 authorizing these loans. (Special types of SBA loans are discussed in Chapter 10.) These loans are slated for businesses that need financing for business construction, expansion, acquisition of equipment or facilities, or working capital. While most types of businesses are eligible for 7(a) loans, speculative businesses, nonprofit businesses, newspapers, lending or investment businesses, and a few others are not.

There are two basic types of 7(a) loans—guaranty loans and SBA direct loans.

Guaranty Loans

As mentioned earlier, most SBA loans are made by private lenders and guaranteed by the SBA. Guaranty loans account for the majority of SBA loans made. In recent years, SBA raised the guaranteed portion of the loans it backed from $500,000 to $750,000. The SBA will guarantee up to 90 percent of a loan, depending on how much the loan is for. The maturity of these loans can be up to 25 years. For loans greater than $155,000, the maximum guaranty is $155,000. Guaranty loans average $175,000 and have a maturity of 8 years.

While the SBA's guaranteed loan cap is $750,000, it will sometimes make exceptions. The first $1 million SBA-guaranteed loan given under the guaranty loan program was to Rocco & His Brothers, a family-run restaurant in the Soho section of Manhattan. The private lender in the deal was The Money Store Investment Corporation, one of the largest lenders of SBA loans, accounting for more than $140 million in SBA loans in 1988 alone.[5]

Loans under the SBA loan program are made in one of two ways, either as *participation loans,* in which the bank puts up at least 25 percent of the money being loaned and the SBA the rest, or as straight *guaranty loans,* in which the bank puts up all the money and the SBA guarantees 90 percent of it in the event that the borrower defaults on the loan.

The principal parties to an SBA guaranty loan are:

1. The SBA
2. The business applicant
3. The private lender

The lender is at the heart of the SBA lending process. The prospective borrower submits its application to the lender, who reviews the application and decides whether or not to forward it to the SBA for analysis. The local SBA office decides whether or not to approve the loan. If it approves it, the lender then closes the loan and disburses the money to the borrower.

Direct Loans

The SBA makes relatively few direct loans. The maximum available is $150,000. These direct loans, which come from SBA money, are available only to prospective borrowers who were not able to get a loan under the guaranty loan program. To apply for an SBA direct loan, the

---

[5]"First $1 Million SBA Loan Given," *Bankers Middle Market Lending Letter,* May 1989, p. 8.

prospective borrower has to apply for financing from the bank where he or she has an account and, in cities with populations greater than 200,000, from at least one other lender. The prospective borrower must present the letters of denial from the two sources to the SBA when applying for a direct loan. The letters must list the amount requested and the reason for denial. Because direct loan funds are limited, they are sometimes targeted to specific types of borrowers, which may include low-income, disabled, Vietnam veteran, or disabled veteran borrowers.

Special Lenders

One of the positive outcomes of the barrage of paperwork that plagues government agencies has been the development of what the SBA refers to as its "Certified Lenders Program" and its "Preferred Lenders Program." About 700 private lenders are active in the Certified Lenders Program. Under SBA supervision, these certified lenders take on the task of reviewing a borrower's financial status as well as handling a lot of the necessary paperwork in the loan process. The desired result is to speed up the lending process. About 170 private lenders are part of the Preferred Lenders Program. Preferred lenders handle all the paperwork for loan processing on their own, as well as processing and servicing. You can find out who the certified lenders and preferred lenders are in your area by consulting an SBA field office.

Applying for an SBA Loan

Applying for an SBA loan is a lot like applying for any other loan. The SBA publishes guidelines on how to apply for an SBA loan; these guidelines are equally useful for approaching a private lender who is not part of the SBA lending program. (See Chapter 11 for a walk through an SBA loan application package.)

The steps include:

1. *Preparing a current business balance sheet that lists all assets and liabilities and establishes a net worth.* If you are a new business owner, you should prepare an estimated balance sheet that begins on the day the business started. You should also indicate the amount of money that you or others have available or have designated to invest in the business.

2. *Submitting income (profit and loss) statements for the current period and for the last 3 fiscal years.* If you are a new business owner, you

should prepare a detailed projection (including a monthly cash flow) of your earnings and expenses for the first year of operation.

3. *Preparing a personal financial statement for the owner or owners as well as for any stockholders who hold more than 20 percent of the stock in your business.*

4. *Listing collateral that you will offer as security, including an estimate of the current market value for each item and the money still owed on each item.*

5. *Stating how much of a loan you want and what you will use it for.*

6. *Taking these materials to the lender and determining whether or not he or she will make the loan.* There is usually a fee of around $500 for processing the loan application. Check to make sure the fee is refundable if the loan is denied. If it is not refundable, you should determine whether or not the lender will work with you to apply for a loan under the SBA guaranty loan program. If these approaches do not work out for you, explore the SBA direct loan program. You should call your nearest SBA field office about the direct loan program as well as with any questions about the guaranty loan program.[6]

Terms of SBA Loans

The maturity of SBA loans for working capital usually range between 5 and 7 years. While the maximum maturity is 25 years, you can get a longer maturity if you are using the loan to finance fixed assets like the purchase or renovation of a business site.

The lender and the borrower negotiate the interest rates just as they would in any lending arrangement. But with an SBA loan, the lender and borrower must work within the SBA guidelines for interest rate maximums. The SBA restrictions restrict interest rates on loans with maturities greater than 7 years to a maximum of 2.75 percentage points over the New York prime lending rate. For loans with maturities of less than 7 years, the interest rates can't be greater than 2.25 percent over the New York prime rate. The interest rate on direct loans is arrived at quarterly and depends on the cost of money to the federal government at the time.

---

[6]"Business Loans from the SBA," Office of Public Communications, OPC-6, U.S. Small Business Administration, Washington, 1986.

SBA Collateral

SBA loans are secured loans, and borrowers must pledge collateral to secure the SBA loans they have taken. The owners and chief executive officer of the business must provide personal guaranties. If there are not enough business assets to secure a loan, liens may be required on the principals' personal assets.

Time for Approval

It usually takes between 3 and 8 weeks to process a loan application, unless there is something missing from the application. It takes about 1 week after a loan is approved to receive the loan money.

SBA Publications and Assistance

There are several helpful booklets and broadsides available from the SBA about its services and loan processes. Besides the *Handbook for Small Business,* mentioned above in this chapter, a good general overview of the services provided by the SBA is *Your Business and the SBA.*[7] It should be available from your nearest SBA field office. Other helpful publications are listed in the Bibliography and mentioned throughout the text of this book.

If you have a touch-tone phone, you can call the Small Business Answer Desk of the SBA Office of Advocacy for recorded messages featuring information on management and financing, and other tips on starting and operating a business.[8]

---

[7]Office of Public Communication, U.S. Small Business Administration, Mail Code: 2550, 1441 L Street, N. W., Washington, DC 20416.
[8]Call 800-368-5855 or, if you live in Washington, D.C., 202-653-7561.

10
Special Channels

Special Loan Programs of the SBA

Besides the Section 7(a) guaranty and direct loan programs, which are the mainstays of the SBA loan program, there are many special loan programs and sources of financing available through the Small Business Administration. Several are discussed in this chapter.

Development Company Loans

The SBA measures economic growth by the creation and retention of jobs. To foster economic growth in rural and urban areas, the SBA makes loans to approved development organizations. The development companies use the loans to help small businesses acquire, build, convert, or expand facilities, equipment, and machinery. Two major types of development company loans are Local Development Company loans (referred to as "LDCs" or "502 loans") and Certified Development Company loans (referred to as "CDCs" or "504 loans").

Local Development Company Loans

LDCs or 502 loans are designed to foster economic growth in rural and urban areas by helping small businesses to acquire, construct, convert, or expand plants and acquire necessary equipment. Borrowers must substantiate that their businesses will have a positive economic impact on their areas by creating jobs, stimulating the economy, or achieving some other desired goal stipulated by the SBA.

The 502 loan is a guaranty loan (see Chapter 9) with a maturity of up to 25 years. The maximum amount of each loan is $750,000. There is a maximum guarantee of 90 percent, depending on how much the loan is for, to the lender making the loan. Loans must be secured.

Interest rates for the 502 loan are set the same way the rates for the regular 7(a) loans are set, but a 1 percent charge is levied on the guaranteed part of the loan. The borrower must provide 10 percent of the cash necessary to complete the project.

Certified Development Company Loans

CDCs or 504 loans are also made to foster economic growth in rural and urban areas by helping small business convert, construct, or expand plants and acquire equipment. These 504 loans are a three-way marriage between the SBA, a certified development company, and a private lender, who join forces to offer 10- or 20-year term financial packages to small businesses. The SBA can provide up to 40 percent or $750,000 of the total package. It provides this by offering 100 percent guaranteed debentures (bonds), sold on the capital market. The 504 loans have the same requirements for use and qualifications as do the 502 loans.[1]

Small General Contract Loans

The SBA provides financing to small general contractors who have short-term needs. The loans can be used for construction of residential or commercial properties or for rehabilitation of property. The loans cannot be used to purchase and own investment real estate.

Usually these loans have maturities of 12 months, but if a large contract is being financed, the SBA might approve an 18-month maturity. The applicant must meet the same requirements as applicants for regular 7(a) loans, and they also have to have been in business for at least 1 year at the time their application is filed.

[1]*Your Business and the SBA,* Office of Public Communication, U.S. Small Business Administration, Mail Code: 2550, 1441 L Street, N.W., Washington, DC 20416, p. 5.

Seasonal Line of Credit Guaranties

The SBA makes seasonal lines of credit available for businesses that have seasonal financing needs because of a seasonal increase in their business. These are for short-term financing needs, and are repaid from cash flow. The requirements and eligibility status are the same as for the regular 7(a) business loan program. Applicants must have been in business for a year at the time of application. The lines of credit are typically for a 12-month period from the time the line is first drawn on.

Energy Loans

The SBA makes loans to small businesses that manufacture, sell, install, service, or develop energy services or products. The requirements and eligibility status are the same as for the regular 7(a) business loan program.

Handicapped Assistance Loans

The SBA provides handicapped assistance loans to small business owners who are handicapped, and to nonprofit businesses that employ the handicapped or operate on behalf of the handicapped.

Handicapped assistance loans have a maximum maturity of 15 years, depending on how the loan proceeds will be used. The interest rate is 3 percent annually on an SBA direct loan or on the SBA part of a participation loan. The handicapped borrower must provide a statement from a doctor or counselor about the nature of his or her disability.

Vietnam-Era and Disabled Veteran Loans

When financing is not available from other sources, Vietnam-era and disabled veterans can apply for direct loans up to $150,000. The veteran must meet basic criteria, such as equity in the business and a reasonable expectation of being able to pay back the loan from the cash flow of the business. The applicant must submit evidence that loans for financing were not available elsewhere.

Vietnam-era veterans are defined as those who served for more than 180 days, part of which must have been between August 5, 1964, and May 7, 1975. They must not have been dishonorably discharged. *Disabled veterans* are defined as (1) Vietnam-era veterans who were discharged because of a service-connected disability, (2) veterans who have a 30 percent or more compensable disability (as defined by the federal government), and (3) veterans who received a disability discharge. The veteran must own at least 51 percent of the company, participate in the company on a day-to-day basis, and demonstrate an ability to run a business successfully.

The interest rates on these loans are the same as interest rates on SBA direct loans.[2]

Export Revolving Lines of Credit

The SBA provides export revolving lines of credit (in which loans are provided up to a set amount for a set period) to exporting businesses that have been in business for at least a year, to help them export their products to foreign markets. The criteria are the same as for the regular 7(a) business loan program. The maximum term of the line of credit is 18 months.

International Trade Loans

The SBA can make international trade loans of up to $1 million to businesses to allow them to acquire, construct, renovate, modernize, improve, or expand buildings or equipment that will be used in the United States to produces goods or services for international trade.

Section 7A(11) Loans

Section 7A(11) loans, formerly known as "Economic Opportunity Loans," are designed to offer financing to businesses in high-employment or low-income locations. The eligibility requirements for

---

[2]"Loans for Vietnam-Era and Disabled Veterans," *Fact Sheet No. 53,* rev. ed., Washington: U.S. Small Business Administration, June 1988.

7A(11) loans are different from those for the Section 7(a) loan program. Prospective borrowers must show that 50 percent or more of their business is owned by a person or people whose annual income (not including any government assistance) cannot cover the financial needs of the owners. They must also show that they have exhausted all other financing avenues open to them.

Disaster Assistance

When the President of the United States or the administrator of the SBA declares an area to be a disaster area because of such natural disasters as hurricanes, floods, tornados, or earthquakes, the SBA can offer *Physical Disaster Loans* or *Economic Injury Disaster Loans.* The SBA sets up on-site offices in the disaster area and staffs them with personnel who help process the loans.

Physical Disaster Loans are made to help replace or repair homes, personal property, or businesses that have been destroyed in a disaster area. The loans are made to home owners, renters, or business owners.

Economic Injury Disaster Loans are made to small business owners who have suffered economic injury as a result of a disaster. The borrowed money can be used for working capital or to make payments that the small business owner would have been able to meet if the disaster had not occurred.

Pollution Control Financing

The SBA will loan a maximum of $1 million through the guaranty loan program to businesses that need long-term financing to plan, design, and install pollution control facilities and equipment. The SBA will guarantee up to 90 percent of the loan.

Surety Bond Guarantee Program

The Surety Bond Guarantee Program allows the SBA to make the bonding process available to small and emerging contractors, who otherwise may not have bonding available. The SBA can guarantee to a qualified surety as much as 90 percent of losses due to a contractor's default. The guarantee is for contracts up to $1.25 million. The loans may be for construction, supplies, manufacturing, or services that a prime contractor or subcontractor provides for government or nongovernment work. The SBA's ten regional offices (with field offices in every state) and surety companies throughout the country participate in the Surety Bond Guarantee Program.

Small Business Investment Companies

The Small Business Investment Act of 1958 gave the SBA the power to license, regulate, and help provide financial assistance to privately and publicly owned SBICs. SBICs can furnish equity capital and long-term unsecured (or not fully collateralized) loans to small businesses. The capital for SBICs is raised privately, but SBICs can get financial leverage from the SBA. SBICs are in business as profit-making enterprises, and typically do not make very small investments.

An SBIC can give a loan to a business, or it can make an equity investment through which it acquires ownership or the potential for future ownership of a business. The SBIC also can furnish management advice to a small business.

Minority Enterprise Small Business Investment Companies, formerly referred to as MESBICs but now officially known as Section 301(d) SBICs, were licensed by the SBA to help small businesses that were owned by socially or economically disadvantaged people.

To finance a small business, an SBIC may use a variety of financing methods, which include:

- Purchasing debentures convertible into stock of the small business
- Purchasing capital stock in the small business
- Purchasing debt securities
- Using other traditional instruments of equity financing
- Making long-term loans to the business

To be eligible for SBIC financing, the business must qualify as a *small business,* defined as a business that is independently owned and operated, has a net worth no greater than $6 million, meets the business loan guidelines under the traditional SBA guaranty loan program mentioned in Chapter 9, and has an average after-tax net income less than $2 million for the prior 2 years.

There is a list of SBICs in Appendix B, and a list of MESBICs in Appendix C. The most current SBIC list is available from any SBA office. *Pratt's Guide to Venture Capital Sources* also lists many SBICs in its directory of venture capital sources.[3]

---

[3]Stanley E. Pratt and Jane K. Morris (eds.), *Pratt's Guide to Venture Capital Sources*, 11th ed. Needham, Mass.: Venture Economics, 1987.

11
The Paperwork

The SBA
Loan Application

The SBA loan application is similar to many bank loan applications. Special forms are provided, however, which the SBA loan applicant must complete. In this chapter, we'll walk you through a typical SBA loan application package.

Contents of a Typical SBA
Loan Package

Usually a loan application package for an SBA loan will consist of the following forms:

- SBA form 4, Application for Business Loan
- SBA form 413, Personal Financial Statement
- SBA form 912, Statement of Personal History
- SBA form 1261, Statements Required by Laws and Executive Orders
- A business plan for your business

There are some additional forms you may have to submit with your loan application if your particular situation warrants them. These include:

- SBA form 159, Compensation Agreement for Services in Connection with Application and Loan from the SBA

- SBA form 641, Request for Counseling

If you are applying for a direct loan from the SBA, your loan application package must also include two loan decline letters from lenders who are part of the SBA lenders program.

All the forms that you will need to apply for an SBA loan should be available from the lender. You can contact your local SBA office for these applications, but in most cases they will direct you to an SBA lender for the forms.

Most of the applications are quite straightforward. You should not have a great deal of difficulty in figuring out how to fill them out. Here are some suggestions, however, that might make the process easier.

SBA Form 4, Application for Business Loan

Most of the loan form is clear. There's a question in the top right-hand side of the first page (see Figure 11-1) that asks you to list the number of employees in your business at the time of application and the number you expect to have if the loan is approved. The second number will no doubt be largely guesswork on your part. Sure, you can make educated predictions, but how can you really know how many employees you will ultimately hire? The best thing to do is be optimistic, yet realistic. The SBA won't look favorably on ridiculous estimates, but they will likely look kindly on a business that is expected to generate a number of jobs.

In the section of the loan form headed "Use of Proceeds," be as accurate in your estimates as possible. Likewise, in the section next to it headed "Collateral," list the values of all your collateral carefully and accurately. The bank will be able to double-check what you write against your personal financial statements, so be consistent. Show the lender and the SBA that you have nothing to hide and are dealing squarely with them.

On the third page of the loan application, item 17 is listed under the heading "Direct Loans Only." If you are applying for a direct loan from the SBA in cities with populations of 200,000 or more, you must provide two bank declination letters. In cities with populations of 200,000 or less, one letter is acceptable. Remember to include these letters with your loan application package if you are applying for a direct loan.

Read all the points listed on the second and third pages of the application. Make sure that you provide all the applicable information that the SBA requires for the type of loan you are seeking. Be forthright in answering all these questions, even the ones that may be tough, like

U.S. Small Business Administration

Application for Business Loan

Applicant	Full Address

Name of Business	Tax I.D. No.

Full Street Address	Tel. No. (Inc. A/C)

City	County	State	Zip	Number of Employees (Including subsidiaries and affiliates)
Type of Business			Date Business Established	At Time of Application _____
Bank of Business Account and Address				If Loan is Approved _____
				Subsidiaries or Affiliates _____ (Separate from above)

Use of Proceeds: (Enter Gross Dollar Amounts Rounded to Nearest Hundreds)	Loan Requested	SBA USE ONLY	Collateral
Land Acquisition			If your collateral consists of (A) Land and Building, (D) Accounts Receivable and/or (E) Inventory, fill in the appropriate blanks. If you are pledging (B) Machinery and Equipment, (C) Furniture and Fixtures, and/or (F) Other, please provide an itemized list (labeled Exhibit A) that contains serial and identification numbers for all articles that had an original value greater than $500. Include a legal description of Real Estate offered as collateral.
New Construction/ Expansion/Repair			
Acquisition and/or Repair of Machinery and Equipment			
Inventory Purchase			

	Loan Requested	SBA USE ONLY		Present Market Value	Present Loan Balance	SBA Use Only Collateral Valuation
Working Capital (Including Accounts Payable)						
Acquisition of Existing Business			A. Land and Building	$	$	$
Payoff SBA Loan			B. Machinery & Equipment			
Payoff Bank Loan (Non SBA Associated)			C. Furniture & Fixtures			
Other Debt Payment (Non SBA Associated)			D. Accounts Receivable			
All Other			E. Inventory			
Total Loan Requested			F. Other			
Term of Loan			Totals	$	$	$

PREVIOUS SBA OR OTHER GOVERNMENT FINANCING: If you or any principals or affiliates have ever requested Government Financing, complete the following:

Name of Agency	Original Amount of Loan	Date of Request	Approved or Declined	Balance	Current or Past Due
	$			$	
	$			$	

SBA Form 4 (2-85) Previous Editions Obsolete

Figure 11-1. SBA form 4, Application for Business Loan.

INDEBTEDNESS: Furnish the following information on all installment debts, contracts, notes, and mortgages payable. Indicate by an asterisk (*) items to be paid by loan proceeds and reason for paying same (present balance should agree with latest balance sheet submitted).

To Whom Payable	Original Amount	Original Date	Present Balance	Rate of Interest	Maturity Date	Monthly Payment	Security	Current or Past Due
	$		$			$		
	$		$			$		
	$		$			$		
	$		$			$		

MANAGEMENT (Proprietor, partners, officers, directors and all holders of outstanding stock — 100% of ownership must be shown). Use separate sheet if necessary.

Name and Social Security Number	Complete Address	% Owned	*Military Service From	To	*Race	*Sex

* This data is collected for statistical purposes only. It has no bearing on the credit decision to approve or decline this application.

ASSISTANCE   List the name(s) and occupation(s) of any who assisted in preparation of this form, other than applicant.

Name and Occupation	Address	Total Fees Paid	Fees Due
Name and Occupation	Address	Total Fees Paid	Fees Due

Signature of Preparers if Other Than Applicant

THE FOLLOWING EXHIBITS MUST BE COMPLETED WHERE APPLICABLE. ALL QUESTIONS ANSWERED ARE MADE A PART OF THE APPLICATION.

For Guaranty Loans please provide an original and one copy (Photocopy is Acceptable) of the Application Form, and all Exhibits to the participating lender. For Direct Loans submit one original copy of application and Exhibits to SBA.

Submit SBA Form 1261 (Statements Required by Laws and Executive Orders). This form must be signed and dated by each Proprietor, Partner, Principal or Guarantor.

1. Submit SBA Form 912 (Personal History Statement) for each person e.g. owners, partners, officers, directors, major stockholders, etc.; the instructions are on SBA Form 912.

2. Furnish a signed current personal balance sheet (SBA Form 413 may be used for this purpose) for each stockholder (with 20% or greater ownership), partner, officer, and owner. Social Security number should be included on personal financial statement. Label this Exhibit B.

3. Include the statements listed below: 1, 2, 3 for the last three years; also 1, 2, 3, 4 dated within 90 days of filing the application; and statement 5, if applicable. This is Exhibit C (SBA has Management Aids that help in the preparation of financial statements.) All information must be signed and dated.

1. Balance Sheet   2. Profit and Loss Statement
3. Reconciliation of Net Worth
4. Aging of Accounts Receivable and Payable
5. Earnings projections for at least one year where financial statements for the last three years are unavailable or where requested by District Office.
(If Profit and Loss Statement is not available, explain why and substitute Federal Income Tax Forms.)

4. Provide a brief history of your company and a paragraph describing the expected benefits it will receive from the loan. Label it Exhibit D.

ALL EXHIBITS MUST BE SIGNED AND DATED BY PERSON SIGNING THIS FORM.

SBA Form 4 (2-85) Previous Editions Obsolete

Figure 11-1. (Continued)

5. Provide a brief description of the educational, technical and business background for all the people listed under Management. Please mark it Exhibit E.

6. Do you have any co-signers and/or guarantors for this loan? If so, please submit their names, addresses and personal balance sheet(s) as Exhibit F.

7. Are you buying machinery or equipment with your loan money? If so, you must include a list of the equipment and cost as quoted by the seller and his name and address. This is Exhibit G.

8. Have you or any officers of your company ever been involved in bankruptcy or insolvency proceedings? If so, please provide the details as Exhibit H. If none, check here: ☐ Yes ☐ No

9. Are you or your business involved in any pending lawsuits? If yes, provide the details as Exhibit I. If none, check here: ☐ Yes ☐ No

10. Do you or your spouse or any member of your household, or anyone who owns, manages, or directs your business or their spouses or members of their households work for the Small Business Administration, Small Business Advisory Council, SCORE or ACE, any Federal Agency, or the participating lender? If so, please provide the name and address of the person and the office where employed. label this Exhibit J. If none, check here: ☐ Yes ☐ No

11. Does your business, its owners or majority stockholders own or have a controlling interest in other businesses? If yes, please provide their names and the relationship with your company along with a current balance sheet and operating statement for each. This should be Exhibit K.

12. Do you buy from, sell to, or use the services of any concern in which someone in your company has a significant financial interest? If yes, provide details on a separate sheet of paper labeled Exhibit L.

13. If your business is a franchise, include a copy of the franchise agreement and a copy of the FTC disclosure statement supplied to you by the Franchisor. Please include it as Exhibit M.

CONSTRUCTION LOANS ONLY

14. Include a separate exhibit (Exhibit N) the estimated cost of the project and a statement of the source of any additional funds.

15. File the necessary compliance document (SBA Form 601).

16. Provide copies of preliminary construction plans and specifications. Include them as Exhibit O. Final plans will be required prior to disbursement.

DIRECT LOANS ONLY

17. Include two bank declination letters with your application. These letters should include the name and telephone number of the persons contacted at the bank, the amount and terms of the loan, the reason for decline and whether or not the bank will participate with SBA. In cities with 200,000 people or less, one letter will be sufficient.

EXPORT LOANS

18. Does your business presently engage in Export Trade?
Check here ☐ Yes ☐ No

19. Do you plan to begin exporting as a result of this loan?
Check here ☐ Yes ☐ No

20. Would you like information on Exporting?
Check here ☐ Yes ☐ No

AGREEMENTS AND CERTIFICATIONS

Agreements of Nonemployment of SBA Personnel: I/We agree that if SBA approves this loan application I/We will not, for at least two years, hire as an employee or consultant anyone that was employed by the SBA during the one year period prior to the disbursement of the loan.

Certification: I/We certify: (a) I/We have not paid anyone connected with the Federal Government for help in getting this loan. I/We also agree to report to the SBA office of the Inspector General, 1441 L Street N.W., Washington, D.C. 20416 any Federal Government employee who offers, in return for any type of compensation, to help get this loan approved.

(b) All information in this application and the Exhibits are true and complete to the best of my/our knowledge and are submitted to SBA so SBA can decide whether to grant a loan or participate with a lending institution in a loan to me/us. I/We agree to pay for or reimburse SBA for the cost of any surveys, title or mortgage examinations, appraisals etc., performed by non-SBA personnel provided I/We have given my/our consent.

I/We understand that I/We need not pay anybody to deal with SBA. I/We have read and understand Form 394 which explains SBA policy on representatives and their fees.

If you make a statement that you know to be false or if you over value a security in order to help obtain a loan under the provisions of the Small Business Act, you can be fined up to $5,000 or be put in jail for up to two years, or both.

If Applicant is a proprietor or general partner, sign below:

By: _____
                                                  Date

If Applicant is a Corporation, sign below:

_____
Corporate Name and Seal   Date

By: _____
                 Signature of President

Attested by: _____
             Signature of Corporate Secretary

ALL EXHIBITS MUST BE SIGNED AND DATED BY PERSON SIGNING THIS FORM.

Figure 11-1. (*Continued*)

question 8 (on the third page) about bankruptcy. Being honest about the bankruptcy of a former business venture will not necessarily ruin your chances of getting an SBA loan. However, if you lie and get caught, not only will your chances be ruined, you'll face federal prosecution and be subject to up to a $5000 fine, up to 2 years in jail, or both.

SBA Form 413, Personal Financial Statement

SBA form 413 (Figure 11-2) is a personal financial statement from which the SBA can get information on your personal finances. Be as thorough as you can. On the first page, the right-hand column asks for your net worth. Arrive at this figure by subtracting your liabilities from your assets; the result is your net worth. The information in the assets and liabilities sections should reflect your personal, not your business, assets and liabilities. On the second page, under section 5, "Other Personal Property," you should list furniture, jewelry, artwork, and other belongings of value. Your spouse's valuables should be included here, since this is a joint statement. Both you and your spouse should sign the personal financial statement.

SBA Form 912, Statement of Personal History

Read the instructions for this form carefully. As stated there, this form must be filled out in triplicate for each small business owner. The purpose of this form is to give the SBA and lenders a sense of your personal character. While a former arrest or conviction must be listed, it will not necessarily disqualify you for an SBA loan. Consider the following questions carefully:

  6. Are you presently under indictment, or parole or probation?
  7. Have you ever been charged with or arrested for any criminal offense other than a minor motor vehicle violation?
  8. Have you ever been convicted of any criminal offense other than a minor motor vehicle violation?

If you answer yes to any of these questions, make sure to include a detailed statement explaining the circumstances. Use another sheet of paper if you need to. Again, it is important to be honest.

PERSONAL FINANCIAL STATEMENT

As of _____ 19 ____

Complete this form if 1) a sole proprietorship by the proprietor; 2) a partnership by each partner; 3) a corporation by each officer and each stockholder with 20% or more ownership; 4) any other person or entity providing a guaranty on the loan.

Name _____ Residence Phone _____

Residence Address _____

City, State, & Zip _____

Business Name of Applicant/Borrower _____

ASSETS		LIABILITIES	
	(Omit Cents)		(Omit Cents)
Cash on hand & in Banks.................$_____		Accounts Payable.......................$_____	
Savings Accounts......................... _____		Notes Payable (to Bk & Others	
IRA...................................... _____		(Describe in Section 2)................ _____	
Accounts & Notes Receivable		Installment Account (Auto)	
(Describe in Section 6)................. _____		Mo. Payments $_____	
Life Insurance—Cash		Installment Account (Other)	
Surrender Value Only................... _____		Mo. Payments $ _____	
Stocks and Bonds		Loans on Life Insurance................. _____	
(Describe in Section 3).................. _____		Mortgages on Real Estate............... _____	
Real Estate		(Describe in Section 4)................ _____	
(Describe in Section 4).................. _____		Unpaid Taxes	
Automobile—Present Value............... _____		(Describe in Section 7)................ _____	
Other Personal Property................... _____		Other Liabilities	
(Describe in Section 5).................. _____		(Describe in Section 8)................ _____	
Other Assets........................... _____			
(Describe in Section 6)................. _____		Total Liabilities........................... _____	
		Net Worth.............................. _____	
Total..........................$_____		Total..........................$_____	

Section 1. Source of Income		Contingent Liabilities	
Salary........................... $_____		As Endorser or Co-Maker...........................$_____	
Net Investment Income.............. _____		Legal Claims & Judgments........................... _____	
Real Estate Income............... _____		Provision for Fed Income Tax........................ _____	
Other Income (Describe)*.......... _____		Other Special Debt............................... _____	

Description of Items Listed in Section I _____

*(Alimony or child support payments need not be disclosed in "Other Income" unless it is desired to have such payments counted toward total income.)

Section 2. Notes Payable to Banks and Others

Name & Address of Noteholder	Original Balance	Current Balance	Payment Amount	Terms (Monthly-etc.)	How Secured or Endorsed—Type of Collateral

(Response is required to obtain a benefit)

Figure 11-2. SBA form 413, Personal Financial Statement.

Section 3. Stocks and Bonds: (*Use separate sheet if necessary*)

No. of Shares	Names of Securities	Cost	Market Value Quotation/Exchange	Date Amount

Section 4. Real Estate Owned. (*List each parcel separately. Use supplemental sheets if necessary. Each sheet must be identified as a supplement to this statement and signed*).

Address—Type of property	Title is in name of	Date Purchased	Original Cost	Present Value	Mortgage Balance	Amount of Payment	Status of Mortgage

Section 5. Other Personal Property. (*Describe, and if any is mortgaged, state name and address of mortgage holder and amount of mortgage, terms of payment, and if delinquent, describe delinquency.*)

Section 6. Other Assets, Notes & Accounts Receivable (Describe)

Section 7. Unpaid Taxes. (*Describe in detail, as to type, to whom payable, when due, amount, and what, if any, property the tax lien attaches*)

Section 8. Other Liabilities. (*Describe in detail*)

Section 9. Life Insurance Held (*Give face amount of policies—name of company and beneficiaries*)

SBA/Lender is authorized to make all inquiries deemed necessary to verify the accuracy of the statements made herein and to determine my/our creditworthiness.
(I) or (We) certify the above and the statements contained in the schedules herein are a true and accurate statement of (my) or (our) financial condition as of the date stated herein. This statement is given for the purpose of: (*Check one of the following*)

☐ Inducing S.B.A. to grant a loan as requested in the application, to the individual or firm whose name appears herein.
☐ Furnishing a statement of (my) or (our) financial condition, pursuant to the terms of the guaranty executed by (me) or (us) at the same time S.B.A. granted a loan to the individual or firm, whose name appears herein.

Signature	Signature	Date

SOCIAL SECURITY NO.	SOCIAL SECURITY NO.

SBA Form 413 (10-86)

Figure 11-2. (*Continued*)

Please Read Carefully - Print or Type

United States of America

SMALL BUSINESS ADMINISTRATION

STATEMENT OF PERSONAL HISTORY

Each member of the small business concern requesting assistance or the development company must submit this form in TRIPLICATE for filing with the SBA application. This form must be filled out and submitted by:

1. If a sole proprietorship by the proprietor.
2. If a partnership by each partner.
3. If a corporation or a development company, by each officer, director, and additionally by each holder of 20% or more of the voting stock.
4. Any other person including a hired manager, who has authority to speak for and commit the borrower in the management of the business.

Name and Address of Applicant (Firm Name)(Street, City, State and ZIP Code)	SBA District Office and City
	Amount Applied for:

1. Personal Statement of: (State name in full, if no middle name, state (NMN), or if initial only, indicate initial). List all former names used, and dates each name was used. Use separate sheet if necessary.	2. Date of Birth: (Month, day and year)
	3. Place of Birth: (City & State or Foreign Country).
First Middle Last	U.S. Citizen? ☐ YES ☐ NO If no, give alien registration number:

4. Give the percentage of ownership or stock owned or to be owned in the small business concern or the Development Company	Social Security No.

5. Present residence address:	City	State
From: To: Address:		
Home Telephone No. (Include A/C):	Business Telephone No. (Include A/C):	
Immediate past residence address:		
From: To: Address:		

BE SURE TO ANSWER THE NEXT 3 QUESTIONS CORRECTLY BECAUSE THEY ARE IMPORTANT.

THE FACT THAT YOU HAVE AN ARREST OR CONVICTION RECORD WILL NOT NECESSARILY DISQUALIFY YOU. BUT AN INCORRECT ANSWER WILL PROBABLY CAUSE YOUR APPLICATION TO BE TURNED DOWN.

6. Are you presently under indictment, on parole or probation?

☐ Yes   ☐ No   If yes, furnish details in a separate exhibit. List name(s) under which held, if applicable

7. Have you ever been charged with or arrested for any criminal offense other than a minor motor vehicle violation?

☐ Yes   ☐ No   If yes, furnish details in a separate exhibit. List name(s) under which charged, if applicable

8. Have you ever been convicted of any criminal offense other than a minor motor vehicle violation?

☐ Yes   ☐ No   If yes, furnish details in a separate exhibit. List name(s) under which convicted, if applicable

9. Name and address of participating bank

The information on this form will be used in connection with an investigation of your character. Any information you wish to submit, that you feel will expedite this investigation should be set forth

Whoever makes any statement knowing it to be false, for the purpose of obtaining for himself or for any applicant, any loan, or loan extension by renewal, deferment or otherwise, or for the purpose of obtaining, or influencing SBA toward, anything of value under the Small Business Act, as amended, shall be punished under Section 16(a) of that Act, by a fine of not more than $5000, or by imprisonment for not more than 2 years, or both.

Signature	Title	Date

It is against SBA's policy to provide assistance to persons not of good character and therefore consideration is given to the qualities and personality traits of a person, favorable and unfavorable, relating thereto, including behavior, integrity, candor and disposition toward criminal actions. It is also against SBA's policy to provide assistance not in the best interests of the United States, for example, if there is reason to believe that the effect of such assistance will be to encourage or indirectly, activities inimical to the Security of the United States. Anyone concerned with the collection of this information, as to its voluntariness, disclosure or routine uses may contact the FOIA Office, 1441 "L" Street, N.W., and a copy of §9 "Agency Collection of Information" from SOP 40 04 will be provided.

SBA FORM 912 (6-85) SOP 9020 PREVIOUS EDITIONS ARE OBSOLETE   **1. SBA FILE COPY**

Figure 11-3. SBA form 912, Statement of Personal History.

United States of America

SMALL BUSINESS ADMINISTRATION

NAME CHECK

Please Read Carefully - Print or Type

Each member of the small business concern requesting assistance or the development company must submit this form in TRIPLICATE for filing with the SBA application. This form must be filled out and submitted by:

1. If a sole proprietorship by the proprietor.
2. If a partnership by each partner.
3. If a corporation or a development company, by each officer, director, and additionally by each holder of 20% or more of the voting stock.
4. Any other person including a hired manager, who has authority to speak for and commit the borrower in the management of the business.

Name and Address of Applicant (Firm Name)(Street, City, State and ZIP Code)

SBA District Office and City

Amount Applied for:

---

1. Personal Statement of: (State name in full, if no middle name, state (NMN), or if initial only, indicate initial) List all former names used, and dates each name was used. Use separate sheet if necessary

First   Middle   Last

2. Date of Birth: (Month, day and year)

3. Place of Birth: (City & State or Foreign Country)

U.S. Citizen? ☐ YES ☐ NO
If no, give alien registration number:

---

4. Give the percentage of ownership or stock owned or to be owned in the small business concern or the Development Company

Social Security No.

---

5. Present residence address
From: To: Address:

City   State

Home Telephone No. (Include A/C):

Business Telephone No. (Include A/C):

Immediate past residence address
From: To: Address:

BE SURE TO ANSWER THE NEXT 3 QUESTIONS CORRECTLY BECAUSE THEY ARE IMPORTANT.

THE FACT THAT YOU HAVE AN ARREST OR CONVICTION RECORD WILL NOT NECESSARILY DISQUALIFY YOU. BUT AN INCORRECT ANSWER WILL PROBABLY CAUSE YOUR APPLICATION TO BE TURNED DOWN.

6.
☐ Yes ☐ No

7.
☐ Yes ☐ No

8.
☐ Yes ☐ No

9. Name and address of participating bank

The information on this form will be used in connection with an investigation of your character. Any information you wish to submit, that you feel will expedite this investigation should be set forth.

Whoever makes any statement knowing it to be false, for the purpose of obtaining for himself or for any applicant, any loan, or loan extension by renewal, deferment or otherwise, or for the purpose of obtaining, or influencing SBA toward, anything of value under the Small Business Act, as amended, shall be punished under Section 16(a) of that Act, by a fine of not more than $5000, or by imprisonment for not more than 2 years, or both.

Signature   Title   Date

SBA FORM 912 (6-85) SOP 9020 PREVIOUS EDITIONS ARE OBSOLETE

2. This copy to be submitted to:
SBA, OFFICE OF INVESTIGATIONS
1441 L ST., N.W., WASHINGTON, D.C. 20416

Figure 11-3. *(Continued)*

Please Read Carefully - Print or Type

United States of America

SMALL BUSINESS ADMINISTRATION

IDENTIFICATION DIV.

Each member of the small business concern requesting assistance or the development company must submit this form in TRIPLICATE for filing with the SBA application. This form must be filled out and submitted by:

1. If a sole proprietorship by the proprietor.
2. If a partnership by each partner.
3. If a corporation or a development company, by each officer, director, and additionally by each holder of 20% or more of the voting stock.
4. Any other person including a hired manager, who has authority to speak for and commit the borrower in the management of the business.

Name and Address of Applicant (Firm Name)(Street, City, State and ZIP Code)	SBA District Office and City
	Amount Applied for:

1. Personal Statement of: (State name in full, if no middle name, state (NMN), or if initial only, indicate initial. List all former names used, and dates each name was used. Use separate sheet if necessary.	2. Date of Birth: (Month, day and year)
	3. Place of Birth: (City & State or Foreign Country)
First Middle Last	U.S. Citizen? ☐ YES ☐ NO If no, give alien registration number:

4. Give the percentage of ownership or stock owned or to be owned in the small business concern or the Development Company	Social Security No.

5. Present residence address:	City	State
From: To: Address:		

Home Telephone No. (Include A/C):   Business Telephone No. (Include A/C):

Immediate past residence address:
From: To: Address:

BE SURE TO ANSWER THE NEXT 3 QUESTIONS CORRECTLY BECAUSE THEY ARE IMPORTANT.

THE FACT THAT YOU HAVE AN ARREST OR CONVICTION RECORD WILL NOT NECESSARILY DISQUALIFY YOU. BUT AN INCORRECT ANSWER WILL PROBABLY CAUSE YOUR APPLICATION TO BE TURNED DOWN.

6.

☐ Yes ☐ No

7.

☐ Yes ☐ No

8.

☐ Yes ☐ No

9 Name and address of participating bank

The information on this form will be used in connection with an investigation of your character. Any information you wish to submit, that you feel will expedite this investigation should be set forth.

Whoever makes any statement knowing it to be false, for the purpose of obtaining for himself or for any applicant, any loan, or loan extension by renewal, deferment or otherwise, or for the purpose of obtaining, or influencing SBA toward, anything of value under the Small Business Act, as amended, shall be punished under Section 16(a) of that Act, by a fine of not more than $5000, or by imprisonment for not more than 2 years, or both.

Signature	Title	Date

SBA FORM 912 (6-85) SOP 9020 PREVIOUS EDITIONS ARE OBSOLETE

3. This copy to be submitted to:
SBA, OFFICE OF INVESTIGATIONS
1441 L ST., N.W., WASHINGTON, D.C. 20416

Figure 11-3. *(Continued)*

SBA Form 1261, Statements Required by Laws and Executive Orders

As part of your loan package, you must sign SBA form 1261, (Figure 11-4) to indicate that you have read the information about various laws that affect the SBA's business loan programs. The forms are straight-forward. Your signature indicates that the SBA has met its legal obligation to provide you with information about these regulations.

Other Forms and Materials that Accompany the Loan Package

In addition to the forms mentioned above, you must also include your complete business plan and two declination letters from banks if you are applying for a direct loan in an area with a population of greater than 200,000, or one declination letter in an area of less than 200,000.

If you have hired someone to help you fill out your loan applications, you will also have to include SBA form 159, which indicates that you have agreed to pay someone for this purpose. If you wish, you can also fill in SBA form 641 (see Figure 11-5), which is a request for counseling from the SBA.

In addition to providing financing, the SBA also provides free nonfinancial assistance to small businesses. It is worthwhile to take the time to look into the assistance provided to see if you and your business might benefit from the advice. Chapter 12 discusses some of the nonfinancial assistance available.

Federal executive agencies, including the Small Business Administration, are required to withhold or limit financial assistance, to impose special conditions on approved loans, to provide special notices to applicants or borrowers and to require special reports and data from borrowers in order to comply with legislation passed by the Congress and Executive Orders issued by the President and by the provisions of various inter-agency agreements. SBA has issued regulations and procedures that implement these laws and executive orders and they are contained in Parts 112, 113 and 116, Title 13 Code of Federal Regulations Chapter 1, or SOPs.

This form contains a brief summary of the various laws and executive orders that affect SBA's business and disaster loan programs and gives applicants and borrowers the notices required by law or otherwise. The signatures required on the last page provide evidence that SBA has given the necessary notices.

Freedom of Information Act
(5 U.S.C. 552)

This law provides that, with some exceptions, SBA must supply information reflected in agency files and records to a person requesting it. Information about approved loans that will be automatically released includes, among other things, statistics on our loan programs (individual borrowers are not identified in the statistics) and other information such as the names of the borrowers (and their officers, directors, stockholders or partners), the collateral pledged to secure the loan, the amount of the loan, its purpose in general terms and the maturity. Proprietary data on a borrower would not routinely be made available to third parties. All requests under this Act are to be addressed to the nearest SBA office and be identified as a Freedom of Information request.

Privacy Act
(5 U.S.C. 552a)

Disaster home loan files are covered by this legislation because they are normally maintained in the names of individuals. Business loan files are maintained by business name or in the name of individuals in their entrepreneurial capacity. Thus they are not files on individuals and, therefore, are not subject to this Act. Any person can request to see or get copies of any personal information that SBA has in the request's file. Requests for information about another party may be denied unless SBA has the written permission of the individual to release the information to the requester's or unless the information is subject to disclosure under the Freedom of Information Act. (The "Acknowledgement" section of this form contains the written permission of SBA to release information when a disaster victim requests assistance under the family and individual grant program.)

NOTE: Any person concerned with the collection of information, its voluntariness, disclosure or routine use under the Privacy Act or requesting information under the Freedom of Information Act may contact the Director, Freedom of Information/Privacy Acts Division, Small Business Administration, 1441 L Street, N.W., Washington, D.C. 20416, for information about the Agency's procedures on these two subjects.

SBA FORM 1261 (12-86) REF: SOP 50 10 Previous Editions Obsolete

Figure 11-4. SBA form 1261, Legal Notification.

Right to Financial Privacy Act of 1978

(12 U.S.C. 3401)

This is notice to you, as required by the Right to Financial Privacy Act of 1978, of SBA's access rights to financial records held by financial institutions that are or have been doing business with you or your business, including any financial institution participating in a loan or loan guarantee. The law provides that SBA shall have a right of access to your financial records in connection with its consideration or administration of assistance to you in the form of a Government loan or loan guaranty agreement. SBA is required to provide a certificate of its compliance with the Act to a financial institution in connection with its first request for access to your financial records, after which no further certification is required for subsequent accesses. The law also provides that SBA's access rights continue for the term of any approved loan or loan guaranty agreement. No further notice to you of SBA's access rights is required during the term of any such agreement.

The law also authorizes SBA to transfer to another Government authority any financial records included in an application for a loan, or concerning an approved loan or loan guarantee, as necessary to process, service or foreclose a loan or loan guarantee or to collect on a defaulted loan or loan guarantee. No other transfer of your financial records to another Government authority will be permitted by SBA except as required or permitted by law.

Flood Disaster Protection Act

(42 U.S.C. 4011)

Regulations issued by the Federal Insurance Administration (FIA) and by SBA implementing this Act and its amendments. These regulations prohibit SBA from making certain loans in an FIA designated floodplain unless Federal flood insurance is purchased as a condition of the loan. Failure to maintain the required level of flood insurance makes the applicant ineligible for any future financial assistance from SBA under any program, including disaster assistance.

Executive Orders -- Floodplain Management and Wetland Protection

(42 F.R. 26951 and 42 F.R. 2961)

The SBA discourages any settlement in or development of a foodplain or a wetland. This statement is to notify all SBA loan applicants that such actions are hazardous to both life and property and should be avoided. The additional cost of flood preventive construction must be considered in addition to the possible loss of all assets and investments in future floods.

Lead-Based Paint Poisoning Prevention Act

(42 U.S.C. 4821 et seq.)

Borrowers using SBA funds for the construction or rehabilitation of a residential structure are prohibited from using lead-based paint (as defined in SBA regulations) on all interior surfaces, whether accessible or not, and exterior surfaces, such as stairs, decks, porches, railings, windows and doors, which are readily accessible to children under 7 years of age. A "residential structure" is any home, apartment, hotel, motel, orphanage, boarding school, dormitory, day care center, extended care facility, college or other school housing, hospital, group practice or community facility and all other residential or institutional structures where person reside.

Equal Credit Opportunity Act

(15 U.S.C. 1691)

The Federal Equal Credit Opportunity Act prohibits creditors from discriminating against credit applicants on the basis of race, color, religion, national origin, sex, marital status or age (provided that the applicant has the capacity to enter into a binding contract); because all or part of the applicant's income drives from any public assistance program, or because the applicant has in good faith exercised any right under the Consumer Credit Protection Act. The Federal agency that administers compliance with this law concerning this creditor is the Federal Trade Commission, Equal Credit Opportunity, Room 500, 633 Indiana Avenue, N.W., Washington, D.C. 20580.

Figure 11-4. (Continued)

Civil Rights Legislation

All businesses receiving SBA financial assistance must agree not to discriminate in any business practice, including employment practices and services to the public, on the basis of categories cited in 13 C.F.R., Parts 112 and 113 of SBA Regulations. This includes making their goods and services available to handicapped clients or customers. All business borrowers will be required to display the "Equal Employment Opportunity Poster" prescribed by SBA.

Executive Order 11738 -- Environmental Protection

(38 F.R. 25161)

The Executive Order charges SBA with administering its loan programs in a manner that will result in effective enforcement of the Clean Air Act, the Federal Water Pollution Act and other environmental protection legislation. SBA must, therefore, impose conditions on some loans. By acknowledging receipt of this form and presenting the application, the principals of all small businesses borrowing $100,000 or more in direct funds stipulate to the following:

1. That any facility used, or to be used, by the subject firm is not listed on the EPA list of Violating Facilities.

2. That subject firm will comply with all the requirements of Section 114 of the Clean Air Act (42 U.S.C. 7414) and Section 308 of the Water Act (33 U.S.C. 1318) relating to inspection, monitoring, entry, reports and information, as well as all other requirements specified in Section 114 and Section 308 of the respective Acts, and all regulations and guidelines issued thereunder.

3. That subject firm will notify SBA of the receipt of any communication from the Director of the Environmental Protection Agency indicating that a facility utilized, or to be utilized, by subject firm is under consideration to be listed on EPA List of Violating Facilities.

Occupational Safety and Health Act

(15 U.S.C. 651 et seq.)

This legislation authorizes the Occupational Safety and Health Administration in the Department of Labor to require businesses to modify facilities and procedures to protect employees or pay penalty fees. In some instances the business can be forced to cease operations or be prevented from starting operations in a new facility. Therefore, in some instances SBA may require additional information from an applicant to determine whether the business will be in compliance with OSHA regulations and allowed to operate its facility after the loan is approved and disbursed.

In all instances, signing this form as borrower is a certification that the OSHA requirements that apply to the borrower's business have been determined and the borrower is, to the best of its knowledge, in compliance.

Debt Collection Act of 1982   Deficit Reduction Act of 1984

(31 U.S.C. 3701 et seq. and other titles)

These laws require SBA to aggressively collect any loan payments which become delinquent. SBA must obtain your taxpayer identification number when you apply for a loan. If you receive a loan, and do not make payments as they come due, SBA may take one or more of the following actions:

- Report the status of your loan(s) to credit bureaus
- Hire a collection agency to collect your loan
- Offset your income tax refund or other amounts due to you from the Federal Government
- Suspend or debar you or your company from doing business with the Federal Government
- Refer your loan to the Department of Justice or other attorneys for litigation
- Foreclose on collateral or take other action permitted in the loan instruments.

Figure 11-4. (Continued)

Consumer Credit Protection Act

(15 U.S.C. 1601 et seq.)

This legislation gives an applicant who is refused credit because of adverse information about the applicant's credit, reputation, character or mode of living an opportunity to refute or challenge the accuracy of such reports. Therefore, whenever SBA declines a loan in whole or in part because of adverse information in a credit report, the applicant will be given the name and address of the reporting agency so the applicant can seek to have that agency correct its report, if inaccurate. If SBA declines a loan in whole or in part because of adverse information received from a source other than a credit reporting agency, the applicant will be given information about the nature of the adverse information but not the source of the report.

Within 3 days after the consummation of the transaction, any recipient of an SBA loan which is secured in whole or in part by a lien on the recipient's residence or household contents may rescind such a loan in accordance with the "Regulation Z" of the Federal Reserve Board.

Applicant's Acknowledgement

My (our) signature(s) acknowledge(s) receipt of this form, that I (we) have read it and that I (we) have a copy for my (our) files. My (our) signature(s) represents my (our) agreement to comply with the requirements the Small Business Administration makes in connection with the approval of my (our) loan request and to comply, whenever applicable, with the hazard insurance, lead-based paint, civil rights or other limitations contained in this notice.

My (our) signature(s) also represent written permission, as required by the Privacy Act, for the SBA to release any information in my (our) disaster loan application to the Governor of my (our) State or the Governor's designated representative in conjunction with the State's processing of my (our) application for assistance under the Individual and Family Grant Program that is available in certain major disaster areas declared by the President.

Business Name

_____   By _____
Date   Name and Title

Proprietor, Partners, Principals and Guarantors

_____   _____
Date   Signature

_____   _____
Date   Signature

_____   _____
Date   Signature

_____   _____
Date   Signature

SBA Form 1261 (12-86) U.S. Government Printing Office:

Figure 11-4. (Continued)

U.S. SMALL BUSINESS ADMINISTRATION

REQUEST FOR COUNSELING

Please Print

Name of Company	Name of Inquirer	Telephone #

Street	City	State	County	Zip

Employer ID #	Social Security Number	Veteran	Vietnam Era Veteran
		Yes ☐ No ☐	Yes ☐ No ☐ Discharged:

Are you presently:	Yes	No	Can you furnish		Yes	No
In Business?	☐	☐	a recen,:	Balance Sheet?	☐	☐
Starting a Business?	☐	☐		Profit & Loss Statement?	☐	☐
SBA Borrower?	☐	☐				

Kind of business/services (Please specify)

Retail (Selling) _____   Construction _____

Service (Kind) _____   Wholesale (Selling) _____

Manufacturing (Product) _____   Other (Specify) _____

Check the problem areas for which you seek assistance.

☐ 1. Starting a New Business   ☐ 9. Recordkeeping and Accounting

☐ 2. Sources of Credit and Financing   ☐ 10. Financial Statements

☐ 3. Increasing Sales   ☐ 11. Office or Plant Management

☐ 4. Advertising & Sales Promotion   ☐ 12. Personnel

☐ 5. Market Research   ☐ 13. Engineering and Research

☐ 6. Selling to the Government   ☐ 14. Inventory Control

☐ 7. Bidding and Estimating   ☐ 15. Purchasing

☐ 8. International Trade   ☐ 16. Credit & Collections

Please describe how SBA may be of assistance.

I request management assistance from the Small Business Administration. I understand that this assistance is free of charge. I agree to cooperate should I be selected to participate in surveys designed to evaluate SBA assistance services. I authorize SBA to furnish relevant information to the assigned management counselor although I expect that information to be held in strict confidence by him/her.

I further understand that any counselor has agreed not to: (1) recommend goods or services from sources in which he/she has an interest and (2) accept fees or commissions developing from this counseling relationship. In consideration of SBA's furnishing management or technical assistance, I waive all claims against SBA personnel or counselors arising from this assistance.

Signature and Title of Requestor	Date

SBA Form 641 (7-87) Use 12-86 edition until exhausted

Figure 11-5. SBA form 641, Request for Counseling.

12

Beyond Money, There Is Help

Nonfinancial SBA Assistance

Although the main focus of this book is on financing, an exploration of some helpful nonfinancial assistance offered by the SBA is also interesting and useful. Most of the professional services that the SBA furnishes are free.

Organizationally, the SBA has three operational levels. The central office in Washington, D.C., is responsible for determining SBA policy. Loans and management assistance are not provided through the central office. The central office does, however, administer the SBIC program. There are ten regional SBA offices located in major cities in the United States. Regional offices direct district offices within their region; they do not make loans or provide management assistance. It is through the district offices, which are located throughout the country, that you can seek information on loans and management counseling. The telephone numbers and addresses of SBA district offices are given in Appendix A.

Business Development Assistance

The SBA's business development programs have at their core many resources that provide training, counseling, and information to small businesses. The management training done through SBA programs focuses on planning, finance, organization, and marketing. Often, the programs are presented in conjunction with schools or colleges, chambers of commerce, or trade associations. These resources are based in many of the communities in which small businesses may be located. The services are designed to help the small business owner avoid failure and succeed in his or her venture, ultimately improving the economic environment in which the businesses are based.

The SBA believes that the primary reason for most small business failures is poor management. While this point can be argued, since other experts will hold that undercapitalization is the primary reason, the SBA is committed to trying to help business owners and managers improve their management ability. The SBA holds prebusiness workshops for prospective owners on a regular basis, as well as other training programs focusing on a variety of needs from rural development to international trade.

The business development programs come in the forms of individual counseling, SBA-sponsored courses, conferences and workshops, and publications. These programs are available to people who are just starting businesses, to business owners who are facing problems in their ongoing businesses, and to owners or managers who want advice on long-term plans for their businesses.

Business counseling is done primarily through the Service Corps of Retired Executives (SCORE), Small Business Institutes (SBIs), Small Business Development Centers (SBDCs), and a variety of other associations. The SBA tries to find a center that will match the needs of the business owner in search of counseling.

Service Corps of Retired Executives

SCORE is staffed by more than 13,000 retired executives who provide management counseling to business owners and managers. The SBA attempts to match the expertise of the SCORE volunteers with the needs of the businesses seeking counseling. There are more than 750 SCORE locations in the United States. You can find out where the nearest one is by calling the SBA field office closest to you. SCORE counseling can be done on a one-to-one basis or through workshops and training sessions. If you can find a SCORE volunteer who understands your business and can provide good management counseling, you will save thousands of dollars in consulting fees that you might have had to pay an outside firm for advice. There is no fee for SCORE counseling. The quality of advice will vary depending on the volunteer who is assigned to you, but there's a good chance that you can benefit from the wisdom of someone who has been in a similar business situation.

Small Business Institutes

SBIs were begun in 1972 as a cooperative venture of the SBA, more than 500 colleges and universities around the country, and the small business community. The SBIs fall under the supervision of the university and SBA staffs. At each SBI site, senior and graduate business students, working under the tutelage of their faculty advisers, dispense management advice to small business owners. The students receive guidance from their faculty and from SBA business development staff, and get academic credit for their participation in the program. The small business owner benefits from free advice, while the students benefit from having been in the "real-world" position of acting as consultants to businesses.

Small Business Development Centers

SBDCs were begun in 1976 to draw on the resources of colleges and universities; the private sector; local, state, and federal governments; and other federal agencies to furnish management training and technical assistance to small business owners. There are 53 "lead" SBDCs that provide full service, and 600 SBDC service locations throughout the United States. The addresses of these SBDCs are available through SBA field offices. The focus of SBDCs may vary from location to location, but primarily they are concerned with providing technical advice, research materials, and other specialized assistance to small business owners. The SBDCs are usually located at universities or colleges.

Small Business Innovation Research Program

The Small Business Innovation Research (SBIR) program is an outgrowth of the Small Business Innovation Development Act of 1982. The SBIR program is designed to use federal money to fund qualified high-technology small businesses. The funds are drawn from the federal agencies with the largest research and development budgets. The agencies are mandated to set aside a required percentage for these funds every year.

The Small Business Innovation Development Act of 1982 identified the SBA as the agency responsible for coordinating the SBIR activities. The SBA must report on the results of the SBIR program to Congress every year. The SBIR Pre-Solicitation Announcement (PSA) is published quarterly by the SBA to give information on the SBIR program. To find out if your business qualifies for SBIR funds, you should call the SBA Office of Innovation, Research, and Technology in Washington, D.C., at 202-653-7875.

Procurement Assistance

Billions of dollars in contracts for goods and services are awarded every year to all businesses of all sizes. The SBA works with other federal agencies to provide procurement assistance to small business owners so that they can have a chance of receiving some of these contracts.

Among the programs in the SBA procurement assistance programs are the following:

- *Prime contract assistance.* Procurement center representatives (PCRs) are located at major federal government buying installations around the country. These PCRs counsel small business owners with advice on how to get prime contracts or subcontracts from the federal government. PCRs also guide small business owners to the government agencies that buy that businesses products or services; aid small business owners in getting their names on bidders' lists; and help them get solicitations, drawings, and specifications for proposed purchases.

  Contracts or portions of contracts are set aside by government purchasing officers for exclusive small business bidding. The PCRs work with the contracting agencies to make sure that they meet the criteria for these set-aside contracts. The PCRs are to act as advocates for full and open competition for procurement of government goods and services.

- *Subcontract assistance.* The SBA refers qualified small businesses to large prime contractors. Many of these prime contractors have agreed through the SBA to offer small businesses the opportunity to bid on subcontract work.

- *Certificates of Competency (COCs).* When a small business is the lowest bidder for a contract and a contracting officer questions the small business's ability to fulfill the terms of the contract, the contracting officer has to refer the small business to the SBA for a Certificate of Competency. The small business then must apply for a COC. In response, the SBA makes an on-site inspection of the business' facilities, management, performance record, and production capabilities to determine whether or not the small business is capable of fulfilling the contract. If the SBA establishes that the small business is capable of completing the contract within the desired time constraints, the SBA issues a COC. The contracting officer is then obligated to award the contract to the small business. The COC is a good program for small businesses, because once a small business is deemed capable of meeting contract requirements, the contracting agency is essentially forced to award the contract to the small business.

- *Procurement Automated Source System (PASS).* PASS was developed to give corporations data on small businesses that are interested in bidding on federal contracts and subcontracts. PASS is a computerized database system listing the names, addresses, and capabilities of more than 130,000 small businesses. It enables federal procurement officers and prime contractors to identify small businesses that might be potential contractors and subcontractors on a contract job. Any SBA office can give small businesses interested in being listed on the PASS system the necessary forms to fill out. (See Figure 12-1.)

- *Natural resources sales assistance.* The federal government sells surplus real property, personal property, and natural resources every year. The SBA works with other federal government agencies to try to ensure that small businesses will have chances to buy these surplus goods.

SBA Office of Advocacy

In 1976, the SBA Office of Advocacy was created within the federal government to be a watchdog agency for small businesses. The president appoints and the Senate confirms the chief counsel for advocacy. The office was created by Public Law 94-305, which among other things listed its functions as:

- Researching how federal laws, programs, regulations, and taxations affect small business. The Office of Advocacy uses this research information to recommend adjustments that will meet small business needs.

- Preparing research and position reports analyzing and making eco-

The enclosed company profile is ☐ a new listing or ☐ an updated listing.
PROCUREMENT AUTOMATED SOURCE SYSTEM (PASS) – COMPANY PROFILE

IDENTIFICATION PASS is designed only for small businesses organized for profit and independently owned and operated.

COMPANY NAME _____ EMPLOYER IDENTIFICATION NO. (if avail.) _____

_____ DUNS NO. (if available) _____

MAILING ADDRESS _____ TOTAL SALES LAST FISCAL YEAR _____

CITY _____ STATE ____ ZIP _____ YEAR BUSINESS ESTABLISHED _____

PHONE _____ NAME OF CONTACT _____

Area Code   Number

BUSINESS TYPES: PASS is divided into 4 types of businesses. Please estimate the percentage of your business allocated to the
following (total must equal 100%) and complete the appropriate Section(s).

MANUFACTURING/SUPPLIES	%	**CONSTRUCTION**	%

CHECK APPLICABLE BOX(ES)   MAXIMUM CURRENT BONDING LEVEL if avail. $_____

☐ Manufacturer   ☐ Dealer   ☐ Wholesale Distributor   MAXIMUM OPERATING RADIUS_____ Miles

Anywhere in U.S., Enter 3999 Above

MANUFACTURING FACILITY SIZE _____ SQ. FT.   Anywhere in the World, Enter 9999 Above

RESEARCH & DEVELOPMENT	%	**SERVICES**	%

No. of Engineers & Scientists _____ MAXIMUM CURRENT BONDING LEVEL if avail. $ _____

Expertise of key personnel _____ MAXIMUM OPERATING RADIUS_____ Miles

_____ Anywhere in U.S., Enter 3999 Above

Anywhere in the World, Enter 9999 Above

CAPABILITIES/EQUIPMENT (Limit 32 words; avoid abbreviations)

List products, equipment, services, special capabilities, and important categories under which you want your business listed. The system searches
businesses based on the capabilities you list in this section. _____

_____

CODES (if not available, leave blank)

Standard Industrial Classification (SIC) Code(s):   Federal Supply Classification/Commodity/Product Service Code(s):

MANUFACTURING QUALITY ASSURANCE INFORMATION | **EXPORTS (check one box ✓)**

☐ MIL-I-45208   ☐ ACTIVE EXPORTER
☐ MIL-Q-9858   ☐ INTERESTED IN EXPORTS
☐ OTHER (Please Identify) _____   ☐ NOT INTERESTED IN EXPORTS

OWNERSHIP (check all applicable boxes) ✓ | **IF MINORITY OWNER, check ✓**

Company is at least 51%   ☐ VETERAN(S)   ☐ BLACK AMERICAN   ☐ HISPANIC AMERICAN
OWNED, CONTROLLED and   ☐ CHECK IF ANY SERVICE   ☐ NATIVE AMERICAN (includes American Indian, Eskimo,
ACTIVELY MANAGED BY   WAS IN THE VIETNAM ERA   Aleut & Native Hawaiian)
        (1964-1975)   ☐ ASIAN-INDIAN AMERICAN (includes India, Pakistan,
        ☐ WOMAN/WOMEN   Bangladesh)
        ☐ MINORITY PERSON(S)   ☐ ASIAN-PACIFIC AMERICAN (includes Asia, Indian Sub
        continent & Pacific Islands & Orientals)

SIGNATURE Important! Signature is required!

CERTIFICATION – I certify that this is a small business and information supplied herein (including all pages attached) is correct and that neither the
applicant nor any person (or concern) in any connection with the applicant as a principal or officer, so far as is known, is now debarred or otherwise
declared ineligible by any agency of the Federal Government from making offers for furnishing materials, supplies, or services to the Government or
any agency thereof.

Information Contained In This Profile May Be Disclosed At The Discretion Of The Small Business Administration.

PLEASE SIGN HERE ➡

Signature of Company Officer _____ Title _____ Date _____

Figure 12-1. Procurement Automated Source System (PASS)—company profile.

nomic evaluations of the impact of public policy issues and legislative
proposals on small businesses.

▪ Evaluating future opportunities, needs, and problems facing small
business, based on economic studies and statistical research performed by the Office of Advocacy.

▪ Assisting small business owners with information about federal laws,
regulations, and programs.

▪ Working with small businesses to furnish information and insight into
small business issues.

- Serving as a liaison between the small business community and the federal government; suggesting and commenting on federal policy affecting small businesses.

One of the best books on small business in the United States, which comes out annually and is prepared by the SBA Office of Advocacy, is *The State of Small Business.*[1] It is packed with research done by the Office of Advocacy, and features dozens of tables of statistics on how small businesses performed in the previous year. The insight and analysis is quite useful for the small business owner who wants to get a feel for the outlook for small business in this country. The book is for sale at any U.S. government bookstore or you can get information on price and availability by writing to the Superintendent of Documents, U.S. Government Printing Office, Washington, DC 20402. Refer to the book by name and ask for the current edition. The year on the cover indicates the year in which the information is published. It always reflects information current up to and including the prior year.

Minority Small Business Owner Assistance

All the programs that the SBA offers are available to minority business owners. But the federal government, recognizing that Americans who are members of a minority group may have difficulty entering the economic mainstream, has also developed special programs through the SBA to help minority group members who want to start or expand small businesses.

In 1978, Congress approved a capital ownership development program for minorities. The program falls under the direction of the SBA's associate administrator for minority small business and capital ownership development. Essentially, this is an outreach program in which the program's staff works with local business development organizations to explain SBA's services and how the SBA can serve their needs as business owners.

Getting a little more specific in help, the SBA, under Section 8(a) of the Small Business Act, works with procurement officials in other federal agencies, serves as a prime contractor for purchase of federal goods and services, and subcontracts the work to small businesses that are

---

[1]SBA Office of Advocacy, *The State of Small Business: A Report of the President.* Washington: U.S. Government Printing Office, 1989.

owned by "socially and economically disadvantaged persons."[2] For a small business to be eligible for the Section 8(a) program, it must be at least 51 percent owned by a U.S. citizen who is a member of a group that has been "subjected to racial or ethnic prejudice or cultural bias because of their identity as a member of a group without regard to their individual qualities." The government identifies these groups as "socially disadvantaged: Black Americans, Hispanic Americans, Native Americans (American Indians, Alaskan Natives, Eskimos, Aleuts, or Native Hawaiians), Asian Pacific Americans (originating from Japan, China, the Philippines, Vietnam, Korea, Samoa, Guam, U.S. Trust Territory of the Pacific Islands, Northern Marianas, Laos, Cambodia, and Taiwan), Asian Americans (originating from India, Pakistan, Bangladesh, and Sri Lanka)." The SBA can be flexible enough to designate other groups from time to time as falling into this category. To participate in the program, you must also show your economic disadvantage, demonstrate that a socially and economically disadvantaged person will be engaged in the day-to-day operation of the business, and generally show that your business has a chance for success. Brokers and packagers are ineligible for the Section 8(a) program.

Each participant in the Section 8(a) program is subject to a program participation term of 9 years from the date of certification as a program participant. Applications to the Section 8(a) program can be made at any SBA field office.

Under the Section 7(j) Management and Technical Assistance Program, the SBA can give grants, agreements, and contracts to individuals, firms, state and local governments, colleges and universities, Indian tribes, and nonprofit institutions to allow them to furnish management and technical advice to small businesses which are situated in areas of high employment. Recipients of this advice can be SBA-certified 8(a) firms, as well as socially and economically disadvantaged people located in high unemployment areas.

In the summer of 1989 (the legislation took effect August 15, 1989), the SBA announced a new set of rules for the Section 8(a) program, which were instituted to try to ensure that companies in the program would survive in the marketplace and to try to safeguard against abuses of the program. (The new rules were instituted in the shadow of the Wedtech scandal, a minority defense contractor in New York that was deemed to have abused the program, among other things.)

The new rules require that the net worth of applicants, excluding home and business equity, be no more than $250,000 instead of the pre-

---

[2]"Section 8(a) Program," *Fact Sheet No. 36.* Washington: U.S. Small Business Administration, revised, February 1989.

vious ceiling of $750,000. During the 9 years a participant is in the program, the net-worth requirements are adjusted. After the first 4 years, the net-worth cap is $500,000; in the ninth year, $750,000. By the end of their involvement in the program, the original legislation called for firms to have won at least 75 percent of their contracts from outside the 8(a) program; SBA officials, however, were quoted as saying they realistically only expected 55 percent to come from outside the 8(a) program.[3]

Women-Owned Businesses

Women are eligible for all SBA programs. The SBA states that one of its major goals is to help women to become successful entrepreneurs. The SBA defines a *woman-owned business* as one that a woman owns at least 51 percent of, and one in which one or more women owners have a day-to-day role in the operation and control of the company.

The growth of women-owned businesses has indeed grown in recent years. In 1985, the number of women-owned firms was a little more than 3.7 million. A year later, that number had grown 10.3 percent to greater than 4.1 million firms. (There were a total of 13.8 million nonfarm sole proprietorships in the United States in 1986.) The total number of sole proprietorships between 1980 and 1986 increased 41.8 percent, while the number of women-owned sole proprietorships grew by 62.6 percent. The receipts from women-owned nonfarm sole proprietorships amounted to $71.6 billion at the end of 1986 (out of a total $553.7 billion). By 1986, women-owned sole proprietorships accounted for 12.9 percent of the total business receipts for that year.[4]

Clearly, women business owners are a growing and driving force in the economy today. Too often in the past, women were not treated with the same seriousness as men when they approached bankers or other lenders for financing. Even today, the situation is not totally resolved. Some successful businesswomen still feel it necessary to take a male financial professional with them when they seek financing, not for his advice, but simply in hopes that the presence of a male will ensure square treatment.

For bankers to put capable businesswomen in demeaning situations is not only myopic but also self-destructive. Like the programs for the handicapped, disabled veterans, and "economic and socially disadvan-

---

[3]Jeanne Saddler, "SBA Sets New Rules on Minority Program," *The Wall Street Journal,* August 16, 1989, p. B2.
[4] SBA Office of Advocacy, op. cit., pp. 26–27.

taged" (e.g., minorities), the government programs designed to help women cannot legislate away condescension and patronizing attitudes. Unenlightened lenders would be wise to wake up and follow the lead of lenders who know a good business deal when they see one, regardless of gender, race, or handicap. Small business owners who currently are secure in their financing relationships would be doing a service to their small business community by avoiding doing business with lenders who discriminate against prospective borrowers.

To combat some of the troubles women have had in getting into business, the SBA has had a nationwide women's business-owner program in effect since 1977. It also began organizing a series of seminars and workshops in 1983 for women business owners or prospective business owners. The seminars focus on business planning and development, credit, and procurement. In 1988, the Women's Business Ownership Act was passed to assist women-owned businesses. The act focuses on improved collection of government data on women's business ownership and improved accessibility of SBA programs to women business owners.

SBA Management Assistance Publications

The SBA has many publications that are designed to help current and prospective small business owners. Appendix D lists the titles of many of these booklets, along with their prices and the address from which you can order them. The books are short, inexpensive, and basic. They are very good sources for the small business owner who is looking for information on a particular topic. The best thing about these little volumes is that they do not include a lot of extraneous information or opinionated passages. For the busy small business owner, the delivery of just the facts is a blessing.

PART 4

Pulling It All Together

Understanding the Business Proposal, Loan Package, and Financial Ratios

13
Thinking It Through:

The Business Plan

A well-thought-out business plan can serve many purposes. Two of its chief purposes are: (1) it can provide you with a tool for starting and running your business successfully, and for making it grow, and (2) you can use it to shop your business idea around for financing. There are no fixed rules about precisely what form your business plan should take. Certainly, there are some common, essential elements that all business plans must have, but business plans, like business ideas, will vary from business to business.

You should write your own business plan rather than hiring outside consultants to package it for you. One of the strongest arguments that can be made for doing it this way is that going through the process will force you to become intimately familiar with the ins and outs of your business: what the business idea is, how it might work, who and where the markets are, how much money it will take to get off and running, and so on. If you participate in the process of putting together your business plan, your personality and strengths will be reflected in the final plan. You'll also be in a position to show a prospective lender or investor that you really know your business inside and out, when it comes time to discuss your plans.

Some lenders or investors have standard requirements that they insist on seeing in a business plan. Be sure to check with a prospective financing source to make sure you cover all the appropriate bases in your plan.

In this chapter, we'll look at what goes into a full-fledged business plan. In Chapter 14, we'll look at a shorter loan proposal that incorporates some, but not all, of the information you may have already used in your business plan. How much information you present to the financing source depends on who the financing source is and how much they want to see. For example, an initial loan proposal for an SBA loan would probably be a lot briefer than a proposal for venture capital funding. The SBA lender may ask to see your complete business plan somewhere down the line, but probably won't need to see it right away.

Venture capital investors, on the other hand, will want to see an elaborately thought out business plan. Unlike bank lenders, venture capitalists will likely have no standard application forms for you to fill out. There's a good chance they will be considering making an equity investment, in which they become part owners of your business. To win them over, you had better show them you know your stuff. A well-wrought business plan can prove that you know the business you're getting into.

There are countless examples of companies that have taken off like crazy and then failed due to a lack of planning. One such company was Have a Heart, founded by Lucy Mackall in 1977. In 1981, Mackall hooked onto the idea of making shoelaces with hearts on them, in keeping with the heart motif that emblazoned all the products she sold in her store. Shoelace mania caught on, to the point that sales hit the $10 million mark a year later. But Mackall had no systems in place, no inventory planning, no controls. In spite of burgeoning sales, the business failed.[1] Had Mackall taken the time to put together a well-thought-out business plan, she might have been prepared to handle the ebb and flow of orders and the snags she hit with manufacturing.

The Format

There is no set format for successful business plans, but there are some good outlines. One school of thought has it that business plans should be as brief and to the point as possible, covering all the bases but not belaboring the point. Sometimes that's fine. But the best business plan I have ever seen—in terms of content and writing style—was close to 300 pages long. It worked because the business founders were presenting not only a business plan but a plan for a new business concept. So they certainly had some selling to do to prospective financing sources to convince them that this business idea could really fly. They did their job well and got the financing they wanted. Even investment bankers who

[1]Peyton Petty, "The Rise and Fall of Lucy Mackall," *Boston Woman*, April 1987, p. 28.

decided against making an investment in the business still comment years later about the quality of this plan.

What made this plan so good? Simply stated, it did its job by explaining the business, the market, the projections for the future, and so on, in a way that was not only convincing but also easy to follow because of its simple format.

Here is a basic outline for the format of a business plan that can really do two jobs: It can help the business owner to understand why he or she is in business, and it can help the prospective financing source to understand why this business is worth a risk.

    Cover Sheet
    Table of Contents

      I. Executive Summary
     II. History of the Business
    III. General Philosophy
    IV. The Market
     V. The Competition
    VI. The Business (the Product or Service)
   VII. The Management Team
  VIII. The Operating Plan
    IX. The Marketing Plan
     X. Business Risks
    XI. Summary Financial and Operating Statements
   XII. Operating Statements
  XIII. Balance Sheets
       Appendixes

Since business plans differ from business to business, and can number well over 300 pages when all the support material and financials are included, we will not include a complete sample business plan in this book. There are plenty of good sources for this information. *Starting and Managing the Small Business,*[2] by Arthur H. Kuriloff and John M. Hemphill, Jr., has an excellent sample business plan in its appendix. Many books listed in the Bibliography also include good sample business plans. The SBA publishes five separate booklets on writing business plans for specific industries. They are: *Business Plan for Small Manufacturers, Business Plan for Small Construction Firms, Business Plan for Retailers, Business Plan for Small Service Firms,* and *The Business Plan for Homebased Business.* (Information on how to obtain these

[2]New York: McGraw-Hill, 1988.

SBA booklets is given in Appendix D.) You can also ask a financial professional with whom you do business to show you an example of a good business plan.

Included in this chapter are synopses of the sections of a solid business plan, to give you an idea how these are important to finding money to start and operate a business. Remember that business plans are highly individual documents, and as such, they differ from business owner to business owner. Some basics that you should try to include are described below.

Cover Sheet

The cover sheet for a business plan need not be too elaborate. Simply state the name of the business; the date; some notation, if necessary, about the confidentiality of the business plan (Bethany Bagel Shops, a fictional example we will be studying in this chapter, might state, "This business plan is confidential information. It should not be distributed without the permission of Max Nilges, president, Bethany Bagel Company."); and the name, address, and telephone number of the business owner who is submitting the plan. (If there is more than one owner, give the names, addresses, and telephone number of all the owners.)

Table of Contents

To make your business plan easy for a prospective financing source to follow, a detailed table of contents is an important feature. Different financing sources will look for different things when they are deciding to lend or invest. A detailed table of contents allows them to turn to their areas of greatest concern first, whether it be the financial projections, the management team, or the market analysis of the product or service.

When you are writing your business plan, remember that you may be trying to woo a prospective lender or investor with it; make it as easy to follow as possible. An added benefit will be the ease with which you yourself and the officers of your business can refer to specific sections of the business plan when it comes time to run your business.

In our business plan for Bethany Bagel Shops, a complete section in the table of contents might read as follows:

XI. Summary Financial and Operating Statements
Bethany Bagel Shop Opening Plan
Shop Opening Expenses

Shop Operations
Shop Overhead
Operating Statement
Single Shop Operating Statement
Balance Sheet Assumptions
Summary Balance Sheet

Executive Summary

The executive summary should be a brief synopsis of the business concept. It should give the prospective financing source an idea of the business and its validity. The writer should leave all extraneous information out of this section, and should get right to the point. This section should run about 5 to 10 pages, but there are no hard-and-fast rules about length. Remember, this is just a summary. Make it clear that the information presented here is discussed at length later in the business plan. The executive summary should include the following information:

- *A paragraph or two stating the nature of the business being proposed, what, if anything, makes it unique in the marketplace, and what features of this business will make it work.*

- *A paragraph giving brief information on the founders.* Don't go into great detail here. Give the name, age, and a brief sentence on the background of each founder.

- *A brief description of the business.* For example, you might write: "The Bethany Bagel Shops will be a chain of 2000-square-foot shops on locations accessible primarily by pedestrian foot traffic in areas near major employers in downtown locations." In the same paragraph, give a rough estimate of average sales volume for the business, as well as estimated profits. Also give an estimate of financing needs. For Bethany Bagel, you might estimate the financing needs for each shop, including such items as equipment, fixtures, and leasehold improvements; inventory costs; preopening and start-up costs; and rents. You can also give a brief projected operating statement. State that this paragraph includes summaries of items that will be elaborated upon in appropriate sections of the business plan. An example such as Table 13-1 may be included here.

- *A statement about how much equity or debt is needed to finance the business.* Be as specific as you can about how much is needed and what form you see it taking (e.g., equity, bank line of credit, equipment loan, and so on).

Table 13-1. Bethany Bagel Shops
Projected Operating Statement

Year	1	2	3	4	5
Sales ($000)	$1,375	$4,045	$6,188	$10,998	$17,591
Gross profit*($000)	$ 315	$ 958	$1,518	$ 2,791	$ 4,315
Gross margin†	22.9%	23.7%	24.5%	25.4%	24.5%
Wages	5.2%	3.9%	3.8%	3.5%	3.2%
Advertising	7.5%	4.4%	3.7%	3.2%	3.3%
Overhead	18.0%	4.9%	5.4%	3.8%	2.7%
Profit (or loss) before interest and taxes($000)	($ 261)	$ 30	$ 212	$ 750	$ 1,540
Percentage of profit (or loss) be- fore interest and taxes	(19%)	0.7%	3.4%	6.8%	8.7%
No. of shops at year-end	4	4	7	12	17

*Gross profit is calculated by subtracting the cost of goods sold from net sales.
†Gross margin is calculated by dividing gross profit by sales.

- *A brief statement of why you and the other cofounders decided upon this particular business.* Follow this with your reasons in a bulleted or numbered list. Try to answer the following questions:

What is the industry you are entering?
How will your business serve the market that exists for this business?
How big is the industry that you are entering?
How fast is the industry growing every year?
What has accounted for the growth?
Does the growth show signs of continuing?
Are there any special concepts about your proposed business that need explaining?
Who are your primary target customers? Why?
Who are your secondary targets? Why?
How will your business service these target markets better than your competition?
Are there critical business events that must occur to enable you to succeed in your business concept? (For example, will you need attractive pricing from suppliers? New construction near your sites?)
What are the sales volumes you project? What percentage of market share does this represent for your business in your primary market? What percentage in your secondary market?
Is your business concept susceptible to competitors moving in on the concept?
Is there anything about your business concept, the people starting the business, or other aspects of the business that limit its prospects of success?

After completing your list, focusing on the issues above, sum up briefly by writing that these are the reasons you, as founders, are committed to the success of the business. The executive summary is a good place to state whether or not you have identified any of the proposed sites for business or for a central office for the business.

- *A statement of the names and background of any other key senior executives who will be involved in running the business.*

- *A brief summary reiterating that the business has been researched exhaustively.* This demonstrates that there is room for success in the marketplace, and that the key executives are experienced enough and have good enough track records to ensure the success of the business.

History of the Business

The contents of the "History of the Business" section of the business plan are pretty self-explanatory. Here is where you tell the background of the business—how you came upon the idea for the business, how the founders' backgrounds match the business's needs, what assumptions you are making about the potential marketplace that might increase the likelihood of success, what other kinds of businesses in different market segments have succeeded with similar concepts, and so on.

Go on to specifically lay out how you designed your business and what criteria you used. The questions listed below will serve as guidelines.

- How large does the potential market have to be in the location in which you set up your business?
- What kind of needs will your customers have, and how will you meet them?
- How can your business be duplicated if this is a franchisable or chain store idea?
- What kind of distribution or pricing issues are critical to your business's success?
- After you identified your criteria for a business, how did you settle on the particular concept? Did your research point to this type of business more clearly than other types? How?
- Who is your primary target market?
- How did you arrive at this primary target market?
- Are there any statistics you can use to briefly back up your decision about your primary target market?
- Who are your secondary target markets?
- How did you discover these secondary target markets? Back up your decision.

Unless the business you are proposing is highly technical and requires a great deal of technical explanation, the section on the history of your business should probably run about five to ten pages tops. Make it as brief as you can, but back up all the conclusions you make.

General Philosophy

In this section, you will lay out your general philosophy of doing business. The questions listed below will serve as guidelines.

- What principles will you use to run your business? Will you keep it lean and mean?
- How much will you invest in the latest technology of your industry?
- Will you wait to see how the business does before pouring a great deal of money into it?
- What kind of overhead costs will you have?
- Will you staff up immediately, or will you make use of outside consultants who might cost less in the long run than full-time employees?
- If you plan for expansion, how will you dedicate the funds you are seeking for financing?
- Will you invest a good deal of money in marketing to drive up short-term sales, or will you keep overhead low to protect long-term profitability?
- If you keep the business overhead bare-bones, how will you provide for expansion when you decide it is time?
- Are there challenges facing your entry into the marketplace?
- Is your product or service new or unfamiliar?
- Will you need to change the behavior of your market?
- How will you overcome these hurdles?

The general philosophy section of your business plan need not be longer than two to five pages. Be clear and focused, and get to the point.

The Market

The section of your business plan focusing on the market will likely be longer than the earlier sections discussed. Here, you will begin to present convincing evidence that your business is likely to meet with success in the market place. This section will detail your market as you see it, using numbers derived from the research you have done in developing your business idea.

First off, you'll want to present some hard numbers. List the total market for your product or service in the United States (and in foreign countries if appropriate). If your business can be broken down into different categories, list the total market for each category. Also list the total market in dollars.

Then give any statistics or support that shows how the market has continued to grow over the last 5 to 10 years. You can state the growth as a percentage or in total dollar volume. Here you will be giving your potential financing source an indication that your business is one that is on a growth track and is likely to continue growing in the future. After presenting the numbers, draw any conclusions that you can substantiate about the potential for future growth of the type of business you are proposing.

List any market characteristics that support your business concept. Be as thorough as possible. If you are aware of a demographic trend that leads to the conclusion that the population will be needing more of your product or service, indicate that in this section. If any shifts in the economy make it likely that your business will prosper, this is the place to substantiate that claim.

Present outside support from any studies or research you have done indicating that the market will be receptive to your business. If you need to quote extensive portions of background material, do so in an appendix. Present a synopsis of your research findings here.

- How are the types of businesses you are going into currently run?

- What distribution methods are used?

- How is pricing done?

- Will your business be different from other similar businesses in ways that will make your business more efficient in delivering the product to the market at a profit to you?

- How do your prospective customers currently buy from the businesses that now exist to serve their needs?

- What kind of dollar volume passes through these businesses?

- What are the traditional channels of distribution for your business?

Who are your target customers? List the primary target markets. If businesses in your primary target market fall within the Standard Industry Classification (SIC) system that the federal government uses to categorize businesses by industry, you can include these SIC codes in an appendix to your business plan. Within these primary market businesses, who is typically the decision maker about purchases from a company like yours? Is there anything about your business concept that will change the way these decision makers will have to do business with your company? How will you educate these people to become comfortable with your business concept? Will you use advertising? Seminars? Or some other technique?

Who are the secondary target markets for your business? Again, who makes the buying decisions within these companies? Will these decision makers be receptive to your business idea? How will the CEOs, chief financial officers (CFOs), controllers, or other financial decision makers view your business?

The same questions are applicable to consumer products. Who are the decision makers in the consumer market who buy your type of product? How might they receive what you are offering them?

What is the demand for your product or service? How much does your prospective market make use of your product (in dollars) every year? Present background research or numbers that back up your demand estimates. If appropriate, you can analyze a specific segment within your potential primary market to illustrate how products or services like those you will offer are currently used.

Conclude with tables or charts, if possible, that support your claims about the potential market for your product.

The Competition

Obviously, competition varies from business type to business type. The section on competition in your business plan should focus specifically on your major competitors. You may want to include a diagram showing the channels of distribution (i.e., how the product moves from manufacturer to ultimate user) and where your business or service is located on the diagram. Discuss each of the major competitors you have outlined in the diagram that serve a similar function to the one you see your business serving.

Take the competitors one by one. For each competitor company, present the following information:

- The types of profits it experiences
- Its sales volume
- Its return on investment
- Where it is located
- How profitable it is
- How many and what types of employees it has
- How much sales per employee it averages
- How it is set up as a business (e.g., sole proprietorship, partnership, corporation)

Add any other information that you think might help a reader understand how these businesses work. If you can, also include the following industry figures:

- Total sales
- Cost of goods sold
- Gross profits
- Selling expenses
- Leasehold expenses
- Inventory expenses
- Office and computer expenses
- Administrative expenses
- Tax expenses (payroll, property, and taxes other than federal)
- Miscellaneous expenses
- Net profits before income taxes

If you have researched specific major competitors, include any relevant information on how they do business and how successful they have been. Report the findings of any market research you have done. What does the competition think of your business concept? If your business differs from the competition in any significant way, whether financial or distribution, how do you justify this difference?

Discuss any other sources of competition you see in the marketplace. Give sales figures, growth rates, and as much of the information mentioned above as you can for each of these.

It is a good idea to clearly state how your business will compare with the competition. You can do this as you discuss each of the major competitors, or in list format toward the end of the discussion of competition.

Include a survey of what competitors charge for the type of product or service you are proposing. List how your prices will compare with competitors' prices.

The section on competition can vary widely in length, depending largely on how much competition there is and how much information is available on it. Use your judgment. Don't overload the reader with too much information, but give him or her enough to make a convincing case that you understand and can succeed among the competition.

The Business: The Product or Service

This section gives you a chance to make the case for your product or service. This will be a highly personal section, but one that is backed up by a thorough working out of how you see your business concept working.

How did you arrive at your concept? Was it part of an existing business? Did you analyze market needs and arrive at a business that met those needs? Outline the concept of your business thoroughly in this section.

If you were opening the Bethany Bagel Shops, for example, you might state your objective as serving the needs of consumers in highly trafficked business districts in downtown locations. You might also state your objective as providing bagels at a specific savings over the competition. You might then go on to briefly state your target market as consumers on their way to work and your secondary market as businesses in need of food for breakfast or lunch meetings. Then you could talk about the bagel shops themselves. For example:

- How will each shop be designed?
- Will there be seating?
- What types of bagels will you carry?
- Will you also sell other items, such as orange juice, cream cheese, coffee, and tea?
- In other words, what type of product will you stock in your shops?
- How extensive will service be?
- What will be the hours of operation?
- What kind of payment will you accept?
- Will you provide catering services?

In this section you should also talk about your projected sales and gross profit margins. A *gross profit margin* is the price you get for your product or service less your costs. You can present this information in spreadsheet format or in a summary statement. You will be presenting more detailed financial statements later in the business plan.

Talk about any particular aspect of your business that will make it unique. Is pricing going to make your business special? How about distribution or location? Spell out any special aspects of your business here.

Are there foreseeable problems that may affect your business in the future? Are you avoiding doing something now that you may have to address at a later date? Discuss any such issues in this section, and be clear about your reasons for choosing the particular way you intend to do business.

The Management Team

Your section on the management team should not consist of just the résumés of the members of the management team; it should be more than that. In fact, the résumés can be included in the appendix to the business plan. Here you want to give a narrative discussion of each member of the management team and how he or she will contribute to the success of the business. Your discussion should cover the following information for each team member.

- What position will the person hold?
- What relevant education and experience has the person had?
- What specific business experiences might lend insight into this new venture?
- What successes has the person had in previous businesses that are hopeful indications of success in your business?

For a start-up business, it is often the case that not everyone is in place in the management team. Often there are prospects for the positions, however. Once you are clear that these people are candidates for positions on your team, you can go ahead and give their backgrounds.

Also discuss any consultants you plan to use in running your business, including accountants, lawyers, personnel specialists, and advertising firms.

Include a section on how you see management evolving in your business. Many small businesses do not have a large layer of management, and so this section may be short. But you can talk about how you plan to train employees, what types of employees you plan to hire to start with, and what types you plan to add as the business grows.

If your business is going to have a board of directors, include the names of the members of the board of directors and brief background information on them. If you know the types of people you are looking for to serve on your board but have not yet identified the individuals, you can write about this situation here, including your plans for finding the appropriate individuals.

The length of the section on the management team will obviously vary depending on how many people will be involved in your business. But a safe bet is that it will run between 5 and 15 pages, unless your business is to be a sole proprietorship, in which case the section is likely to be much shorter.

The Operating Plan

This portion of the business plan lays out how you plan to operate your business. It should cover:

- Where you plan to locate your business and why you have chosen that location
- Where and when you plan to open subsequent locations, if any
- Your projections for sales volume, based on your location or locations
- What criteria you will use for selection of a site, if you are opening a retail establishment
- The size of the site
- The design of the site, both interior and exterior
- What kind of operating systems you will use, including computer systems for sales, invoicing, and inventory control, if appropriate
- What kind of personnel you will bring on board
- How you will open new branches if the need arises
- Any other issues that pertain to operating your business on a day-to-day basis

The operations of different types of businesses will obviously differ. What you are trying to spell out in this portion of the business plan is a scheme by which you can try to plan for all operations needs so that your business can run smoothly once you get it up and going. Include costs where you can. Planning for most contingencies will help you to be prepared to handle the arduous task of running a business, and prospective financing sources will see that you have thought out your business in quite some detail. The length of this section of your business plan will vary greatly depending on the type and size of business you are planning. Make it long enough to show yourself and other appropriate parties that you have a solid grasp of what it will take to operate the business you are planning.

The Marketing Plan

The marketing plan is the section of the business plan in which you will lay out how you intend to market your great concept to the end user. It should be straightforward, and should cover at the very least the following areas:

- *Business marketing objectives.* What is your marketing objective for your business? Is it to get 30 percent of your primary target market to buy products or services from you within the first 6 months or 1 year? Is it the desire to project a particular image to your target market? What are your sales objectives? How much of the primary target market's business are you trying to capture? How much of the secondary market's business? Spell out these objectives here. Be as specific as you can, and support your objectives by referring to other parts of the business plan, if necessary. But you should be able to state the marketing objectives of your business in one or two succinct paragraphs. As hard as it may be, you must try to make these statements as good and as specific as possible. The sharper your handle on the objectives, the more likely you will be to have a firm grasp on what you're trying to accomplish.

- *The customer.* Recap your primary market. Refer to any analytical studies or research that supports your identification of your market, but if you are going to include detailed studies, use them as appendixes rather than including them here. Devote 5 to 15 paragraphs to a discussion of your primary target market and how customers within it make purchasing decisions about products or services like those you are offering. Be as specific as you can and back up your conclusions with evidence.

  Discuss, as part of this section, whether you will need salespeople, account representatives, or other sales support staff in your business. Also discuss the functions of these people in relation to your target customer.

  Discuss how your business concept will meet the needs of your target customers better than your competitors' concepts are doing it. Include charts, sales-volume comparisons, service comparisons, and anything else that will make a distinction between you and your competitors.

  Recap your primary target market and your secondary target market briefly (in one or two paragraphs each). Refer to any support material you are including in appendixes that will give target market information in detail (e.g., SIC codes).

- *Marketing communications strategy.* In three or four paragraphs, discuss what the communications efforts you are planning must do to be successful. Must they explain a new concept to the target customer? Will they differentiate you from the competition? What benefits will you try to get across in your communications efforts? How was the name of your business chosen? Does the name do anything to help you achieve your communications objectives?

- *Pricing.* Describe in two to four paragraphs your pricing strategy for the goods or services you will be offering. Will you offer any trade discounts? Will you offer credit financing? Is there anything unique about the way you will price your goods or services?

- *Advertising.* What kind of advertising mix can you use to best reach your target market? Mention some specifics. If you or your advertising agency has developed a media plan, include it as an appendix to the business plan. Describe it briefly in this section.

- *Creative strategy.* What creative strategy will you use to get your point across to your target market? Are there other advertising campaigns similar to the one you have in mind? If so, you might want to include some examples in an appendix.

- *Advertising and public relations agency selection.* What are your major criteria for an advertising agency or public relations agency? If you have talked to some prospective agencies, describe them briefly in this section and point out what you perceive to be their strengths and weaknesses.

- *Internal communications.* Briefly describe any internal communications vehicles you will use. Visualizing internal communications may be easier for a retail establishment than for a service business. Include items such as internal newsletters and employee communications that ultimately will aid your marketing efforts.

- *Promotions.* If appropriate, discuss promotional strategies you will use. Will you use giveaways? Hold special events to promote your business? Give discounts for referrals? Include any strategies you think might work for your business.

For a thorough discussion of marketing and how it can be used in a small business, a good reference is *The McGraw-Hill 36-Hour Marketing Course.*[3]

Business Risks

In this section of the business plan, try to point out as many of the potential business risks you are facing in opening your small business as you can think of. If you can answer questions about these risks, it will show that you have thought out ways to overcome some major obstacles. Some owners write this section in a question-and-answer format, pre-

---

[3]Jeffrey L. Seglin, *The McGraw-Hill 36-Hour Marketing Course.* New York: McGraw-Hill, 1990.

senting each risk as a question and their plans for dealing with it as the answer. If this format works well for you, use it.

Try to address as many issues as you can think of. If your business is based on a new concept, address the question of whether or not your target market will be willing to try something new. How will you convince prospective customers to change their current way of thinking? Discuss what you plan to do if you do not meet your projections for sales or profits. What if your competition tries to undermine your entry into the field? What operating problems might occur? How will you deal with them?

Summary Financial and Operating Statements

Financial and operating statements differ greatly depending on the type of business. The operating plan for a chain of bagel shops will look significantly different from a plan for a public relations business. For the bagel shops, you would include store-opening plans that would be inapplicable in operating plans for the public relations business. The main concern in the summary financial and operating statements is that you include summaries of all operating statements and financial statements that are appropriate to your type of business. For the financials, you should consult with your accountant. The operating statements should be based on your research and knowledge of the type of business you are going into.

In putting together the summary financial and operating statements section of your business plan for the Bethany Bagel Shops, you might start this section of your business plan by making a statement such as, "The shop-opening schedule for Bethany Bagel Shops is to have 17 shops open after year 5, with sales volume at the end of year 5 at $17.591 million" (a figure derived from Table 13-1). This could be followed by a statement that you believed you had made conservative assumptions in keeping with your expectations of market receptance, expenses, and other factors. You might follow with specific details of your plans for opening the bagel shops quarter by quarter during the 5-year period.

In this section you can use a table similar to, but more detailed than, Table 13-1, which was used as an example in the executive summary. Here it's a good idea to specify in detail why you think you can reach your predicted sales volume by following this particular plan.

If you are opening a manufacturing or a service business, this is the place to detail the costs, schedule, and plan for opening your plant or offices. Include your sales expectations and details of your reasons for choosing your specific plan of action for operations.

In retail, manufacturing, and service businesses, you should include information on the costs of start-up. For the Bethany Bagel Shops, you would include items such as fixtures, equipment, and leasehold improvements; inventory; preopening training, utilities, and rent; and postopening payroll and advertising. Include all expenses of getting your business up and going. For a public relations business, this might include little more than Fax machine, computer, telephone, rent, and utilities. For a manufacturing firm, the costs would be heavy in equipment, leasehold improvements, inventory, and other related costs.

Next, you should include a subsection that focuses more narrowly on operations. For a retail operation, focus on the following items:

- Sales-volume potentials for your stores
- How those volumes will increase as you open more stores
- How profits will be affected by more stores openings
- How much you project sales to increase every year
- Gross profit margins for each store
- Wages you will be paying out for hourly employees as well as store management
- The cost of benefits (as a percentage of payroll)
- Rent costs
- Utility costs
- Costs of any discounts you will offer
- Charge card fees
- Supplies
- Depreciation expenses for any fixtures or equipment
- Advertising expenses

For service and manufacturing businesses, you should include operating expenses applicable to your type of business, such as truck leasing expenses, and depreciation of major equipment.

You should include information about your overhead expenses—expenses that aren't directly related to the production or sale of your goods or services. These might include such items as advertising agency fees, high-level management salaries and benefits, consultants, and software for computer systems. Get an accountant or an accounting firm to work with you to produce a detailed operating statement including all this information; this statement can be attached it to the business plan as

160

part of this section or as an appendix. You may want to detail some major expenses in the operating plan. For the Bethany Bagel Shops, these might be as shown below.

	Annual cost
President	$95,000
Controller	55,000
Marketing manager	45,000
Vice president, purchasing	55,000
Advertising agency	75,000

You could follow this table with a list of other major expenses that you expect as part of overhead, including such items as computerized cash register systems, food industry consultants, and public relations fees.

In this section of the business plan, you should also include a summary profit and loss statement, referring the reader to a more elaborate statement attached to the business plan as an appendix. The summary profit and loss statement might be as shown in Table 13-2.

If you are opening a multiple-store retail outlet or a business that you project will have many different offices, attach a complete operating statement for each location that you expect to be open by the end of year 1.

In this section of your business plan, you should also detail any assumptions you are making on your balance sheet. These might include the following items:

- Any cash you plan to have on hand in each retail outlet
- Accounts receivables expected (e.g., 10 days worth of charges on 20 percent of sales)
- Inventory turnover assumptions, with support for how you arrived at the figures
- Plant, property, and equipment expenses, as well as depreciation
- Accounts payable assumptions (e.g., 10 days on 60 percent of purchases, 25 days on 40 percent of purchases, which tells the reader how long you plan to take to pay off your accounts payables)

At the end of this section you should also include a summary balance sheet for years 1 through 5 of your business. You can include a more detailed quarterly balance sheet as an appendix to which you refer the reader for more detail. The summary balance sheet can be based on year-end and can provide the basics to give the reader a sense of how

Table 13-2. Bethany Bagel Shop
Summary Profit and Loss Statement, Years 1 through 5

Year	Preopening	1	2	3	4	5
Sales ($000)		1,375	4,045	6,188	10,998	17,591
Gross profit ($000)		315	958	1,518	2,791	4,315
		(22.9%)	(23.7%)	(24.5%)	(25.4%)	(24.5%)
Wages ($000)		71.5	157.75	235	385	563
		(5.2%)	(3.9%)	(3.8%)	(3.5%)	(3.2%)
Advertising ($000)		103	178	229	352	580.5
		(7.5%)	(4.4%)	(3.7%)	(3.2%)	(3.3%)
Overhead ($000)	55	247.5	198	334	418	475
		(18.0%)	(4.9%)	(5.4%)	(3.8%)	(2.7%)
Net earnings:						
Pretaxes ($000)	(55)	(248)	(18)	149	701	1,504
Net after taxes($000)	(55)	(248)	(18)	149	543	752
No. of shops at year-end		4	4	7	12	17
Year-end investment ($000)		787	756	961	865	774
Bank Debt* ($000)		173	97	358†	262	141

*Assumes $650,000 in equity financing prior to opening. The remaining investment will be financed through borrowing against equipment and inventory.
†Represents bank debt at its peak.

you see your whole business. It can also give you a touchstone upon which to measure your own business. The balance sheet would most likely include the items shown in Table 13-3. Your own accountant may suggest other items or formats more appropriate for your business.

Operating Statements

If you prefer, you can present all your detailed operating statements in this section, rather than adding them as appendixes. If you do choose to make them appendixes, however, place them at the beginning of your

Table 13-3. [Business Name]
Balance Sheet, Year-End

Year	1	2	3	4	5
Assets					
Current assets					
Cash					
Accounts receivable					
Inventory					
Total current assets					
Property, plant and equipment					
Less depreciation					
Total assets					
Liabilities and Equity					
Current liabilities					
Accounts payable					
Bank notes payable					
Total current liabilities					
Equity					
Preferred stock					
Retained earnings* (or deficit)					
Total equity					
Total liabilities and equity					

*Retained earnings are those net profits a business accumulates after all dividends are paid.

appendix section, so that potential financing sources can have easy access to them.

Balance Sheets

Detailed balance sheets can be included as a final section of your business plan or as appendixes. If you do decide to make them appendixes, place them immediately after the operating statements appendixes. You could put the detailed operating statements and the detailed balance sheets together as part of the main plan, or you could put them together as appendixes. In either event, don't separate them. Make it easy for a potential financing source to get to these spreadsheets and study them.

Appendixes

Besides, possibly, the spreadsheets discussed above, your appendixes should include any items that you believe are relevant to your business plan and will work as support material. Some likely candidates are marketing research data, SIC codes, surveys of competitors' pricing, résumés of the management team, a media plan, sample advertising programs, and consulting firm reports.

Your business plan in its final form should take a thorough look at every aspect of your business. Financing sources should be able to get a strong sense from it of whether or not you have an understanding of your business and a realistic grasp of what it will take to make it succeed. They should also be able to get a sense, from concept to financing needs, of whether or not this is a venture to which they would like to commit funds. For you, the benefit of a well-prepared business plan is that you will have a working tool on which you can base the growth of your business. It will enable you to measure your progress and to make changes as the needs arise.

Your business plan will go a long way toward helping you find the type of financing you want. Most venture capital companies, investment bankers, and others who might make an equity investment will scrutinize your business plan thoroughly to decide whether or not to invest in you. If they need specific information besides what you've included in the business plan, in order to make a decision, they will request it.

If bank financing's what you're looking for, you'll find the next chapter, which focuses on putting together a bank loan package, particularly instructive.

14

Banking On It

Preparing
the Loan Package

Like small business owners, each banker has his or her own way of doing business. The basics may be the same, but some bankers will look for one thing in a loan proposal package, while others will stress something else. Most lenders have their own specific requirements for all prospective borrowers. These requirements may take the form of standard forms, personal histories, tax returns, and so on. Be sure to ask a prospective lender what he or she expects to see in the loan proposal package.

Most lenders, however, want some pretty routine information. In this chapter we'll look at what you should have to pull together to present a solid loan proposal. Some of these forms are more appropriate for some types of businesses than others. Seasoned companies with a proven track record, for example, are better able to present detailed past financial information for their business than are start-up businesses. These situations will become clear as you read about them in this chapter.

While the loan package needn't be as elaborate as a business plan, it must be thorough and well-supported. Use footnotes if necessary. If you make a claim about revenues or expenses in your financial statements, be sure to include any needed explanation or elaboration. It is a mistake to present incomplete or misleading information to a prospective lender. Such a presentation can lead to outright dismissal of the loan request, or even to legal problems if you are caught trying to conceal information or being dishonest on your financial statement. Do not conceal from the lender such matters as bankruptcies or other business tragedies of your past business life. If you are up-front and truthful now, lapses will not come back to haunt you later. From an ethical standpoint, being dishonest is wrong. It's also simply bad business.

Another bad business practice is presenting an unprofessional-looking loan package. This may seem like a needless reminder, but it's worth repeating: Take the time to make your loan proposal look professional. Have it typed or printed out on a letter-quality or laser printer. Check for grammatical mistakes. Have someone proofread the loan package to check for inconsistencies, misspellings, or other errors. You are applying for financing that may spell the difference between a flying start and a slow-paced crawl for your business. Take the time to give it that professional look it deserves. If you need some help with writing, there are plenty of good books around that can guide you in good usage and grammar. One, published by the American Management Association (AMA), is *The AMA Handbook of Business Letters.*[1] It not only features tips on writing, grammar, and usage, but also includes the "Grammar Hotline Directory," listing the telephone numbers of college English departments around the country staffed by people who are willing and able to help you through the tough spots with your writing.

The contents of a basic loan proposal package may vary slightly from bank to bank, but it always consists of some pretty standard information. In addition to the applications the bank will require you to fill out, the standard information you will have to provide includes the following:

- Company history
- Principals' résumés
- Statement about use of loan proceeds
- Business financial statements
- Projected cash-flow statements
- Corporate tax returns
- Personal financial statement and personal guaranty
- Personal tax return
- Schedules of equipment and inventory
- Aging of accounts receivable and accounts payable

[1]Jeffrey L. Seglin, *The AMA Handbook of Business Letters.* New York: AMACOM, 1989.

- Customer and supplier lists

A loan package should be significantly shorter than a business plan. Some lenders will ask to see your business plan in addition to the basic loan proposal package. The loan proposal should be as brief and to the point as possible, providing all the information necessary or requested, but not going overboard with excess details. It should be easy to follow, so as to enable the prospective lender to get the information needed to make a lending decision.

Company History

Included in your loan proposal package, right after the bank's loan application forms, should be a brief company history that gives basic information about your business: when it was started; its purpose (if appropriate, you can include its mission statement); its record of growth; your plans for the future of the business; and economic, demographic, or market trends that have a bearing on your business's future.

You don't need to get too elaborate or technical. Present the company history in accessible language so that the prospective lender can get a feel for what you do and what you plan to do. The purpose of this section is to give the lender a clear indication that you are in control of your business and that your business is a solid financial risk. You should explain any down years you have experienced, especially if they show up in your financials, and tell what safeguards you have installed to ensure against future down ticks in your business.

The company history section of your loan proposal need not be longer than one or two double-spaced typewritten pages. It might read something like this:

Company History

Bethany Bagel Shops was incorporated on March 20, 1989. We opened our first shop on 312 West Main Street in Boston, Massachusetts. When we opened the first shop, we had only six employees other than the two founding principals, but our business plan spelled out our goals for the future of our business. Our goals were as follows: to have four shops at the end of the first year of operations; to generate revenues of just over $1 million; and to provide bagels and other food items to downtown pedestrian customers who were looking for high-quality food, reasonable prices, and fast, efficient service. Our bagels are all baked using top-grade ingredients at our main bakery in south Boston.

Within the first 6 months of business, it became clear that we were on-line with our business plan projections. We had three stores open, with a total of 12 employees on payroll, and we had taken over additional bakery space in the building we were leasing in South Boston.

At the same time, our corporate catering business had begun to take off. This market, which is a secondary target market for us, had been increasing in volume at a faster rate than we had anticipated. We had hired a new salesperson to focus solely on corporate accounts, and we had also designated a section of our bakery facilities to be used solely for corporate catering.

The market reception to the Bethany Bagel Shop concept has been phenomenal. We are optimistic that, with proper financing, Bethany Bagel Shops will continue to grow and will compete vigorously with the muffin and donut shops that, until now, have been the main source of competition for us in the marketplace.

Principals' Résumés

You should feature résumés or personal histories for each high-level executive in your business. Most of these résumés should be no longer than one page. You needn't present the personal histories in traditional résumé format, but may instead choose a more readable narrative style. If you choose to use a résumé format, write the résumés for all the key players using the same format, instead of including a collection of already-existing résumés. Using the same format will give the impression that you took the time to prepare the loan package specifically for this lender and also will make it easier for the lender to glance through the résumés and pull out some chief items that might be of interest.

There are some basics, of course, that you should include: education and employment history, chief among them. The résumés should give the lender the clear message that here is a business run by sound, levelheaded, responsible businesspeople who are capable of making this business succeed.

Include résumés for all the principals of the business as well as high-level decision makers, such as chief financial officer, controller, and director of marketing. You might also include other corporate officers or stockholders whose work in the company may ensure repayment of loan proceeds. If you have an active board of directors, you may decide to include their résumés as well, particularly if their involvement will have some bearing on your chances of success.

If your company is just starting up, you will obviously have no financial record on which the lender can make a lending decision; thus your personal histories section will be even more important than if your business were already well established. The lender will have to make a decision on whether or not you and other key executives in your business are a good risk. Take the time to prepare a well-written, well-thought-out personal history section that clearly gives a prospective lender reason to believe in you and your chances for success.

In the discussion of Small Business Administration loan programs in Chapter 11 we mentioned that the SBA requires prospective borrowers to fill out a form entitled Statement of Personal History (see Figure 11-3). Other lenders will also require forms like this. Do not assume, however, that such a form can take the place of your own résumé or personal history statement. The advantage of including your own résumé is that you can use it to stress the items *you* believe are indicative of your chances for success in your business.

Statement about Use of Loan Proceeds

As part of the loan proposal package, you should include a statement about how you will use the loan proceeds. The simplest approach is to use a straightforward list format. You can cite each category for which you plan to use the proceeds, state the amount you will use for each item, and add brief statements about specifics, if appropriate. This list will obviously differ from borrower to borrower, depending upon needs, but it may include the following:

- *Working capital.*
- *Equipment.* Name the specific equipment you plan to lease or purchase, and state how it will help your business.
- *Real estate purchases.*
- *Real estate construction.*
- *Leasehold improvements.*
- *Real estate leasing.* Since you may be paying back a loan over a several-year period, you should include a copy of your lease with the loan package, explaining what you plan to do when the lease expires.
- *Inventory.*
- *Repayment of debt.*

You should be as accurate with your figures as you can, so that the lender will know you that have thought through these items and will understand your motives for borrowing.

Business Financial Statements

It is generally worth the investment to have your financial statements prepared by an accountant. The accountant should usually write a cover letter for the financial statements, explaining any assumptions made on the balance sheet and verifying that the statements accurately reflect your business's financial condition. To allow the lender to make an analysis of your business's financials, you should include income statements and balance sheets for the last 3 full years of business, as well as for the most recent quarter. Make sure that the quarterly statement is not more than 90 days old; if it is, the lender will most likely want to see a more current interim statement. The financial statements should be as comprehensive and clear as possible so that the lenders will not have to ask you for more information. If lenders sense that information is missing or hidden, they may question your motives. They will want to see how you have handled paying off past debt and how your company's cash flow looks, to help them to evaluate your prospects of meeting future financial obligations.

Different lenders will look for different items on your income statements and balance sheets, but there are some things you can be sure that any lender will focus on: your net profit and your cost of goods as a percentage of sales on your income statement. They will likely compare this information with assumptions about what businesses like yours should be doing in these categories. If you know that there are aberrations on your income statement, use a footnote to state why your percentages may have strayed from reasonable expectations for a specific period on your statements.

Lenders will also look at specific items on your balance sheet to get a sense of where you are, financially. They will look at your *current ratio*— the ratio of current assets to current liabilities (see Chapter 15 for a more complete discussion of financial ratios)—to see how highly leveraged you are. While a ratio of 2 to 1 is ideal, since it indicates that you would be likely to liquidate assets to pay off liabilities if necessary, lenders will make loans if the ratio is smaller. Some companies that have low inventory levels and easily collected accounts receivable can operate quite nicely on a lower ratio. Again, you should footnote any reasons for an unusual current ratio.

The lender will also look at the balance sheet for your *net worth,* or total assets minus total liabilities. Some lenders follow rules of thumb for how much debt they like to see a business take on in relation to net worth. In the past, it was assumed that you could only hope to get a loan that was 2.5 times greater than your net worth. Nowadays, however, some lenders are less stringent about net worth, and will look at other items when making a loan. It is often possible to get financing that exceeds the 2.5 to 1 ratio of net worth to debt.

The lender will examine your accounts receivable to see how quickly the money is coming in, and your accounts payable to see how quickly your bills are paid. If your accounts payable exceed 90 days, explain in a footnote why this is the case. Lenders will be highly skeptical about the quality of accounts payable that exceed 90 days and will often assume that these accounts have become bad debt. You'll have to make a good argument for why these accounts payable are still good and why you have allowed them to go as long as they have.

Lenders will interpret items on the financial statements differently depending on what type of business is applying for a loan. For example, a manufacturing firm's financial statements might be studied carefully for details of equipment costs, while a retail business's inventory figures will likely be given intense scrutiny. A lender will focus on items that give a good sense of how well you are performing for the type of business you are in.

The format for a balance sheet and an income statement will vary slightly depending on who is preparing it, but they will all basically feature similar items. A simple balance sheet would look something like the one shown in Table 14-1. A very basic income statement might look like the one shown in Table 14-2.

New businesses that are seeking money for start-up will obviously not be able to provide financial statements that reflect several years of business. Lenders will want to see projections, customer lists, and other support materials indicating that you are likely to be a good credit risk. If you have large prospective customers who have made a commitment to using your products or services, a letter of intent from some of these prospects might help convince a prospective lender that your sales potential is likely to be good.

Projected Cash-Flow Statements

As part of your loan package, you should provide a projected cash-flow statement for the coming year. This projection will be a month-by-month analysis of your cash position. You should indicate your anticipated sales each month, your collections, and your month-to-month expenses. By looking at the cash you have available each month, a lender can get a feel for your capability of paying back the loan.

Table 14-1. Edward Manufacturing
Projected Balance Sheet (as of December 31, 19XX)

Assets		
Current assets:		
Cash	$125,000	
Accounts receivable—current	$338,000	
Inventory	$137,000	
Other current assets	$ 10,000	
Total current assets		$610,000
Fixed assets:		
Equipment, machinery, trucks	$105,000	
Reserve for depreciation	$(26,000)	
Total fixed assets		$ 79,000
Other assets:		
Deposits on orders	$ 22,500	
Total other assets		$ 22,500
Total assets		$711,500
Liabilities		
Current liabilities:		
Accounts payable	$167,500	
Truck Loan	$ 22,000	
Federal taxes	$63,000	
Other taxes	$39,500	
Total taxes	$102,500	
Total current liabilities		$292,000
Other liabilities:		
Loans to officers	$32,750	
Total other liabilities		$ 32,750
Total liabilities		$324,750
Net worth		$386,750

Make the projections as realistic as you can. Don't overstate your sales potential. If a lender senses that you are inflating projections, it will likely hesitate to approve financing.

Make sure, however, that your cash-flow statement shows some indication that you are capable of paying back the loan. It may be realistic to project that your cash flow will grow by 10 or 20 percent. If you show a larger increase than that, be prepared to explain the reason for your projection of stellar growth. The lender won't dismiss the possibility if you can substantiate your reasoning.

Table 14-2. Edward Manufacturing
Projected Profit and Loss Statement

	4th quarter, 1988		1989
Income—sales		$315,000	$1,790,000
Cost of sales:			
Cost of goods sold and labor		$204,000	$1,020,300
Gross profit		$111,000	$ 769,700
Expenses:			
Advertising	$ 1,220	$ 14,640	
Truck fleet	3,650	35,800	
Depreciation	3,880	15,520	
Delivery	6,040	17,900	
Utilities	3,020	15,530	
Telephone	6,475	25,900	
Insurance	2,500	23,350	
Accounting	1,725	10,350	
Office expenses	865	6,500	
Supplies	4,350	17,120	
Officers' salaries	12,950	103,600	
Payroll taxes	20,750	70,590	
Travel	8,050	14,175	
Miscellaneous	3,150	7,775	
Total expenses		78,625	378,750
Net profit before taxes		32,375	390,950
Corporate taxes		(6,750)	(75,750)
Net profit		$ 25,625	315,200

Corporate Tax Returns

You should provide corporate federal tax returns for the last 3 complete years of business. The financial information on your tax returns should match up with the financial information on the year-end financial statements you provide the lender. If the numbers don't jibe, you will have some explaining to do. Of course, there may be a legitimate reason for valuing your assets according to one legal method for the Internal Revenue Service and according to a different method for your lenders, stockholders, or others. You should explain any discrepancy to the prospective lender in writing.

Personal Financial Statement and Personal Guaranty

Most lenders will require that you and other principals in your business supply personal guaranties for the loans you receive. This, of course, places the principals at risk, as well as the corporation. Should something happen to your business, the lender could hold the principals responsible for paying back the loan. By providing a personal guaranty for a loan, you give the lender a signal that you are willing to take a significant risk on your business venture. You are willing to put your money where your mouth is. Since most lenders are extremely risk-aversive, anything you can do to convince them that their risk is diminished helps. A personal guaranty on a loan can serve to boost a lender's confidence that the loan will be repaid. Figure 5-2 is a sample of a personal guaranty form used by a bank. Guaranty forms differ only slightly from bank to bank.

Lenders will want to see personal financial statements for you (and your spouse if you are married) and other principals of the business, to get an idea of your net worth. Personal financial statements were discussed in Chapter 5, and Figure 5-1 shows a typical personal financial statement. These statements give the lender, and often the borrower, a clear idea of the borrower's net worth by taking stock of his or her assets (including everything from house and cars to jewelry and cash) and liabilities and coming up with a personal net-worth figure.

Personal Tax Return

To verify your personal financial statement, lenders will want to see personal tax returns, usually for the previous 3 years. Do not hesitate to give lenders this personal information, if they need it to make a decision about lending to your business. They are making a decision about whether or not to take a chance on you and your business. They want to get a sense of who you are as a prospect. Some business owners are put off by having to provide personal information for a business loan. Remember that it is perfectly natural, particularly if you have a small business, for lenders to ask for this information. From how you run your personal financial affairs, they can get a sense of how you might run your business financial affairs. Give them the information they need to make a sound lending decision. Obviously, you should explain any aberrations or seeming discrepancies on your personal financial statements.

Schedules of Equipment and Inventory

Depending on the type of business you are in, you may have to provide a schedule of equipment or inventory. If you own a manufacturing company, you probably have a lot of equipment that is needed to keep the business running; you should provide the lender with a detailed accounting of those fixed assets. This will give you a chance to detail the actual value of the equipment you own, rather than just stating the cost less the depreciation—the form in which your equipment may have shown up on your business's financial statement. The actual value of your equipment can become an important issue, if the collateral you have to offer is worth more than the amount you paid for it less depreciation. Be sure to give accurate appraisals of your equipment and its value. You should have an outside professional provide you with an appraisal of the equipment's value plus an estimate of the amount you could get for the equipment should you have to sell it. Provide this appraisal to the lender.

For retail businesses, inventory is usually a far more significant asset than equipment. You should provide a lender with a detailed accounting of all the inventory you have in stock, along with its value. Its actual worth may be higher than you were able to list it as on your business financial statements. Be sure to take this into account. Conversely, also be aware that lenders most likely know as well as you do that some inventory items become obsolete. Give an accurate accounting, substantiating the real value of the inventory.

Aging of Accounts Receivable and Accounts Payable

To give the lender a sense of how you meet your financial obligations, provide a list of all current bills that are due to you during the next year, stating how long each bill has been outstanding (i.e., "age" each accounts receivable bill). Be accurate in your listing and provide the lender with any explanations that are needed. The lender will look at how quickly your customers pay, and at whether you are relying primarily on one or two large customers or on several smaller customers. If you are relying principally on a large customer or two, the lender may become concerned about what would happen should you lose this customer's business. A portion (the full list would obviously be a lot longer) of the aging of an accounts receivable list might be as shown in Table 14-3.

You should also include a list of all bills that you are due to pay within the next year. This is your accounts payable list. You should age this list too, indicating how long each payable has been outstanding. Since most trade bills offer a discount if paid early, and since they are due in full in 30 days, lenders may become alarmed if they see that you have a number of bills aged more than 30 days. Be accurate in your list, and explain any extenuating circumstances or unusual items. Your aging of ac-

Table 14-3. Aging of Accounts Receivable

Customer	Total	0–30 days	30–60 days	60–90 days	90 or more days
Bethany's Kids	$ 560	$ 425		$135	
Eddie's Bikes	3,240	3,000		240	
Grimes Bottomland	6,700	6,000	$ 700		
Kenney's Dogs	125				$ 125
Krauss Fruit	1,235	1,200		35	
Lisa's Treats	980		900	80	
Loren's Fudge	675				675
Mahaffey's Tree	565	565			
McGuffie Books	575	385	190		
Nancy's Nibbles	800		600	200	
Total	$15,455	$11,575	$2,390	$690	$ 800

counts payable list will, in format, look similar to your aging of accounts payable. Obviously, it differs in that in refers to money you owe instead of money owed to you.

Customer and Supplier Lists

To give the lender an idea of your relationships with your customers and suppliers, provide the lender with lists of about five of your best customers and about five of your best suppliers. By "best," I mean those with whom you have the best relationships. As if you were giving references for a job, you should give the names, addresses, and telephone numbers of people who will be honest and informative, yet positive about your business. You should indicate to the bank how long you have done business with each customer or supplier on your list. You should first call the suppliers and customers you want to list to ask their permission to list them as business references. That way, they will be prepared to talk to a prospective lender about your business relationship.

In Chapter 15, we'll take a look at financial ratios and how they can be used by you and a prospective financing source to measure the performance of your business. By understanding financial ratios and having a clear sense of what makes up a good business proposal and thorough loan package, you should be able to approach most any financing source with the confidence that you have thought out your business and its financial needs thoroughly. You will indeed be in an excellent position to find the money to start and operate your own small business.

15
Measuring Up

Understanding
Financial Ratios

Financial ratios have been mentioned throughout this book. They are used in a process called *ratio analysis,* to get a handle on a business's performance. Detailed description of ratio analysis and other financial statement interpretive tools would be somewhat beyond the scope of a book on how to find money to start and operate a small business. However, a brief look at how these financial ratios work will be useful, since many financing sources do use them in making decisions about whether or not to finance a business.

Ratio analysis uses the financial ratios of a business to make business decisions based on a comparison with other similar companies or periods within the business's history. Many financial institutions also compare a business's financial ratios with industry standards.

Standard industry ratios are published by a number of organizations, most notably Dun & Bradstreet and Robert Morris Associates. See Chapter 3 for more details on these publications. Industry trade associations also provide financial ratios of businesses common to their respective industries. A list of some of these associations is given in Appendix E.

The idea of ratio analysis is that it can give business owners the opportunity to use information from their balance sheets and profit and loss statements to interpret the relationships between figures available from the many financial reports a company owner has access to. Since many sources of financing use some of the more common financial ratios, it is a good idea to have a handle on what these are. One unfortunate drawback to financial ratios is that sometimes businesses that are lumped into the same industry classification do business differently, which means that their financial ratios are out of kilter with industry standards. Financing sources comparing these businesses' financial ratios with industry standards may be alarmed. But if a business is truly healthy and the financing source takes the time to understand the business, this misunderstanding can be cleared up.

Financial ratios do not solve businesses problems. They merely take a "snapshot" of where a business is and how it is performing at a given time. If appropriate, they can be compared with ratios of other similar businesses, or with your own financial ratios from earlier periods to get an idea of how your performance has changed over the years. A dramatic change in your financial ratios should serve as a warning sign that something in your business performance has gone awry. In this respect, financial ratios can be a useful mechanism for keeping your business on course.

You should remember that:

- You cannot make apples-to-apples comparisons of two businesses, since they may do calculations differently on their financial statements.

- Some changes in your business's financial ratios may be due to seasonal fluctuations. If you want to get a reading on how your business performs during peak or slow periods of business activity, you will have to compare financial ratios of two or more peak periods or two or more slow periods.

- You can use financial ratios to plan for the future, but remember that financial statements reflect business activity that has occurred in the past. They cannot predict the future. You can only use them to make informed decisions about how your business may perform, based on the financial information you have available.

There are a number of different types of financial ratios available for use by the small business owner. Some measure liquidity, while others measure profitability. Some of the more commonly used financial ratios are discussed below. This discussion is by no means all-inclusive. Instead, it is meant to give the small business owner an overall sense of how financial ratios work and the ability to use some of the more commonly available ones.

Financial Ratios Used to Measure Liquidity

If an asset is easily converted into cash or a cash equivalent without a significant loss in the value of that asset, it is said to be "liquid." For the small business owner, *liquidity* is the capability to pay all the bills due during a given time period. If Samuel Johnson, for example, owner of the Gough Square Supply Company, is trying to determine whether or not he has enough cash (or liquid assets to convert to cash) to pay all his bills during a given accounting period, he is trying to determine his company's liquidity.

The Current Ratio

The *current ratio* is used to measure whether or not a company has enough current assets to pay off its current debts, plus a little extra to handle any emergencies that might arise. It is one of the more commonly used financial ratios.

The current ratio is a company's current assets divided by its current liabilities. For the Gough Square Supply Company, the balance sheet of which is shown in Table 15-1, the current ratio would be calculated as follows:

$$\frac{\text{Current assets}}{\text{Current liabilities}} = \frac{\$280,000}{\$120,000} = 2.3 \text{ (or 2.3 to 1)}$$

Thus stated, this current ratio tells Johnson absolutely nothing. He must go on to determine whether or not this is a good current ratio for his company—but he can't use the current ratio alone to determine whether or not his company's performance is up to snuff. As a general rule of thumb, a good current ratio is 2 to 1, but this can vary, depending on the type of business and its assets and liabilities. For companies with little inventory and with accounts receivable that are easily collectible, a current ratio lower than those of companies with less steady cash flow can nevertheless be considered good.

If owner Johnson decided that his company's current ratio was too low, he could raise it by taking any of a number of different steps: he could pay off some debts, increase his current assets with loans or other borrowed funds that have maturities of a year or greater, increase his current assets by securing new equity contributions, or put profits earned back into the business.

The figures shown in Table 15-2 will give you an idea of how a business can raise or lower its current ratio. If Sam Johnson wanted to increase his inventory by buying $30,000 worth of merchandise, his inventory would add up to $70,000, raising his total current assets to $130,000. His current ratio would drop from 2.0 to 1.6 (current ratios are rounded off to the nearest tenth). If Johnson decided instead to pay $14,000 of his accounts payable (his bills), his current assets

Table 15-1. Gough Square Supply Company
Combined Balance Sheets, January 1 and December 31, 19XX

	December 31, 19XX			January 1, 19XX		
Assets						
Current assets:						
Cash		$ 60,000			$ 60,000	
Accounts receivable	$ 84,000			$ 64,000		
Less allowance for bad debt	4,000			4,000		
		80,000			60,000	
Inventory		120,000			100,000	
Prepaid expenses		20,000			20,000	
Total current assets			$280,000			$240,000
Fixed assets:						
Buildings and equipment	$240,000			$240,000		
Less accumulated depreciation	140,000	$100,000		$120,000	$120,000	
Land		60,000			60,000	
Total fixed assets			160,000			180,000
Goodwill and patents			20,000			
Total assets			$460,000			$420,000
Liabilities						
Current liabilities:						
Accounts payable	$ 60,000			$ 50,000		
Accrued wages and taxes	20,000			20,000		
Estimated income taxes payable	40,000			30,000		
Total current liabilities		$120,000			$100,000	
Fixed liabilities:						
Mortgage bonds, 5 percent		100,000			100,000	
Total liabilities			$220,000			$200,000
Equity						
Common stock (10,000 shares outstanding)		$120,000			$120,000	
Retained earnings		140,000			120,000	
Total owner equity			260,000			240,000
Total liabilities and equity			$480,000			$440,000

Table 15-2. Gough Square Supply Company

Current Ratio Variations

	Original current assets and current liabilities	Inventory bought on account ($30,000)	Cash paid on accounts payable ($14,000)	New capital invested ($20,000)
Current assets:				
Cash	$ 20,000	$ 20,000	$ 6,000	$ 40,000
Accounts receivable	40,000	40,000	40,000	40,000
Inventory	40,000	70,000	40,000	40,000
Total current assets	$100,000	$130,000	$86,000	$120,000
Current liabilities:				
Accounts payable	$ 40,000	$ 70,000	$26,000	$ 40,000
Other	$ 10,000	$ 10,000	$10,000	$ 10,000
Total current liabilities	$ 50,000	$ 80,000	$36,000	$ 50,000
Net working capital	$ 50,000	$ 50,000	$50,000	$ 70,000
Current ratio	2.0	1.6	2.4	2.4

would shrink to $86,000, and his current liabilities to $36,000. His current ratio would then be 2.4.

If Johnson decided to buy more inventory or pay off some bills, there would be no change in his *working capital*, which is calculated by subtracting current liabilities from current assets. If, however, Johnson decided to invest another $20,000 in the business, his working capital would increase to $70,000, and his current ratio would increase to 2.4. Lenders and other financing sources may look at a company's working capital to see whether a company has the working capital available to withstand any unforeseen crises. As part of a loan offering, some lenders, in fact, will require that a business owner keep a specific amount of working capital available.

Acid-Test Ratio

The *acid-test ratio,* also called a "quick ratio" or "quick-asset ratio," is used to measure a company's liquidity. The formula for calculating the acid-test ratio is as follows:

$$\frac{\text{Cash} + \text{marketable securities} + \text{accounts receivables}}{\text{Current liabilities}} = \text{acid-test ratio}$$

The Gough Square Supply Company has no marketable securities, $60,000 in cash, $80,000 in accounts receivable, and current liabilities of $120,000. Thus, the acid-test ratio for Gough Square Supply would be calculated as follows:

$$\frac{\$60,000 + \$80,000}{\$120,000} = 1.2$$

The acid-test ratio for Gough Square would be 1.2, or 1.2 to 1. The advantage of the acid-test ratio over the current ratio is that the acid-test ratio does not include inventories, so it focuses on a company's assets that are truly liquid assets. It gives a good sense of whether or not a business could pay off all its current debts using the easily liquidated funds available.

The prevailing wisdom is that higher acid-test ratios are better than lower acid-test ratios. An acid-test ratio of 1 to 1 is plausible, however, if your accounts receivable collections keep pace with your payment of current liabilities (and you take advantage of early payment discounts), and if there is little chance that anything will thwart your ability to collect accounts receivable. If your business is unable to meet these conditions, however, it is wise to maintain an acid-test ratio higher than 1 to 1.

While lenders and other financing sources might want to see a company maintain a high acid-test ratio as a sign that the company is being run conservatively and safely, it is not usually a good idea to have a lot of cash or accounts receivables and inventories in relation to what you need for sales. Surely, you want to be careful with your resources, but you also want to be able to transform cash and other resources into more sales for your company. In other words, you don't want a lot of excess cash sitting around if you are in desperate need of more modern equipment or if your sales could be improved by a better-stocked inventory. You want to get the most bang for your buck. You want your dollars placed where they do the most to make your business run smoothly. They might be most helpful in cash, but putting them into a better stocked inventory, a more efficient plant, or a new staff member might be better.

The two financial measures that you can use to get a read on how well you are using your financial resources are the average collection period and the inventory turnover, discussed below.

Average Collection Period

To find out how many days sales are tied up in accounts receivable, you can calculate the *average collection period* by using information found on your balance sheet and your profit and loss statement, as shown in Table 15-3. To calculate the average sales per day, use the following formula:

$$\frac{\text{Net sales}}{\text{Days in accounting period}} = \frac{\$690,000}{365} = \$1,890 \infty \text{average sales per day} \times$$

Next, calculate the average collection period, or how long sales are tied up in receivables, by using the following formula:

$$\frac{\text{Receivables}}{\text{Average sales per day}} = \frac{\$80,000}{\$1,890} = 42 \infty \text{average collection period} \times$$

The average collection period gives a business owner and creditors an idea of how a business is doing at collecting on accounts receivable. The

Table 15-3. Gough Square Supply Company
Condensed Profit and Loss Statement, Year Ended December 31, 1989

Gross sales	$696,900
Less returns and allowances	6,900
Net sales	690,000
Cost of goods sold	414,000
Gross margin	276,000
Operating expenses	179,400
Operating profit	96,600
Interest expense	4,600
Income before taxes	92,000
Estimated income tax	46,000
Net profit	$ 46,000

figure can give you an idea of the quality of the accounts receivable (if the average collection period is quite long, the quality diminishes), and how well your company is doing at collecting money due.

The rule of thumb is that the average collection period shouldn't be greater than 1⅓ times the credit terms you are offering your accounts. If Gough Square Supply gives its accounts 30 days to pay, its average collection period should be 40 days. Sam Johnson and other members of the management committee may want to find out why it is taking 42 days instead of the optimal 40 days to collect.

The calculation for average collection period can vary from business to business. For even greater accuracy, companies may employ some or all of the following techniques.

- Use total credit sales figures instead of the total sales figure.

- Use an average receivables figure by adding together the accounts receivables figures for the beginning and the ending of the accounting period, and then dividing the sum in half.

- Calculate the average collection period on a monthly basis. This calculation allows a company to pinpoint the times during the year when the slow collections problems occur and thus to determine whether the problems are due to seasonal aberrations.

- Use 250 or 260 business days for a business year instead of 365, since most businesses do not attempt to make collections on weekends.

Inventory Turnover

Inventory turnover is a financial ratio that tells you how many times inventory has been "turned over" (i.e., sold and restocked) during a particular accounting period. It gives the business owner an idea of how fast products are selling and how much capital has been tied up in inventory to keep the company's operations going during a particular accounting period.

To calculate inventory turnover, divide the cost of goods sold by the average inventory. Gough Square Supply Company, for example, had an inventory of $100,000 at the beginning of the year and $120,000 at the end of the year. Its inventory turnover is calculated as follows:

$$\frac{\text{Cost of goods sold}}{\text{Average inventory}} = \frac{\$414,000}{0.5(120,000 + 100,000)} = 3.8$$

During the year, Gough Square Supply used up inventory that was equal to 3.8 times its average investment in inventory. It turned over its inventory 3.8 times.

Traditionally, a high inventory turnover rate is viewed as best, since a high number usually indicates that the business has been able to continue operations without making a terribly large inventory investment, and that the inventory is moving and therefore marketable. One caveat, however, is that too high an inventory turnover could result in inability to meet customer demand because of short supplies. Only a careful balance makes it possible to turn over inventory efficiently while also having it available to meet demand. There are no general rules for how high inventory turnover should be. The best balance will vary widely from business to business. You can get an idea from looking at inventory turnover ratios in businesses like yours. Many industry associations publish ratio analysis information for their respective industries. As mentioned earlier, a list of some of these associations is found in Appendix E.

Inventory turnover can give a better idea of your business's performance than the size of your inventory can. Large inventories are not always good; in fact, a large inventory can be either a plus or a minus for a business. In some instances, it may be wise to keep a large inventory so as to be able to meet customer demand. Conversely, a large and growing inventory may indicate that your sales are way off. Keeping track of your inventory turnover ratio will give you an idea of whether or not inventory turnover is changing dramatically in proportion to sales. If your inventory grows faster than your sales, you may have problems on your hands. The inventory turnover ratio can be a useful tool for small business owners, enabling them to be alert to potential problems.

Because of the seasonal nature of many businesses, it is generally a good idea to calculate inventory turnover on a monthly basis. A cumulative record can keep you abreast of the inventory turnover throughout the year. Some business owners will find it useful to calculate monthly inventory turnover ratios for particular products or product lines, to see how well the different products are selling and how much stock should be kept on hand to meet customer demand. This practice will also give business owners a sense of which products are not selling well, so that they can make informed decisions about discontinuing such items.

Financial Ratios Used to Measure Profitability

Business owners and possible sources of financing want to know whether a company is making enough profit, considering how much they've invested in that company. There are many financial ratios that businesses and financing sources traditionally use to make such judgments. Among them are asset earning power, owner's return on equity, net profit on sales, investment turnover, and return on investment (ROI).

Asset Earning Power

To get a sense of the earning power of your company's assets, one of the best ratios to use is *asset earning power*, which looks at operating profit (i.e., earnings before interest and taxes are deducted) in relation to total assets. To calculate the asset earning power of Gough Square Supply Company, you would proceed as follows:

$$\frac{\text{Operating profit}}{\text{Total assets}} = \frac{\$96,600}{\$460,000} = 0.21 \ (21 \text{ percent})$$

Two things this ratio does not do is to account for whose (i.e., the owner's or the investors') assets are making how much in proportion to one another, and what effect a company's tax bracket will have on profits.

Owner's Return on Equity

If Sam Johnson, the owner of Gough Square Supply Company, wants to know how much return he has received on his own investment, he can use a financial ratio that measures the *owner's return on equity*. To make the calculation, the following formula is used:

$$\frac{\text{Net profit}}{\text{Total owner's equity}} = \text{owner's return on equity}$$

In this formula, an average equity figure is used. A business owner can use either the average of 12 months or beginning-of-year and end-of-year figures. Sam Johnson's equity in his business was $240,000 at the beginning of the year and $260,000 at the end of the year. His average equity investment was $250,000, so the owner's return on equity ratio for Gough Square Supply would be calculated as follows:

$$\frac{\text{Net profit}}{\text{Total owner's equity}} = \frac{\$46,000}{\$250,000} = 0.18 \text{ (18 percent)}$$

There is also a ratio that makes the same calculation by substituting *tangible net worth*—owner's equity minus intangible assets (e.g., goodwill, patents, trademarks, licenses, software programs, copyrights, and so on)—for owner's equity. Obviously the two figures will be the same if there are no intangible assets.

Net Profit on Sales

Net profit on sales looks at the amount of money coming into your business and how much you spend to conduct business. Operating costs and pricing procedures have the largest impact on this ratio. Lowering prices to try to increase total sales or failing to increase prices at a time when costs have risen may result in a lower net profit on sales, for example.

Sam Johnson would calculate his net profit on sales for Gough Square Supply by doing the following:

$$\frac{\text{Net profit}}{\text{Net sales}} = \frac{\$46,000}{\$690,000} = 0.067 \text{ (6.7 percent)}$$

For every dollar of goods that Gough Square Supply has sold, it has made 6.7 cents in profit.

Net profit on sales ratios are used by businesses to get an idea of where they stand in relation to other similar businesses, or where they stand historically in relation to their own businesses. Like the inventory turnover ratio, the net profit on sales ratio can be used on individual products or product lines to see how much profit separate products are making. If a product's profitability has dropped way off and is pulling the profitability of the overall company down, a business owner may decide to discontinue the product. He or she might also decide to push more aggressively those products or product lines that are showing a tremendous net profit on sales.

Investment Turnover

The *investment turnover* ratio is calculated by dividing net sales by total assets. It looks at annual net sales in proportion to the total investment in the company—in terms of sales for each dollar that has been invested in the company's assets.

The investment turnover for Gough Square Supply Company is calculated as follows:

$$\frac{\text{Net sales}}{\text{Total assets}} = \frac{\$690,000}{\$460,000} = 1.5$$

Return on Investment

Small business owners can use the rate of *return on investment* to get a good idea of how profitable their businesses are. To calculate return on investment, profit is divided by investment. A business owner must first decide which figure he or she will use from the financial statements to represent profit and which one will represent investment. Profit could be any one of a variety of items, among them net operating profit, net profit before taxes, and net profit after taxes. Investment could be total assets used in the company, or it could be just equity. The owner must decide which figures best meet the needs of the company—a subjective decision based on the type of business and perhaps the requests of any lenders who want to see specific figures. Consistency is the key. Once the small business owner has decided which figures to use to calculate ROI, it is important to be consistent (to continue using the same figures), so that accurate comparisons can be made from one accounting period to another.

Say, for example, that Sam Johnson has decided to calculate ROI for Gough Square Supply. He has decided to use net profit after taxes as the profit figure and total assets as the investment figure. He calculates ROI as follows:

$$\frac{\text{Net profit}}{\text{Total assets}} = \frac{\$46,000}{\$460,000} = 0.10 \text{ (10 percent)}$$

The ROI figure is useful in comparing company performance within industries as well as product line performance. It allows investors and other financing sources to see how well their investment is performing in the company. Obviously, you want to have as high a net profit as you can for as few assets invested as possible.

The financial ratios presented in this chapter are by no means exhaustive. They are simply some of the more common financial ratios that small business owners will find useful. They can help the small business owner to look at profitability, accounts receivables, inventory, return on investment, and other issues that are of regular concern. These are the ratios that most business owners should know and use, to get a sense of where they are in comparison to other similar businesses and in relation to where they want to be in the business' growth.

There are many other financial ratios that you can use to monitor your business's performance. Some of these are detailed in a brief but good SBA booklet entitled *Ratio Analysis for Small Business.*[1]

For starters, however, you should put the ratios detailed in this chapter to use in your own business. Become comfortable with them and use them to get a sense of where you are in your business life. While they won't perform magic or provide potions to cure your business ills, they may guide you toward problem areas that you might want to correct, and also point out to you and your financing sources those areas in which you are running your business quite well.

---

[1]Richard Sanzo, *Ratio Analysis for Small Business.* Washington: Small Business Administration, 1977. Available from the U.S. Government Printing Office, Washington, DC 20402.

16
Final
Observations

This book is a starting point for prospective business owners who are looking for ways to finance their business ideas. There is no magic in these pages; rather, they serve as a guide through some of the basic sources of financing that have been used by small business owners for many years. Although there are some new, up-to-the-minute cases and examples here, the foundation of the book is a commonsense approach to finding money to start and operate a small business.

The reason for this approach is simple. Too often, whether because of press glamorization or an overheard conversation at a party, we are tempted to believe that there are shortcuts to business success. Sometimes, indeed, there are ways to use your time more efficiently or spend your dollars more wisely, but in financing your business—particularly if it's a small business—shortcuts are usually myopic at best. To finance a small business, you need a well-thought-out plan for your business that reflects what your business is, how much it will cost you to start and operate, and what chances it has to succeed. Only such a plan can lessen your chances for failure and increase your likelihood of finding adequate resources to get your business up and going in a manner which is acceptable to you and indicative of future success.

Some issues addressed in this book may not be very popular. One chief area that comes to mind is venture capital. Venture capital is indeed a viable source of financing. In fact, some of the country's most successful businesses owe their birth to venture capital funds. Compaq Computer comes readily to mind as a company that was funded by venture capital and that has flourished by introducing innovative new products to meet market demand.

But let's be realistic. The truth is that for most small business owners, particularly in fields that are fairly traditional and show little promise for dramatic growth, venture capital is not going to be readily available. Sure, you may make it through the door to a venture capital fund, which in itself is no easy task, and the fund associates may give you time as they thoroughly analyze your business plan. But unless you have a product or a business that is so innovative that it will almost shake up the world or earn great sums of cash within the next 7 to 10 years, your chances of receiving venture capital money are dim at best. Venture capitalists are not bad people, mind you. But they are in the business to finance growth companies. They aim to maximize returns on their investments by either selling the companies they finance or making a public stock offering. If your company shows little promise of being a profitable sale or a well-accepted public stock offering, my advice is to look elsewhere for financing.

The "elsewhere" is what is documented in this book. For small businesses, traditional sources of financing are still the best bet. Look first to yourself. Your savings or other sources of cash you have available may be the best financing source around. Then look to family and friends and talk to them about your business idea. If you decide you don't want to risk losing a friendship or straining a family relationship by bringing money into the picture, talk to your accountant, your lawyer, or other business owners to get their suggestions about where you can look for financing.

Don't be discouraged if not everyone is as sold on your idea as you are. If you have put together a viable business plan, using reasonable projections for expenses and sales and market receptivity, and if you think the business is worth pursuing, then pursue it. Talk to bankers about financing. If you can't get a bank loan, look into other sources. See if SBA funds are available for your business. If you explore all the options, you are likely to find a source willing to bet with you on your business' success.

The pages that follow include several tools designed to make your search easier. The Glossary features simple definitions for most of the terms you are likely to run into in your search for money. To supplement these simple definitions, pick up a paperback copy of John Downes and Jordan Goodman's *Dictionary of Finance and Investment Terms,*[1] which costs less than $10. Keep it handy when you are preparing your business plan or meeting with a potential source of funds. It is about the best little dictionary of finance terms available and well worth the investment.

The Bibliography lists other books that are good follow-up sources on

[1]Woodbury, N.Y.: Barron's, 1985.

small business management and financing, if you feel a thirst for more information. The titles are quite descriptive, so you'll be able to tell what each book's focus is. The books listed are those that I've found to be useful for small business owners.

Also included here are five appendixes with names and addresses of sources of information and financing that might be of help to you in your search. The SBA regularly publishes updated lists, so if you want the latest list, call your local SBA field office. The numbers for the field offices are listed in Appendix A. If you are convinced that venture capital is the route for you, go to your library and take a look at *Pratt's Guide to Venture Capital Sources.*[2] It comes out annually and is the best directory of venture capital sources available.

A good business idea, determination, adequate financing, and a little bit of luck can greatly enhance your chances of success as a small business owner. If this book helps you to get your business off the ground or to keep it going, then it has accomplished its purpose.

[2]Stanley E. Pratt and Jane K. Morris (eds.), *Pratt's Guide to Venture Capital Sources,* 13th ed. Needham, Mass.: Venture Economics, 1989.

Appendix A

SBA Field Offices

Regional Offices

Region I
60 Batterymarch Street
10th Floor
Boston, MA 02110
617-451-2030

Region II
26 Federal Plaza
Room 31-08
New York, NY 10278
212-264-7772

Region III
Allendale Square
Suite 201
475 Allendale Road
King of Prussia, PA 19406
215-962-3700

Region IV
1375 Peachtree Street, N.E.
5th FloorAtlanta, GA 30367-8102
404-347-2441

Region V
230 South Dearborn Street
Room 510
Chicago, IL 60604-1593
312-353-0359

Region VI
8625 King George Drive
Building C
Dallas, TX 75235-3391
214-767-7643

Region VII
911 Walnut Street
13th Floor
Kansas City, MO 64106
816-426-2989

Region VIII
999 18th Street
Suite 701, North Tower
Denver, CO 80202
303-844-3984

Region IX
450 Golden Gate Avenue
Box 36044
San Francisco, CA 94102
415-556-7487

Region X
2615 Fourth Avenue
Room 440
Seattle, WA 98121
206-442-5676

District, Branch, and Post-of-Duty Offices

Alabama

2121 8th Avenue, North
Suite 200
Birmingham, AL 35203-2398
205-731-1344

Alaska

Federal Building
701 C Street, Box 67
Anchorage, AK 99513
907-271-4022

Arizona

2005 North Central Avenue
5th Floor
Phoenix, AZ 85004
602-261-3732

300 West Congress Street
Room 3V
Box FB-33
Tucson, AZ 85701
602-629-6715

Arkansas

320 West Capitol Avenue
Suite 601
Little Rock, AR 72201
501-378-5871

California

211 Main Street
4th Floor
San Francisco, CA 94105
415-974-0642

350 South Figueroa Street
6th Floor
Los Angeles, CA 90071
213-894-2956

2202 Monterey Street
Suite 108
Fresno, CA 93721
209-487-5189

660 J Street
Suite 215
Sacramento, CA 95814
916-551-1446

880 Front Street
Suite 4-S-29
San Diego, CA 92188
619-557-7252

Fidelity Federal Building
2700 North Main Street
Suite 400
Santa Ana, CA 92701
714-472-2494

Colorado

721 19th Street
Room 420
Denver, CO 80202-2599
303-844-3984

Connecticut

1 Hartford Square West
Hartford, CT 96106
203-240-4700

Delaware

844 King Street
Room 1315, Lockbox 16
Wilmington, DE 19801
302-573-6294

District of Columbia

1111 18th Street, N.W.
6th Floor
Washington, DC 20036
202-634-4950

Florida

400 West Bay Street
Room 261
Box 35067
Jacksonville, FL 32202
904-791-3782

1320 South Dixie Highway
Suite 501
Coral Gables, FL 33134
305-536-5521

700 Twiggs Street
Room 607
Tampa, FL 33602
813-228-2594

5601 Corporate Way South
Suite 402
West Palm Beach, FL 33407
407-689-3922

Georgia

1720 Peachtree Road, N.W.
6th Floor
Atlanta, GA 30309
404-347-2441

Federal Building
Room 225
52 North Main Street
Statesboro, GA 30458
912-489-8719

Guam

Pacific News Building
Room 508
238 O'Hara Street
Agana, Guam 96910
671-472-7277

Hawaii

300 Ala Moana
Room 2213
P.O. Box 50207
Honolulu, HI 96850
808-541-2990

Idaho

1020 Main Street
Suite 290
Boise, ID 83702
208-334-1696

Illinois

219 South Dearborn Street
Room 437
Chicago, IL 60605-1779
312-353-4528

511 West Capitol Street
Suite 302
Springfield, IL 62704
217-492-4416

Indiana

Minton-Capehart Federal Building
Room 578
575 North Pennsylvania Street
Indianapolis, IN 46204-1584
317-269-7272

Iowa

210 Walnut Street
Room 749
Des Moines, IA 50309
515-284-4422

373 Collins Road, N.E.
Room 100
Cedar Rapids, IA 52402
319-399-2571

Kansas

Main Place Building
110 East Waterman Street
Wichita, KS 67202
316-269-6571

Kentucky

Federal Office Building
600 Federal Place
Room 188
Louisville, KY 40202
502-582-5976

Louisiana

Ford-Fisk Building
1661 Canal Street
Suite 2000
New Orleans, LA 70112
504-589-6685

Maine

40 Western Avenue
Federal Building
Room 512
Augusta, ME 04330
207-622-8378

Maryland

Equitable Building
3d Floor
10 North Calvert Street
Baltimore, MD 21202
301-962-4392

Massachusetts

10 Causeway Street
Room 265
Boston, MA 02114
617-565-5590

Federal Building and Courthouse
1550 Main Street
Room 212
Springfield, MA 01103
413-785-0268

Michigan

McNamara Building
477 Michigan Avenue
Room 515
Detroit, MI 48226
313-226-6075

300 South Front Street
Marquette, MI 49885
906-225-1108

Minnesota

610-C Butler Square
100 North 6th Street
Minneapolis, MN 55403-1563
612-370-2324

Mississippi

1 Hancock Plaza
Suite 1001
Gulfport, MS 39501-7758
601-863-4449

Dr. A. H. McCoy Federal Building
100 West Capitol Street
Jackson, MS 39269-0396

Missouri

1103 Grand Avenue6th Floor
Kansas City, MO 64106
816-374-3419

620 South Glenstone Street
Suite 100
Springfield, MO 65805-3200
417-864-7670

815 Olive Street
Room 242
St. Louis, MO 63101
314-425-6600

Montana

301 South Park Avenue
Room 528, Drawer 10054
Helena, MT 5962
406-449-5381

Nebraska

11145 Mill Valley Road
Omaha, NE 68154
402-221-4691

Nevada

301 East Stewart
Room 301
Box 7527, Downtown Station
Las Vegas, NV 89125
702-388-6611

50 South Virginia Street
Room 238
P.O. Box 3216
Reno, NV 89505
702-784-5268

New Hampshire

55 Pleasant Street
Room 210
P.O. Box 1257
Concord, NH 03301-1257
603-225-1400

New Jersey

2600 Mt. Ephrain Avenue
Camden, NJ 08104
609-757-5183

Military Park Building
60 Park Place
4th Floor
Newark, NJ 07102
201-645-2434

New Mexico

Patio Plaza Building
Suite 320
5000 Marble Avenue, N.E.
Albuquerque, NM 87110
505-262-6171

New York

26 Federal Plaza
Room 3100
New York, NY 10278
212-264-4355

445 Broadway
Room 261
Albany, NY 12207
518-472-6300

111 West Huron Street
Room 1311
Buffalo, NY 14202
716-846-4301

Elmira Savings Bank Building
333 East Water Street
Room 412
Elmira, NY 14901
607-734-8130

35 Pinetown Road
Room 102-E
Melville, NY 11747
516-454-0750

Federal Building
Room 601
100 State Street
Rochester, NY 14614
716-263-6700

Federal Building
Room 1071
100 South Cointon Street
Syracuse, NY 13260
315-423-5383

North Carolina

222 South Church Street
Suite 300
Charlotte, NC 28202
704-371-6563

North Dakota

Federal Building
Room 218
657 Second Avenue, North
P.O. Box 3086
Fargo, ND 58108-3086
701-239-5131

Ohio

AJC Federal Building
Room 317
1240 East 9th Street
Cleveland, OH 44199
216-522-4180

Federal Building, U.S. Courthouse
85 Marconi Boulevard
Room 512
Columbus, OH 43215
614-469-6860

John Weld Peck Federal Building
550 Main Street
Room 5028
Cincinnati, OH 45202
513-684-2814

Oklahoma

200 Northwest 5th Street
Suite 670
Oklahoma City, OK 73102
405-231-43-1

Oregon

Federal Building
Room 676
1220 S.W. Third Avenue
Portland, OR 97204-2882
503-221-2682

Pennsylvania

Allendale Square
Suite 201
475 Allendale Road
King of Prussia, PA 19406
215-962-3846

100 Chestnut Street
Room 309
Harrisburg, PA 17101
717-782-384

960 Penn Avenue
5th Floor
Pittsburgh, PA 15222
412-644-2780

Penn Place
20 North Pennsylvania Avenue
Wilkes-Barre, PA 18701
717-826-6497

Puerto Rico

Federico Degatau Federal Building
Room 691
Carlos Chardon Avenue
Hato Rey, PR 00918
809-753-4002

Rhode Island

380 Westminster Mall
Providence, RI 02903
401-528-4586

South Carolina

1835 Assembly Street
Room 358
P.O. Box 2786
Columbia, SC 29202
803-765-5376

South Dakota

101 South Main Avenue
Suite 101
Sioux Falls, SD 57102-0577
605-336-2980, Ext. 231

Tennessee

404 James Robertson Parkway
Suite 1012, Parkway Towers
Nashville, TN 37219
615-736-5881

Texas

1100 Commerce Street
Room 3C-36
Dallas, TX 75242
214-767-0605

Federal Building
300 East Eighth Street
Room 520
Austin, TX 78701
512-482-5288

819 Taylor Street
Room 10A27
Fort Worth, TX 76102
817-334-3613

400 Mann Street
Suite 403
Corpus Christi, TX 78401
512-888-3331

10737 Gateway West
Suite 320
El Paso, TX 79902
915-541-7586

222 East Van Buren Street
Suite 500
Harlingen, TX 78550
512-427-8533

2525 Murworth
Suite 112
Houston, TX 77054
713-660-4420

1611 Tenth Street
Suite 200
Lubbock, TX 79401
806-743-7462

505 East Travis
Room 103
Marshall, TX 75670
214-935-5257

7400 Blanco Road
Suite 200
San Antonio, TX 78216
512-229-4535

Utah

125 South State Street
Room 2237
Salt Lake City, UT 84138-1195
801-524-3209

Vermont

87 State Street
Room 205
Montpelier, VT 05602
802-828-4474

Virgin Islands

Veterans Drive
Room 283
St. Thomas, VI 00801
809-774-8530

4C & 4D Estate Sion Farm
Room 7
P.O. Box 4010
Christiansted
St. Croix, VI 00820
809-778-5380

Virginia

400 North 8th Street
Room 3015
P.O. Box 10126
Richmond, VA 23240
804-771-2617

Washington

Second Avenue
Room 1792
Seattle, WA 98174-1088
206-442-5534

U.S. Courthouse
Room 651
P.O. Box 2167
Spokane, WA 99210
509-456-3786

West Virginia

168 West Main Street
5th Floor
Clarksburg, WV 26301
304-623-5631

550 Eagan Street
Room 309
Charleston, WV 25301
304-347-5220

Wisconsin

212 East Washington Avenue
Room 213
Madison, WI 53703
608-264-5261

Henry S. Reuss Federal Plaza
310 West Wisconsin Avenue
Suite 400
Milwaukee, WI 53203
414-291-3942

500 South Barstow Street
Room 37
Eau Claire, WI 54701
715-834-9012

Wyoming

100 East B Street
Federal Building
Room 4001
P.O. Box 2839
Casper, WY 82602-2839
307-261-5761

Disaster Area Offices

Area 1 (Covers Regions I and II)

15-01 Broadway
Fair Lawn, NJ 07410
201-794-8195

Area 2 (Covers Regions III, IV, and V)

120 Ralph McGill Street
Atlanta, GA 30308
404-347-3771

Area 3 (Covers Regions VI and VII)

2306 Oak Lane
Suite 110
Grand Prairie, TX 75051
214-767-7571

Area 4 (Covers Regions VIII, IX, X)

1825 Bell Street
Suite 208
P.O. Box 13795
Sacramento, CA 95853-4795

Appendix B
Small Business Investment Companies

Alabama

First SBIC of Alabama
16 Midtown Park East
Mobile, AL 36606
205-476-0700

Hickory Venture Capital Corp.
699 Gallatin Street, Suite A-2
Huntsville, AL 35801
205-539-1931

Remington Fund, Inc.
1927 First Avenue North
Birmingham, AL 35202
205-324-7709

Alaska

Alaska Business Investment Corp.
301 West Northern Lights
  Boulevard
P.O. Box 100600
Anchorage, AK 99510
907-278-2071

Arizona

Northwest Venture Partners
88777 East Via de Ventura
Suite 335
Scottsdale, AZ 85258
602-483-8940

Rocky Mountain Equity Corp.
4530 Central Avenue
Phoenix, AZ 85012
602-274-7534

Valley National Investors, Inc.
201 North Central Avenue
Suite 900
Phoenix, AZ 85004
602-261-1577

Wilbur Venture Capital Corp.
4575 South Palo Verde
Suite 305
Tucson, AZ 85714

SBICs and addresses are from the June 1988 issue of the *Directory of Operating Small Business Investment Companies*, published by the U.S. Small Business Administration. For the most recent issue of this publication, contact your nearest SBA field office.

Arkansas

Independence Financial Services,
Inc.
Town Plaza Office Park
P.O. Box 3878
Batesville, AR 72501
501-793-4533

Small Business Investment Capital,
Inc.
10003 New Benton Highway
P.O. Box 3627
Little Rock, AR 72203
501-455-3590

California

AMF Financial, Inc.
4330 La Jolla Village Drive
Suite 110
San Diego, CA 92122
619-546-0167

Atalanta Investment Company,
Inc.
141 El Camino Drive
Beverly Hills, CA 90212
213-273-1730

Bancorp Venture Capital, Inc.
11812 San Vicente Boulevard
Los Angeles, CA 90049
213-820-7222

BankAmerica Ventures, Inc.
555 California Street
San Francisco, CA 94104
415-953-3001

BNP Venture Capital Corp.
3000 Sand Hill Road
Building 1, Suite 125
Menlo Park, CA 94025
415-854-1084

California Capital Investors, Ltd.
11812 San Vincente Boulevard
Los Angeles, CA 90049
213-820-7222

Citicorp Venture Capital, Ltd.
2 Embarcadero Place
2200 Geny Road
Suite 203
Palo Alto, CA 94303
415-424-8000

City Ventures, Inc.
400 North Roxbury Drive
Beverly Hills, CA 90210
213-550-5709

CFB Venture Capital Corp.
530 B Street
3d Floor
San Diego, CA 92101
619-230-3304

CFB Venture Capital Corp.
350 California Street
Mezzanine
San Francisco, CA 94104
415-445-0594

Crosspoint Investment Corp.
1951 Landings Drive
Mountain View, CA 94043
415-968-0930

Developers Equity Capital Corp.
1880 Century Park East
Suite 311
Los Angeles, CA 90067
213-277-0330

Draper Associates
3000 Sand Hill Road
Building 4
Menlo Park, CA 94025
415-854-1712

First Interstate Capital, Inc.
5000 Birch Street
Suite 10100
Newport Beach, CA 92660
714-253-4360

First SBIC of California
650 Town Center Drive
17th Floor
Costa Mesa, CA 92626
714-556-1964

First SBIC of California
5 Palo Alto Square
Suite 938
Palo Alto, CA 94306
415-424-8011

First SBIC of California
155 North Lake Avenue
Suite 1010
Pasadena, CA 91109
818-304-3451

GC&H Partners
1 Maritime Plaza
20th Floor
San Francisco, CA 94110
415-981-5252

Hamco Capital Corp.
235 Montgomery Street
San Francisco, CA 94104
415-986-6567

HMS Capital, Ltd.
555 California Street
Room 5070
San Francisco, CA 94109
415-221-1225

Imperial Ventures, Inc.
9920 South Lacienega Boulevard
Inglewood, CA 90301
P.O. Box 92991
Los Angeles, CA 90009
213-417-5888

Ivanhoe Venture Capital, Ltd.
737 Pearl Street
Suite 201
La Jolla, CA 92037
619-454-8882

Jupiter Partners
600 Montgomery Street
35th Floor
San Francisco, CA 94111
415-421-9990

Latigo Capital Partners, II
1015 Gayley Avenue
Suite 202
Los Angeles, CA 90024
218-208-3892

Marwit Capital Corp.
180 Newport Center Drive
Suite 200
Newport Beach, CA 92660
714-640-6234

Merrill Pickard Anderson &
  Eyre I
2 Palo Alto Square
Suite 425
Palo Alto, CA 94306
415-856-8880

Metropolitan Venture Company,
  Inc.
5757 Wilshire Boulevard
Suite 670
Los Angeles, CA 90036
213-938-3488

Nelson Capital Corp.
1000 Santa Monica Boulevard
Suite 300
Los Angeles, CA 90067
213-556-1944

New West Partners II
4600 Campus Drive
Suite 103
Newport Beach, CA 92660
714-756-8940

New West Partners II
4350 Executive Drive
Suite 206
San Diego, CA 92121
619-457-0723

Peerless Capital Company, Inc.
675 South Arroyo Parkway
Suite 320
Pasadena, CA 91105
818-577-9199

PBC Venture Capital, Inc.
1408 18th Street
P.O. Box 6008
Bakersfield, CA 93386
805-395-3555

Ritter Partners
150 Isabella Avenue
Atherton, CA 94025
415-854-1555

Round Table Capital Corp.
655 Montgomery Street
Suite 700
San Francisco, CA 94111
415-392-7500

San Joaquin Capital Corp.
1415 18th Street
Suite 306
P.O. Box 2538
Bakersfield, CA 93301
805-323-7581

Seaport Ventures, Inc.
525 B Street
Suite 630
San Diego, CA 92101
619-232-4069

Union Venture Corp.
445 South Figueroa Street
Los Angeles, CA 90071
213-236-4092

Vista Capital Corp.
5080 Shoeham Place
Suite 202
San Diego, CA 92122
619-453-0780

VK Capital Company
50 California Street
Suite 2350
San Francisco, CA 94111
415-391-5600

Walden Capital Partners
750 Battery Street
7th Floor
San Francisco, CA 94111
415-391-7225

Westamco Investment Company
8929 Wilshire Boulevard
Suite 400
Beverly Hills, CA 90211
213-652-8288

Colorado

Associated Capital Corp.
4891 Independence Street
Suite 201
Wheat Ridge, CO 80033
303-420-8155

UBD Capital, Inc.
1700 Broadway
Denver, CO 80274
303-863-6329

Connecticut

AB SBIC, Inc.
275 School House Road
Cheshire, CT 06410
203-272-0203

All State Venture Capital Corp.
The Bishop House
32 Elm Street
P.O. Box 1629
New Haven, CT 06506
203-787-5029

Capital Impact Corp.
961 Main Street
Bridgeport, CT 06601
203-384-5670

Capital Resource Co. of
   Connecticut
699 Bloomfield Avenue
Bloomfield, CT 06002
203-243-1114

Dewey Investment Corp.
101 Middle Turnpike West
Manchester, CT 06040
203-649-0654

First Connecticut SBIC
177 State Street
Bridgeport, CT 06604
203-366-4726

First New England Capital
255 Main Street
Hartford, CT 06106
203-249-4321

Marcon Capital Corp.
49 Riverside Avenue
Westport, CT 06880
203-226-6893

Northeastern Capital Corp.
209 Church Street
New Haven, CT 06510
203-865-4500

Regional Financial Enterprises
36 Grove Street
New Canaan, CT 06840
203-966-2800

SBIC of Connecticut, Inc.
1115 Main Street
Bridgeport, CT 06603
203-367-3282

Delaware

Morgan Investment Corp.
902 Market Street
Wilmington, DE 19801
302-651-2500

District of Columbia

Allied Investment Corp.
1666 K Street, N.W.
Suite 901
Washington, DC 20006
202-331-1112

American Security Capital Corp.,
Inc.
730 15th Street, N.W.
Washington, DC 20013

DC Bancorp Venture Capital
Company
1801 K Street, N.W.
Washington, DC 20006
202-955-6970

Washington Ventures, Inc.
1320 18th Street, N.W.
Suite 300
Washington, DC 20036
202-895-2560

Florida

Allied Investment Corp.
Executive Office Center
Suite 305
2770 North Indian River
  Boulevard
Vero Beach, FL 32960
407-778-5556

Caribank Capital Corp.
2400 East Commercial Boulevard
Suite 814
Fort Lauderdale, FL 33308
305-776-1133

First North Florida SBIC
1400 Gadsden Street
P.O. Box 1021
Quincy, FL 32351

Gold Coast Capital Corp.
3550 Biscayne Boulevard
Room 601Miami, FL 33137
305-576-2012

J&D Capital Corp.
12747 Biscayne Boulevard
North Miami, FL 33181
305-893-0303

Market Capital Corp.
1102 North 28th Street
P.O. Box 22667Tampa, FL 33630
813-247-1357

Southeast Venture Capital
 Limited I
3250 Miami Center
100 Chopin Plaza
Miami, FL 33131
305-379-2005

Western Financial Capital Corp.
1380 N.E. Miami Gardens Drive
Suite 225
N. Miami Beach, FL 33179
305-949-5900

Georgia

Investor's Equity, Inc.
2629 First National Bank Tower
Atlanta, GA 30383404-523-3999

North Riverside Capital Corp.
50 Technology Park/Atlanta
Norcross, GA 30092
404-446-5556

Hawaii

Bancorp Hawaii SBIC
111 South King Street
Suite 1060
Honolulu, HI 96813
808-521-6411

Illinois

Alpha Capital Venture Partners
3 First National Plaza
14th Floor
Chicago, IL 60602
312-372-1556

ANB Venture Corp.
33 North LaSalle Street
Chicago, IL 60690
312-855-1554

Business Ventures, Inc.
20 North Wacker Drive
Suite 550
Chicago, IL 60606
312-346-1580

Continental Illinois Venture Corp.
209 South LaSalle Street
Chicago, IL 60693
312-828-8023

First Capital Corp. of Chicago
3 First National Plaza
Suite 1330
Chicago, IL 60670
312-732-5400

Frontenac Capital Corp.
208 South LaSalle Street
Room 1900Chicago, IL 60604
312-368-0047

LaSalle Street Capital Corp.
200 North LaSalle Street
10th Floor
Chicago, IL 60601
312-621-7057

Mesirow Capital Partners SBIC,
 Ltd.
350 North Clark Street
3d Floor
Chicago, IL 60610
312-670-6098

Walnut Capital Corp.
208 South LaSalle Street
Chicago, IL 60604
312-346-2033

Indiana

Circle Ventures, Inc.
2502 Roosevelt Avenue
Indianapolis, IN 46218
317-636-7242

Equity Resource Company, Inc.
1 Plaza Place
202 South Michigan Street
South Bend, IN 46601
219-237-5255

1st Source Capital Corp.
100 North Michigan Street
South Bend, IN 46601
P.O. Box 1602
South Bend, IN 46634
219-236-2180

Raffensperger Hughes Venture
  Corp.
20 North Meridian Street
Indianapolis, IN 46204
317-635-4551

White River Capital Corp.
500 Washington Street
P.O. Box 929
Columbus, IN 47201
812-372-0111

Iowa

MorAmerica Capital Corp.
Suite 200 America Building
Cedar Rapids, IA 52401
319-363-8247

Kansas

Financial Opportunities, Inc.
6060 Dutchman's Lane
Louisville, KY 40205
P.O. Box 35710
Louisville, KY 40232
502-451-3800

Kansas Venture Capital, Inc.
1030 First National Bank Tower
1 Townsite Plaza
Topeka, KS 66603
913-235-3437

Mountain Ventures, Inc.
911 North Main Street
P.O. Box 628
London, KY 40741
606-864-5175

Wilbur Venture Capital Corp.
400 Fincastle Building
3d and Broadway
Louisville, KY 40202
502-585-1214

Louisiana

Capital Equity Corp.
1885 Wooddale Boulevard
Suite 210
Baton Rouge, LA 70806
504-924-9209

Capital for Terrebonne, Inc.
27 Austin Drive
Houma, LA 70360
504-868-3930

Dixie Business Investment
  Company
401½ Lake Street
P.O. Box 588
Lake Providence, LA 71254
318-559-1558

Louisiana Equity Capital Corp.
451 Florida Street
Baton Rouge, LA 70821
504-389-4421

Maine

Maine Capital Corp.
70 Center Street
Portland, ME 04101
207-772-1001

Maryland

First Maryland Capital, Inc.
107 West Jefferson Street
Rockville, MD 20850
301-251-6630

Greater Washington Investments,
  Inc.
5454 Wisconsin Avenue
Chevy Chase, MD 20815
301-656-0626

Jiffy Lube Capital Corp.
6000 Metro Drive
Baltimore, MD 21215
P.O. Box 17223
Baltimore, MD 21203-7223
301-764-3234

Massachusetts

Advent Atlantic Capital Company
45 Milk Street
Boston, MA 02109
617-338-0800

Advent IV Capital Company
45 Milk Street
Boston, MA 02109
617-338-0800

Advent V Capital Company
45 Milk Street
Boston, MA 02109
617-338-0800

Advent Industrial Capital
  Company
45 Milk Street
Boston, MA 02109
617-338-0800

Atlas II Capital Corp.
260 Franklin Street
Suite 1501
Boston, MA 02109
617-439-6160

BancBoston Ventures, Inc.
100 Federal Street
P.O. Box 2016
Boston, MA 02106
617-434-2441

Bever Capital Corp.
260 Franklin Street
15th Floor
Boston, MA 02109
617-439-6160

Boston Hambro Capital Company
160 State Street
9th Floor
Boston, MA 02109
617-523-7767

Business Achievement Corp.
1172 Beacon Street
Suite 202
Newton, MA 02161
617-965-0550

Chestnut Capital International II
45 Milk Street
Boston, MA 02109
617-338-0800

Chestnut Street Partners, Inc.
45 Milk Street
Boston, MA 02109
617-574-6763

First Capital Corp. of Chicago
133 Federal Street
6th Floor
Boston, MA 02110
617-542-9185

First United SBIC, Inc.
135 Will Drive
Canton, MA 02021
617-828-6150

Fleet Venture Resources, Inc.
60 State Street
Boston, MA 02109
617-367-6700

Mezzanine Capital Corp.
45 Milk Street
Boston, MA 02109
617-574-6752

Milk Street Partners, Inc.
45 Milk Street
Boston, MA 02109
617-574-6723

208

Monarch-Narragansett Ventures,
Inc.
1 Financial Plaza
Springfield, MA 01102
413-781-3000

New England Capital Corp.
1 Washington Mall
7th Floor
Boston, MA 02108
617-722-6400

Northeast SBI Corp.
16 Cumberland Street
Boston, MA 02115
617-267-3983

Orange Nassau Capital Corp.
260 Franklin Street
15th Floor
Boston, MA 02109
617-439-6160

Pioneer Ventures Limited
Partnership
60 State Street
Boston, MA 02109
617-742-7825s

Shawmut National Capital Corp.
c/o Shawmut Bank, N.A.
1 Federal Street
Boston, MA 02210
617-292-4128

Stevens Capital Corp.
168 Stevens Street
Fall River, MA 02721
617-679-0044

UST Capital Corp.
40 Court Street
Boston, MA 02108
617-726-7137

Vadus Capital Corp.
260 Franklin Street
15th Floor
Boston, MA 02109
617-439-6160

Michigan

Doan Resources Limited
Partnership
4251 Plymouth Road
P.O. Box 986
Ann Arbor, MI 48106
313-747-9401

Michigan Tech Capital Corp.
Technology Park
601 West Sharon Avenue
P.O. Box 364
Houghton, MI 49931
906-487-2970

Minnesota

FBS SBIC, Limited Partnership
1100 First Bank Place East
Minneapolis, MN 55480
612-370-4764

Hidden Oaks Financial Services, Inc.
4620 West 77th Street
Suite 155
Edina, MN 55435
612-897-3902

Itasca Growth Fund, Inc.
1 Northwest Third Street
Grand Rapids, MN 55744
218-327-6200

North Star Ventures II, Inc.
100 South Fifth Street
Suite 2200
Minneapolis, MN 55402
612-33-1133

Northland Capital Venture
Partnership
613 Missabe Building
Duluth, MN 55802
218-722-0545

Northwest Venture Partners
2800 Piper Jaffray Tower
222 South Ninth Street
Minneapolis, MN 55402
612-372-8770

Norwest Growth Fund, Inc.
2800 Piper Jaffray Tower
222 South Ninth Street
Minneapolis, MN 55402
612-372-8770

Shared Ventures, Inc.
6550 York Avenue, South
Suite 419
Edina, MN 55435
612-925-3411

Mississippi

Vicksburg SBIC
302 First National Bank Building
Vicksburg, MS 39180
601-636-4762

Missouri

Bankers Capital Corp.
3100 Gillham Road
Kansas City, MO 64109
816-531-1600

Capital for Business, Inc.
100 Walnut
18th Floor
Kansas City, MO 64106
816-234-2357

Capital for Business, Inc.
11 South Meramec
Suite 804
Saint Louis, MO 63105
314-854-7427

MBI Venture Capital Investors,
Inc.
850 Main Street
Kansas City, MO 64105
816-471-1700

MorAmerica Capital Corp.
911 Main Street
Suite 2724A
Commerce Tower Building
Kansas City, MO 64105
816-842-0114

United Missouri Capital Corp.
1010 Grand Avenue
Kansas City, MO 64106
P.O. Box 419226
Kansas City, MO 64141
816-556-7333

Nebraska

United Financial Resources Corp.
6211 L Street
P.O. Box 1131
Omaha, NE 68101
402-734-1250

Nevada

Enterprise Finance Capital
Development Corp.
First Interstate Bank of Nevada
Building
1 East First Street
Suite 1100
Reno, NV 89501
702-329-7797

New Hampshire

VenCap, Inc.
1155 Elm Street
Manchester, NH 03101
603-644-6100

New Jersey

Bishop Capital
58 Park Place
Newark, NJ 07102
201-623-0171

ESLO Capital Corp.
212 Wright Street
Newark, NJ 07114
201-242-4488

First Princeton Capital Corp.
5 Garret Mountain Plaza
West Paterson, NJ 07424
201-278-8111

210   Appendix B

Monmouth Capital Corp.
125 Wycoff Road
Midland National Bank Building
P.O. Box 335
Eatontown, NJ 07724
201-542-4927

Tappan Zee Capital Corp.
201 Lower Notch Road
Little Falls, NJ 07424
201-256-8280

Unicorn Ventures II
6 Commerce Drive
Cranford, NJ 07016
201-276-7880

United Jersey Venture Capital, Inc.
301 Carnegie Center
P.O. Box 2066
Princeton, NJ 08540
609-987-3490

New Mexico

Albuquerque SBIC
501 Tijeras Avenue, N.W.
P.O. Box 487
Albuquerque, NM 87103
505-247-0145

Equity Capital Corp.
119 East Marcy Street
Suite 101
Santa Fe, NM 87501
505-988-4273

Southwest Capital Investments, Inc.
The Southwest Building
3500-E Comanche Road, N.E.
Albuquerque, NM 87107
505-884-7161

United Mercantile Capital Corp.
2400 Louisiana Boulevard
Building 4, Suite 101
Albuquerque, NM 87110
P.O. Box 37487
Albuquerque, NM 87176
505-883-8201

New York

American Commercial Capital
Corp.
310 Madison Avenue
Suite 1304
ew York, NY 10017
212-986-3305

American Energy Investment
Corp.
645 Fifth Avenue
Suite 1900
New York, NY 10022
212-688-7307

Amev Capital Corp.
1 World Trade Center
50th Floor
New York, NY 10048
212-775-9100

ASEA—Harvest Partners II
767 Third Avenue
New York, NY 10017
212-838-7776

Atalanta Investment Company,
Inc.
450 Park Avenue
New York, NY 10022
212-832-1104

BT Capital Corp.
280 Park Avenue—10 West
New York, NY 10017
212-850-1916

Boston Hambro Capital Company
17 East 71st Street
New York, NY 10021
212-288-9106

Bridger Capital Corp.
645 Madison Avenue
Suite 810
New York, NY 10022
212-888-4004

Central New York SBIC
351 South Warren Street
Syracuse, NY 13202
315-478-5026

Chase Manhattan Capital Corp.
1 Chase Manhattan Plaza
23d Floor
New York, NY 10081
212-552-6275

Chemical Venture Capital
 Associates
277 Park Avenue
10th Floor
New York, NY 10172
212-310-7578

Citicorp Venture Capital, Ltd.
153 East 53d Street
28th Floor
New York, NY 10043
212-559-1127

Clinton Capital Corp.
79 Madison Avenue
Suite 800
New York, NY 10016
212-696-4334

CMNY Capital
77 Water Street
New York, NY 10005
212-437-7078

Croyden Capital Corp.
45 Rockefeller Plaza
Suite 2165
New York, NY 10111
212-974-0184

Diamond Capital Corp.
805 Third Avenue
Suite 1100
New York, NY 10017
212-838-1255

EAB Venture Corp.
EAB Plaza
Uniondale, NY 11555
516-296-5784

Edwards Capital Company
215 Lexington Avenue
Suite 805
New York, NY 10016
212-686-2568

Fairfield Equity Corp.
200 East 42d Street
New York, NY 10017
212-867-0150

Ferranti High Technology, Inc.
515 Madison Avenue
New York, NY 10022
212-688-9828

Fifty-Third Street Ventures
155 Main Street
Cold Spring, NY 10516
914-265-5167

First New York SBIC
20 Squandron Boulevard
Suite 480
New City, NY 10956
914-638-1550

Franklin Corp.
767 Fifth Avenue
G.M. Building
23d Floor
New York, NY 10153
212-486-2323

Fundex Capital Corp.
525 Northern Boulevard
Great Neck, NY 11021
516-466-8551

Genesee Funding, Inc.
100 Corporate Woods
Rochester, NY 14623
716-272-2332

GHW Capital Corp.
489 Fifth Avenue
New York, NY 10017
212-687-1708

Hanover Capital Corp.
150 East 58th Street
Suite 2710
New York, NY 10155
212-980-9670

Intergroup Venture Capital Corp.
230 Park Avenue
New York, NY 10017
212-661-5428

Interstate Capital Company, Inc.
380 Lexington Avenue
New York, NY 10017
212-986-7333

Irving Capital Corp.
1290 Avenue of the Americas
New York, NY 10104
212-408-4800

Kwiat Capital Corp.
576 Fifth Avenue
New York, NY 10036
212-391-2461

M & T Capital Corp.
1 M & T Plaza
Buffalo, NY 14240
716-842-5881

MH Capital Investors, Inc.
270 Park Avenue
New York, NY 10017
212-286-3222

Multi-Purpose Capital Corp.
31 South Broadway
Yonkers, NY 10701
914-963-2733

NatWest USA Capital Corp.
175 Water Street
New York, NY 10038
212-602-1200

Nelson Capital Corp.
585 Stewart Avenue
Suite 416
Garden City, Long Island, NY
  11530
516-222-2555

Norstar Capital Inc.
1 Norstar Plaza
Albany, NY 12207
518-447-4043

NYBDC Capital Corp.
41 State Street
Albany, NY 12207
518-463-2268

NYSTRS/NV Capital
1 Norstar Plaza
Albany, NY 12207
518-447-4050

Onondaga Venture Capital Fund,
  Inc.
327 State Tower Building
Syracuse, NY 13202
315-478-0157

Preferential Capital Corp.
16 Court Street
Brooklyn, NY 11241
718-855-2728

Pyramid Ventures, Inc.
280 Park Avenue
New York, NY 10015
212-850-1934

Questech Capital Corp.
320 Park Avenue
3d Floor
New York, NY 10022
212-891-7500

R & R Financial Corp.
1451 Broadway
New York, NY 10036
212-790-1441

Rand SBIC, Inc.
1300 Rand Building
Buffalo, NY 14203
716-853-0802

Realty Growth Capital Corp.
331 Madison Avenue
4th Floor East
New York, NY 10017
212-661-8380

Republic SBI Corp.
452 Fifth Avenue
New York, NY 10018
212-930-8639

SLK Capital Corp.
115 Broadway
20th Floor
New York, NY 10006
212-587-8800

Small Business Electronics
 Investment Corp.
1220 Peninsula Boulevard
Hewlett, NY 11557
516-374-0743

767 Limited Partnership
767 Third Avenue
New York, NY 10017
212-838-7776

Southern Tier Capital Corp.
55 South Main Street
Liberty, NY 12754
914-292-3030

Tappan Zee Capital Corp.
120 North Main Street
New City, NY 10956
914-634-8890

Telesciences Capital Corp.
26 Broadway
Suite 841
New York, NY 10004
212-425-0320

TLC Funding Corp.
141 South Central Avenue
Hartsdale, NY 10530
914-683-1144

Vega Capital Corp.
720 White Plains Road
Scarsdale, NY 10583
914-472-8550

Venture SBIC, Inc.
249-12 Jericho Turnpike
Floral Park, NY 11001
516-352-0068

WFG-Harvest Partners, Ltd.
767 Third Avenue
New York, NY 10017
212-838-7776

Winfield Capital Corp.
237 Mamaroneck Avenue
White Plains, NY 10605
914-949-2600

Wood River Capital Corp.
645 Madison Avenue
New York, NY 10022
212-750-9420

North Carolina

Delta Capital, Inc.
227 North Tryon Street
Suite 201
Charlotte, NC 28202
704-372-1410

Falcon Capital Corp.
400 Wst Fifth Street
Greenville, NC 27834
919-752-5918

Heritage Capital Corp.
2095 Two First Union Plaza
Charlotte, NC 28282
704-334-2867

Kitty Hawk Capital
Independence Center
Suite 1640
Charlotte, NC 28246
704-333-3777

NCNB SBIC Corp.
1 NCNB Plaza
Charlotte, NC 28255
704-374-5723

Ohio

A.T. Capital Corp.
900 Euclid Avenue
P.O. Box 5937
Cleveland, OH 44101
216-687-4970

Banc One Capital Corp.
100 East Broad Street
Columbus, OH 43215
614-248-5932

Capital Funds Corp.
800 Superior Avenue
Cleveland, OH 44114
216-344-5774

Clarion Capital Corp.
35555 Curtis Boulevard
Eastlake, OH 44094
216-953-0555

First Ohio Capital Corp.
606 Madison Avenue
Toledo, OH 43604
P.O. Box 2061
Toledo, OH 43603
419-259-7146

Gries Investment Company
1500 Statler Office Tower
Cleveland, OH 44115
216-861-1146

JRM Capital Corp.
110 West Streetsboro Street
Hudson, OH 44236
216-656-4010

National City Capital Corp.
629 Euclid Avenue
Cleveland, OH 44114
216-575-2491

River Capital Corp.
796 Huntington Building
Cleveland, OH 44114
216-781-3655

SeaGate Venture Management, Inc.
245 Summit Street
Suite 1403
Toledo, OH 43603
419-259-8605

Tamco Investors (SBIC), Inc.
375 Victoria Road
Youngstown, OH 44515
216-792-3811

Oklahoma

Alliance Business Investment
Company
17 East Second Street
1 Williams Center, Suite 2000
Tulsa, OK 74172
918-584-3581

Western Venture Capital Corp.
4880 South Lewis
Tulsa, OK 74105
918-749-7981

Oregon

First Interstate Capital, Inc.
227 S.W. Pine Street
Suite 200
Portland, OR 97204
503-223-4334

Northern Pacific Capital Corp.
1201 S.W. 12th Avenue
Suite 608
Portland, OR 97205
P.O. Box 1658
Portland, OR 97207
503-241-1255

Norwest Growth Fund, Inc.
1300 Southwest Fifth Street
Suite 3108
Portland, OR 97201
503-223-6622

Pennsylvania

Capital Corp. of America
225 South 15th Street
Suite 920
Philadelphia, PA 19102
215-732-1666

Enterprise Venture Capital Corp.
of Pennsylvania
227 Franklin Street
Suite 215
Johnstown, PA 15901
814-535-7597

Erie SBIC
32 West Eighth Street
Suite 615
Erie, PA 16501
814-453-7964

Fidelcor Capital Corp.
123 South Broad Street
Philadelphia, PA 19109
215-985-7287

First SBIC of California
P.O. Box 512
Washington, PA 15301
412-223-0707

First Valley Capital Corp.
640 Hamilton Mall
8th Floor
Allentwon, PA 18101
215-776-6760

Franklin Corp.
Plymouth Meeting Executive
 Congress
610 West Germantown Pike
Suite 461
Plymouth Meeting, PA 19462

Meridian Capital Corp.
650 Skippack Pike
Suite 222, Blue Bell West
Blue Bell, PA 19422
215-278-8907

Meridian Venture Partners
The Fidelity Court Building
259 Radnor-Chester Road
Radnor, PA 19087
215-293-0210

PNC Capital Corp.
Pittsburgh National Building
Fifth Avenue and Wood Street
Pittsburgh, PA 15222
412-355-2245

Rhode Island

Domestic Capital Corp.
815 Reservoir Avenue
Cranston, RI 02910
401-946-3310

Fleet Venture Resources, Inc.
111 Westminster Street
Providence, RI 02903
401-278-6770

Moneta Capital Corp.
285 Governor Street
Providence, RI 02906
401-861-4600

Old Stone Capital Corp.
1 Old Stone Square
11th Floor
Providence, RI 02903
401-278-2559

River Capital Corp.
555 South Main Street
Providence, RI 02903
401-861-7470

Wallace Capital Corp.
170 Westminister Street
Suite 300
Providence, RI 02903
401-273-9191

South Carolina

Carolina Venture Capital Corp.
14 Archer Road
Hilton Head Island, SC 29928
803-842-3101

Charleston Capital Corp.
111 Church Street
P.O. Box 328
Charleston, SC 29402
803-723-6464

Floco Investment Company, Inc.
Highway 52 North
Scranton, SC 29561
P.O. Box 919
Lake City, SC 29560

Lowcountry Investment Corp.
4444 Daley Street
P.O. Box 10447
Charleston, SC 29411
803-554-9880

Reedy River Ventures
400 Haywood Road
P.O. Box 17526
Greenville, SC 29606
803-297-9198

Tennessee

Financial Resources, Inc.
2800 Sterick Building
Memphis, TN 38103
901-527-9411

Leader Capital Corp.
158 Madison Avenue
P.O. Box 708
Memphis, TN 38101
901-578-2405

Texas

Alliance Business Investment
  Company
911 Louisiana
1 Shell Plaza, Suite 3990
Houston, TX 77002
713-224-8224

Americap Corp.
7575 San Felipe
Houston, TX 77063
713-780-8084

Ameriway Venture Partners I
7575 San Felipe
Houston, TX 77063
713-780-8084

Brittany Capital Company
1525 Elm Street
2424 LTV Tower
Dallas, TX 75201
214-954-1515

Business Capital Corp.
4809 Cole Avenue
Suite 250
Dallas, TX 75205
214-522-3739

Capital Marketing Corp.
100 Nat Gibbs Drive
P.O. Box 1000
Keller, TX 76248
817-656-7309

Capital Southwest Venture Corp.
12900 Preston Road
Suite 700
Dallas, TX 75230
214-233-8242

Central Texas SBI Corp.
P.O. Box 2600
Waco, TX 76702
817-753-6461

Charter Venture Group, Inc.
2600 Citadel Plaza Drive
Suite 600
Houston, TX 77008
713-863-0704

Citicorp Venture Capital, Ltd.
717 North Harwood Street
Dallas, TX 75201
214-880-9670

Energy Assets, Inc.
4900 Republic Bank Center
700 Louisiana
Houston, TX 77002
713-236-9999

Enterprise Capital Corp.
4543 Post Oak Place
Suite 130
Houston, TX 77027
713-621-9444

FCA Investment Company
3000 Post Oak
Suite 1790
Houston, TX 77056
713-965-0061

First Interstate Capital Corp. of
  Texas
1000 Louisiana
7th Floor
Houston, TX 77002
P.O. Box 3326
Houston, TX 77253 713-224-661

Ford Capital, Ltd.
1525 Elm Street
Dallas, TX 75201
P.O. Box 2140
Dallas, TX 75221
214-954-0688

Mapleleaf Capital Ltd.
55 Waugh
Suite 710
Houston, TX 77007
713-880-4494

MCap Corp.
1717 Main Street
6th Floor
Momentum Place
Dallas, TX 75201
214-939-3131

Mid-State Capital Corp.
510 North Valley Mills Drive
Waco, TX 76710
817-772-9220

MVenture Corp.
1717 Main Street
6th Floor—Momentum Place
Dallas, TX 75201
P.O. Box 662090
Dallas, TX 75266
214-939-3131

Neptune Capital Corp.
5956 Sherry Lane
Suite 800
Dallas, TX 75225
214-739-1414

North Riverside Capital Corp.
400 North St. Paul
Suite 1265
Dallas, TX 75201
214-220-2717

Omega Capital Corp.
755 South 11th Street
Suite 250
P.O. Box 2173
Beaumont, TX 77704
409-832-0221

Republic Venture Group, Inc.
325 North St. Paul
2829 Tower II
Dallas, TX 75201
P.O. Box 655961
Dallas, TX 75265
214-922-3500

Revelation Resources, Ltd.
2929 Allen Parkway
Suite 1705
Houston, TX 77019
713-526-5623

Rust Capital Limited
114 West Seventh Street
Suite 500
Austin, TX 78701
512-482-0806

San Antonio Venture Group, Inc.
2300 West Commerce Street
San Antonio, TX 78207
512-223-3633

SBI Capital Corp.
6305 Beverly Hill Lane
Houston, TX 77057
P.O. Box 570368
Houston, TX 77257
713-975-1188

218

Appendix B

South Texas SBIC
120 South Main Street
P.O. Box 1698
Victoria, TX 77902
512-573-5151

Southwestern Venture Capital of
Texas, Inc.
1250 N.E. Loop 410
Suite 300
San Antonio, TX 78209
512-822-9949

Southwestern Venture Capital of
Texas, Inc.
1336 East Court Street
P.O. Box 1719
Seguin, TX 78155
512-379-0380

Sunwestern Capital Corp.
3 Forest Plaza
12221 Merit Drive
Suite 1300
Dallas, TX 75251
214-239-5650

Sunwestern Ventures Company
3 Forest Plaza
12221 Merit Drive
Suite 1300
Dallas, TX 75251
214-239-5650

Texas Commerce Investment
Company
Texas Commerce Bank Building
30th Floor
712 Main Street
Houston, TX 77002
713-236-4719

Wesbanc Ventures, Ltd.
2401 Fountainview
Suite 950
Houston, TX 77057
713-977-7421

Vermont

Queneska Capital Corp.
123 Church Street
Burlington, VT 05401
802-865-1806

Virginia

Crestar Capital
9 South 12th Street
3d Floor
Richmond, VA 23219
804-643-7358

James River Capital Associates
9 South 12th Street
P.O. Box 1776
Richmond, VA 23219
804-643-7323

Metropolitan Capital Corp.
2550 Huntington Avenue
Alexandria, VA 22303
703-960-4698

River Capital Corp.
1033 North Fairfax Street
Alexandria, VA 22314
703-739-2100

Sovran Funding Corp.
Sovran Center
6th Floor
1 Commercial Plaza
P.O. Box 600
Norfolk, VA 23510
804-441-4041

Tidewater Industrial Capital Corp.
United Virginia Bank Building
Suite 1424
Norfolk, VA 23510
804-622-1501

Tidewater SBI Corp.
1214 First Virginia Bank Tower
101 St. Paul's Boulevard
Norfolk, VA 23510
804-627-2315

Washington

Capital Resource Corp.
1001 Logan Building
Seattle, WA 98101
206-623-6550

Northwest Business Investment
Corp.
929 West Sprague Avenue
Spokane, WA 99204
509-838-3111

Peoples Capital Corp.
1415 Fifth Avenue
Seattle, WA 98171
206-344-5463

Seafirst Capital Corp.
Columbia Seafirst Center
701 Fifth Avenue
P.O. Box 34103
Seattle, WA 98124
206-358-7441

Washington Trust Equity Corp.
Washington Trust Financial
 Center
P.O. Box 2127
Spokane, WA 99210
509-455-4106

Wisconsin

Bando-McGlocklin Capital Corp.
13555 Bishops Court
Suite 225
Brookfield, WI 53005
414-784-9010

Capital Investments, Inc.
Commerce Building
Suite 400
744 North Fourth Street
Milwaukee, WI 53203
414-273-6560

N & I Ventures Corp.
770 North Water Street
Milwaukee, WI 53202
414-765-7910

Marine Venture Capital, Inc.
111 East Wisconsin Avenue
Milwaukee, WI 53202
14-765-2274

MorAmerica Capital Corp.
600 East Mason Street
Milwaukee, WI 53202
414-276-3839

Super Market Investors, Inc.
23000 Roundy Drive
Pewaukee, WI 53072
P.O. Box 473
Milwaukee, WI 53202
414-547-7999

Wisconsin Community Capital,
 Inc.
14 West Mifflin Street
Suite 314
Madison, WI 53703
608-256-3441

Wyoming

Capital Corp. of Wyoming, Inc.
145 South Durbin Street
P.O. Box 3599
Casper, WY 82602
307-234-5351

Appendix C

Minority Enterprise Small Business Investment Companies

Alabama

Alabama Capital Corp.
16 Midtown Park East
Mobile, AL 36606
205-476-0700

Alabama Small Business
Investment Company
206 North 24th Street
Birmingham, AL 35203
205-324-5234

Tuskegee Capital Corp.
Hampton Hall Building
4453 Richardson Road
Montgomery, AL 36108
205-281-8059

Alaska

Calista Business Investment Corp.
503 East Sixth Avenue
Anchorage, AK 99501
907-277-0425

Arkansas

Capital Management Services, Inc.
1910 North Grant Street
Suite 200
Little Rock, AR 72207
501-664-8613

Kar-Mal Venture Capital, Inc.
2821 Kavanaugh Blvd.
Little Rock, AR 72205
501-661-0010

SBICs and addresses are from the June 1988 issue of the *Directory of Operating Small Business Investment Companies*, published by the U.S. Small Business Administration. For the most recent issue of this publication, contact your nearest SBA field office.

Power Ventures, Inc.
829 Highway 270 North
Malvern, AR 72104
501-332-3695

California

ABC Capital Corp.
610 East Live Oak Avenue
Arcadia, CA 91006
818-570-0653

Allied Business Investors, Inc.
428 South Atlantic Boulevard
Suite 201
Monterey Park, CA 91754
818-289-0186

Ally Finance Corp.
9100 Wilshire Boulevard
Suite 408
Beverly Hills, CA 90212
213-550-8100

Asian American Capital Corp.
1251 West Tennyson Road
Suite 4
Hayward, CA 94544
415-887-6888

Astar Capital Corp.
7282 Orangethorpe Avenue
Suite 8
Buena Park, CA 90621
714-739-2218

Bentley Capital
592 Vallejo Street
Suite 2
San Francisco, CA 94133
415-362-2868

Best Finance Corp.
1814 West Washington Boulevard
Los Angeles, CA 90007
213-731-2268

Business Equity and Development
Corp.
767 North Hill Street
Suite 401
Los Angeles, CA 90012
213-613-0351

Charterway Investment Corp.
222 South Hill Street
Suite 800
Los Angeles, CA 90012
213-687-8539

Continental Investors, Inc.
8781 Seaspray Drive
Huntington Beach, CA 92646
714-964-5207

Equitable Capital Corp.
855 Sansome Street
San Francisco, CA 94111
415-434-4114

First American Capital Fundings,
Inc.
38 Corporate Park
Suite B
Irvine, CA 92714
714-660-9288

Helio Capital, Inc.
5900 South Eastern Avenue
Suite 136
Commerce, CA 90040
213-721-8053

LaiLai Capital Corp.
1545 Wilshire Boulevard
Suite 510
Los Angeles, CA 90017
213-484-5085

Magna Pacific Investments
977 North Broadway
Suite 301
Los Angeles, CA 90012
213-680-2505

Myriad Capital, Inc.
328 South Atlantic Boulevard
Suite 200
Monterey Park, Ca 91754
818-570-4548

New Kukje Investment Company
958 South Vermont Avenue
Suite C
Los Angeles, CA 90006
213-389-8679

Opportunity Capital Corp.
1 Fremont Place
39650 Liberty Street
Suite 425
Fremont, CA 94538
415-651-4412

Positive Enterprises, Inc.
399 Arguello Street
San Francisco, CA 94118
415-386-6606

RSC Financial Corp.
323 East Matilija Road
Suite 208
Ojai, CA 93023
805-646-2925

San Joaquin Business Investment
  Group, Inc.
2310 Tulare Street
Suite 140
Fresno, CA 93721
209-233-3580

Colorado

Colorado Invesco, Inc.
1999 Broadway
Suite 2100
Denver, CO 80202
303-293-2431

District of Columbia

Allied Financial Corp.
1666 K Street, N.W.
Suite 901
Washington, DC 20006
202-331-1112

Broadcast Capital, Inc.
1771 N Street, N.W.
Suite 421
Washington, DC 20036
202-429-5393

Consumers United Capital Corp.
2100 M Street, N.W.
Washington, DC 20037
202-872-5274

Fulcrum Venture Capital Corp.
1030 15th Street, N.W.
Suite 203
Washington, DC 20005
202-785-4253

Minority Broadcast Investment
  Corp.
450 M Street, S.W.
Washington, DC 20024
202-479-0878

Syncom Capital Corp.
1030 15th Street, N.W.
Suite 203
Washington, DC 20005
202-293-9428

Florida

Allied Financial Corp.
Executive Office Center
Suite 305
2770 North Indian River
  Boulevard
Vero Beach, FL 32960
407-778-5556

First American Lending Corp.
1926 Tenth Avenue North
Lake Worth, FL 33461
P.O. Box 24660
West Palm Beach, FL 33416
305-533-1511

Ideal Financial Corp.
780 N.W. 42d Avenue
Suite 303
Miami, FL 33126
305-442-4665

Pro-Med Investment Corp.
1380 N.E. Miami Gardens Drive
Suite 225
North Miami Beach, Fl 33179
305-949-5915

Venture Group, Inc.
5433 Buffalo Avenue
Jacksonville, FL 32208
904-353-7313

Georgia

Renaissance Capital Corp.
161 Spring Street, N.W.
Suite 610
Atlanta, GA 30303
404-658-9061

Hawaii

Pacific Venture Capital, Ltd.
222 South Vineyard Street, PH 1
Honolulu, HI 96813
808-521-6502

Illinois

Amoco Venture Capital Company
200 East Randolph Drive
Chicago, IL 60601
312-856-6523

Chicago Community Ventures,
Inc.
104 South Michigan Avenue
Suite 215-218
Chicago, IL 60603
312-726-6084

Combined Fund, Inc.
1525 East 53d Street
Chicago, IL 60615
312-753-9650

Neighborhood Fund, Inc.
1950 East 71st Street
Chicago, IL 60649
312-684-8074

Peterson Finance and Investment
Company
3300 West Peterson Avenue
Suite A
Chicago, IL 60659
312-583-6300

Tower Ventures, Inc.
Sears Tower, BSC 43-50
Chicago, IL 60684
312-875-0571

Kentucky

Equal Opportunity Finance, Inc.
420 Hurstbourne Lane
Suite 201
Louisville, KY 40222
502-423-1943

Louisiana

SCDF Investment Corp.
1006 Surrey Street
P.O. Box 3885
Lafayette, LA 70502
318-232-3769

Maryland

Albright Venture Capital, Inc.
1355 Piccard Drive
Suite 380
Rockville, MD 20850
301-921-9090

Security Financial and Investment
  Corp.
7720 Wisconsin Avenue
Suite 207
Bethesda, MD 20814
301-951-4288

Massachusetts

Argonauts MESBIC Corp.
2 Vernon Street
Framingham, MA 01701
508-820-3430

New England MESBIC, Inc.
530 Turnpike Street
North Andover, MA 01845
617-688-4326

Transportation Capital Corp.
230 Newbury Street
Suite 21
Boston, MA 02116
617-536-0344

Michigan

Dearborn Capital Corp.
P.O. Box 1729
Dearborn, MI 48121
313-337-8577

Metro-Detroit Investment Company
30777 Northwestern Highway
Suite 300
Farmington Hill, MI 48018
313-851-6300

Motor Enterprises, Inc.
3044 West Grand Boulevard
Detroit, MI 48202
313-556-4273

Mutual Investment Company, Inc.
21415 Civic Center Drive
Mark Plaza Building
Suite 217
Southfield, MI 48076
313-557-2020

Minnesota

Capital Dimensions Ventures
  Fund, Inc.
2 Appletree Square
Suite 244
Minneapolis, MN 55425
612-854-3007

Mississippi

Sun-Delta Capital Access Center,
  Inc.
819 Main Street
Greenville, MS 38701
601-335-5291

New Jersey

Capital Circulation Corp.
208 Main Street
Fort Lee, NJ 07024
201-947-8637

Formosa Capital Corp.
605 King George Post Road
Fords, NJ 08863
201-738-4710

Rutgers Minority Investment
  Company
92 New Street
Newark, NJ 07102
201-648-5287

Transpac Capital Corp.
1037 Route 46 East
Clifton, NJ 07013
201-470-0706

Zaitech Capital Corp.
2083 Center Avenue
Fort Lee, NJ 07024
201-944-3018

New Mexico

Associated Southwest Investors,
Inc.
2400 Louisiana N.E.
Building 4, Suite 225
Albuquerque, NM 87110
505-881-0066

New York

American Asian Capital Corp.
130 Water Street
Suite 6-L
New York, NY 10005
212-422-6880

Avdon Capital Corp.
805 Avenue L
Brooklyn, NY 11230
718-692-0950

Capital Investors & Management
Corp.
210 Canal Street
Suite 607
New York, NY 10013
212-964-2480

Cohen Capital Corp.
8 Freer Street
Suite 185
Lynbrook, NY 11563
516-887-3434

Columbia Capital Corp.
79 Madison Avenue
Suite 800
New York, NY 10016
212-696-4334

CVC Capital Corp.
131 East 62d Street
New York, NY 10021
212-319-7210

East Coast Venture Capital, Inc.
313 West 53d Street
3d Floor
New York, NY 10019
212-245-6460

Elk Associates Funding Corp.
600 Third Avenue
38th Floor
New York, NY 10016
212-972-8550

Equico Capital Corp.
1290 Avenue of the Americas
Suite 3400
New York, NY 10019
212-397-8660

Everlast Capital Corp.
350 Fifth Avenue
Suite 2805
New York, NY 10118
212-695-3910

Exim Capital Corp.
290 Madison Avenue
New York, NY 10017
12-683-3375

Fair Capital Corp.
c/o Summit Associates
3 Pell Street
2d Floor
New York, NY 10013
201-608-5866

Freshstart Venture Capital Corp.
313 West 53d Street
3d Floor
New York, NY 10019
212-265-2249

Hanam Capital Corp.
1 Penn Plaza
Suite 3330
New York, NY 10119
212-714-9830

Hop Chung Capital Investors, Inc.
185 Canal Street
Room 303
New York, NY 10013
212-219-1777

Horn & Hardart Capital Corp.
730 Fifth Avenue
New York, NY 10019
212-484-9600

Ibero American Investors Corp.
38 Scio Street
Rochester, NY 14604
716-262-3440

Intercontinental Capital Funding
  Corp.
60 East 42d Street
Suite 740
New York, NY 10165
212-286-9642

International Paper Capital
  Formation, Inc.
2 Manhattanville Road
Purchase, NY 10577
914-397-1578

Japanese American Capital Corp.
19 Rector Street
New York, NY 10006
212-964-4077

Jardine Capital Corp.
8 Chatham Square
Suite 708
New York, NY 10038
212-406-1799

Manhattan Central Capital Corp.
1255 Broadway
Room 405
New York, NY 10001
212-684-6411

Medallion Funding Corp.
205 East 42d Street
Suite 2020
New York, NY 10017
212-682-3300

Minority Equity Capital Company,
  Inc.
275 Madison Avenue
New York, NY 10016
212-686-9710

Monsey Capital Corp.
125 Route 59
Monsey, NY 10952
914-425-2229

New Oasis Capital Corp.
114 Liberty Street
Suite 404
New York, NY 10006
212-349-2804

North American Funding Corp.
177 Canal Street
New York, NY 10013
212-226-0080

North Street Capital Corp.
250 North Street, RA-65
White Plains, NY 10625
14-335-6306

Pan Pac Capital Corp.
121 East Industry Court
Deer Park, NY 11729
516-586-7653

Pierre Funding Corp.
131 South Central Avenue
Hartsdale, NY 10530
914-683-1144

Pierre Funding Corp.
270 Madison Avenue
New York, NY 10016
212-689-9361

Pioneer Capital Corp.
113 East 55th Street
New York, NY 10022
212-980-9090

Situation Venture Corp.
502 Flushing Avenue
Brooklyn, NY 11205
718-855-1835

Square Deal Venture Capital Corp.
805 Avenue L
Brooklyn, NY 11230
718-692-2924

Taroco Capital Corp.
19 Rector Street
35th Floor
New York, NY 10006
212-344-6690

Transportation Capital Corp.
60 East 42d Street
Suite 3126
New York, NY 10165
212-697-4885

Triad Capital Corp. of New York
960 Southern Boulevard
Bronx, NY 10459
212-589-6541

Trico Venture, Inc.
805 Avenue L
Brooklyn, NY 11230
718-692-0950

United Capital Investment Corp.
60 East 42d Street
Suite 1515
New York, NY 10165
212-682-7210

Venture Opportunities Corp.
110 East 59th Street
29th Floor
New York, NY 10022
212-832-3737

Watchung Capital Corp.
431 Fifth Avenue
5th Floor
New York, NY 10016
212-889-3466

Yang Capital Corp.
41-40 Kissena Boulevard
Flushing, NY 11355
516-482-1578

Yusa Capital Corp.
622 Broadway
New York, NY 10012
212-420-1350

Ohio

Center City MESBIC, Inc.
Centre City Office Building
Suite 762
40 South Main Street
Dayton, OH 45402
513-461-6164

Rubber City Capital Corp.
1144 East Market Street
Akron, OH 44316
216-796-9167

Pennsylvania

Alliance Enterprise Corp.
1801 Market Street
3d Floor
Philadelphia, PA 19103
215-977-3925

Greater Philadelphia Venture
  Capital Corp., Inc.
920 Lewis Tower Building
225 South 15th Street
Philadelphia, PA 19102
215-732-3415

Salween Financial Services, Inc.
228 North Pottstown Pike
Exton, PA 19341
215-524-1880

Puerto Rico

North America Investment Corp.
Banco CTR 1710
M Rivera Avenue Stop 34
Hato Rey, PR 00936
P.O. Box 1831
Hato Rey Station, PR 00919
809-751-6178

Tennessee

Chickasaw Capital Corp.
67 Madison Avenue
Memphis, TN 38147
901-523-6404

International Paper Capital
Formation, Inc.
International Place I
6400 Poplar Avenue, 10-74
Memphis, TN 38197
901-763-6282

Tennessee Equity Capital Corp.
1102 Stonewall Jackson Court
Nashville, TN 37220
615-373-4502

Tennessee Venture Capital Corp.
162 Fourth Avenue North
Suite 125
P.O. Box 2567
Nashville, TN 37219
615-244-6935

Valley Capital Corp.
Krystal Building
8th Floor
100 West Martin Luther King
  Boulevard
Chattanooga, TN 37402
615-265-1557

West Tennessee Venture Capital
  Corp.
152 Beale Street
Suite 401
P.O. Box 300
Memphis, TN 38101
901-527-6091

Texas

Chen's Financial Group, Inc.
1616 West Loop South
Suite 200
Houston, TX 77027
713-850-0879

Evergreen Capital Company, Inc.
8502 Tybor Drive
Suite 201
Houston, TX 77074
713-778-9770

MESBIC Financial Corp. of Dallas
12655 North Central Expressway
Suite 814
Dallas, TX 75243
214-991-1597

MESBIC Financial Corp. of
  Houston
811 Rusk
Suite 201
Houston, TX 77002
713-228-8321

Minority Enterprise Funding, Inc.
17300 El Camino Real
Suite 107-B
Houston, TX 77058
713-488-4919

Southern Orient Capital Corp.
2419 Fannin
Suite 200
Houston, TX 77002
713-225-3369

United Oriental Capital Corp.
908 Town and Country Boulevard
Suite 310
Houston, TX 77024
713-461-3909

Virginia

Basic Investment Corp.
6723 Whittier Avenue
McLean, VA 22101
703-356-4300

East West United Investment
  Company
815 West Broad Street
Falls Church, VA 22046
703-237-7200

Washington Finance and
  Investment Corp.
100 East Broad Street
Falls Church, VA 22046
703-534-7200

Wisconsin

Future Value Ventures, Inc.
622 North Water Street
Suite 500
Milwaukee, WI 53202
414-278-0377

Appendix D
Business Development Publications Available from the SBA

The following booklets are available from the SBA. All are brief treatments of the topics described in the titles. To order, indicate the title and the number listed in brackets, and send a check or money order (payable to the U.S. Small Business Administration) to U.S. Small Business Administration, P.O. Box 15434, Fort Worth, TX 76119. For the latest list of publications, call your nearest SBA field office.

Financial Management and Analysis

[FM1] *ABC's of Borrowing* ($1.00)

[FM2] *Profit Costing and Pricing for Manufacturers* ($1.00)

[FM3] *Basic Budgets for Profit Planning* ($.50)

[FM4] *Understanding Cash Flow* ($1.00)

[FM5] *A Venture Capital Primer for Small Business* ($.50)

[FM6] *Accounting Services for Small Service Firms* ($.50)

[FM7] *Analyze Your Records to Reduce Costs* ($.50)

[FM8] *Budgeting in a Small Business Firm* ($.50)

[FM9]   *Sound Cash Management and Borrowing* ($.50)

[FM10] *Recordkeeping in a Small Business* ($1.00)

[FM11] *Breakeven Analysis: A Decision Making Tool* ($1.00)

[FM12] *A Pricing Checklist for Small Retailers* ($.50)

[FM13] *Pricing Your Products and Services Profitably* ($1.00)

General Management and Planning

[MP1]   *Effective Business Communications* ($.50)

[MP2]   *Locating or Relocating Your Business* ($1.00)

[MP3]   *Problems in Managing a Family-Owned Business* ($.50)

[MP4]   *Business Plan for Small Manufacturers* ($1.00)

[MP5]   *Business Plan for Small Construction Firms* ($1.00)

[MP6]   *Planning and Goal Setting for Small Business* ($.50)

[MP7]   *Fixing Production Mistakes* ($.50)

[MP8]   *Should You Lease or Buy Equipment?* ($.50)

[MP9]   *Business Plan for Retailers* ($1.00)

[MP10] *Choosing a Retail Location* ($1.00)

[MP11] *Business Plan for Small Service Firms* ($.50)

[MP12] *Going Into Business* ($.50)

[MP14] *How to Get Started with a Small Business Computer* ($1.00)

[MP15] *The Business Plan for Homebased Business* ($1.00)

[MP16] *How to Buy or Sell a Business* ($1.00)

[MP17] *Purchasing for Owners of Small Plants* ($.50)

[MP18] *Buying for Retail Stores* ($1.00)

[MP19] *Small Business Decision Making* ($1.00)

[MP20] *Business Continuation Planning* ($1.00)

[MP21] *Developing a Strategic Business Plan* ($1.00)

[MP22] *Inventory Management* ($.50)

[MP23] *Techniques for Problem Solving* ($1.00)

[MP24] *Techniques for Productivity Improvement* ($1.00)

[MP25] *Selecting the Legal Structure for Your Business* ($.50)

[MP26] *Evaluating Franchise Opportunities* ($.50)

[MP27] *Starting a Retail Travel Agency* ($1.00)

[MP28] *Small Business Risk Management Guide* ($1.00)

Crime Prevention

[CP1]   *Reducing Shoplifting Losses* ($.50)

[CP2]   *Curtailing Crime—Inside and Out* ($1.00)

[CP3]   *A Small Business Guide to Computer Security* ($1.00)

Marketing

[MT1]   *Creative Selling: The Competitive Edge* ($.50)

[MT2]   *Marketing for Small Business: An Overview* ($1.00)

[MT3]   *Is the Independent Sales Agent for You?* ($.50)

[MT4]   *Marketing Checklist for Small Retailers* ($1.00)

[MT8]   *Research Your Market* ($1.00)

[MT9]   *Selling by Mail Order* ($1.00)

[MT10]   *Market Overseas with U.S. Government Help* ($1.00)

[MT11]   *Advertising* ($1.00)

Personnel Management

[PM1]   *Checklist for Developing a Training Program* ($.50)

[PM2]   *Employees: How to Find and Pay Them* ($1.00)

[PM3]   *Managing Employee Benefits* ($1.00)

New Products, Ideas, and Inventions

[PI1]   *Can You Make Money with Your Idea or Invention?* ($.50)

[PI2]   *Introduction to Patents* ($.50)

Industry Ratio Analysis

Advertising and Marketing

American Association of
Advertising Agencies
666 Third Avenue
13th Floor
New York, NY 10017

American Jewelry Marketing
Association
1900 Arch Street
Philadelphia, PA 19103

Building and Supply

American Supply Association
20 North Wacker Drive
Suite 2260
Chicago, IL 60606

Building Owners and Managers
Association Internation
1250 I Street, N.W.
Suite 200
Washington, DC 20005

Door and Hardware Institute
7711 Old Springhouse Road
McLean, VA 22102

Material Handling Equipment
Distributors Association
201 Route 45
Vernon Hills, IL 60061

Mechanical Contractors
Association of America
5410 Grosvenor Lane
Suite 120
Bethesda, MD 20814

National Association of Electrical
Distributors
28 Cross Street
Norwalk, CT 06851

National Electrical Contractors
Association, Inc.
7315 Wisconsin Avenue
Bethesda, MD 20814

National Electrical Manufacturers
Association
2101 L Street, N.W.
Washington, DC 20037

National Home Furnishings
Association
220 West Gerry Lane
Wood Dale, IL 60191

These industry associations have made studies of financial ratios within their respective industries.

233

National Kitchen Cabinet
Association
P.O. Box 6830
Falls Church, VA 22046

National Lumber and Building
Material Dealers Association
40 Ivy Street, S.E.
Washington, DC 20003

North American Wholesale
Lumber Association, Inc.
2340 South Arlington Heights Road
Suite 680
Arlington Heights, IL 60005

Northeastern Retail Lumbermens
Association
339 East Avenue
Rochester, NY 14604

Painting and Decorating
Contractors of America
7223 Lee Highway
Falls Church, VA 22046

Financial Services

American Financial Services
Association
1101 14th Street, N.W.
Washington, DC 20005

Independent Insurance Agents of
America
100 Church Street
19th Floor
New York, NY 10007

National Association of
Accountants
10 Paragon Drive
P.O. Box 433
Montvale, NJ 07645

Food-Related Industries

American Meat Institute
P.O. Box 3556
Washington, DC 20007

Food Market Institute, Inc.
1750 K Street, N.W.
Suite 700
Washington, DC 20006

Foodservice Equipment
Distributors Association
332 South Michigan Avenue
Chicago, IL 60604

National American Wholesale
Grocers' Association
201 Park Washington Court
Falls Church, VA 22046

National Association of Food
Chains
1750 K Street
Suite 700
Washington, DC 20006

National Beer Wholesalers
Association
5205 Leesburg Pike
Suite 505
Falls Church, VA 22041

National Confectioners Association
of the U.S.
645 North Michigan Avenue
Suite 1006
Chicago, IL 60611

National Grocers Association
1825 Samuel Moore Drive
Reston, VA 22090

National Restaurant Association
311 First Street, N.W.
Washington, DC 20001

National Soft Drink Association
1101 16th Street, N.W.
Washington, DC 20036

United Fresh Fruit and Vegetable
Association
727 North Washington Street
Alexandria, VA 22314

Wine and Spirit Wholesalers of
America, Inc.
1023 15th Street, N.W.
Washington, DC 20005

Manufacturing

Motor and Equipment
Manufacturers' Association
300 Sylvan Avenue
P.O. Box 1638
Englewood Cliffs, NJ 07632

National Association of Furniture
Manufacturers
P.O. Box HP7
High Point, NC 27261

Miscellaneous Associations

American Society of Association
Executives
1575 I Street, N.W.
Washington, DC 20005

Laundry and Cleaners Allied
Trades Association
543 Valley Road
Upper Montclair, NJ 07043

National Art Materials Trade
Association
178 Lakeview Avenue
Clifton, NJ 07011

National Automatic
Merchandising Association
20 North Wacker Drive
Chicago, IL 60606

National Decorating Products
Association
1050 North Lindbergh Boulevard
Saint Louis, MO 63132

National Machine Tool Builders
Association
7901 Westpark Drive
McLean, VA 22102

National Office Products
Association
301 North Fairfax Street
Alexandria, VA 22314

National Paint and Coatings
Association
1500 Rhode Island Avenue, N.W.
Washington, DC 20005

National Parking Association
1112 16th Street, N.W.
Suite 2000
Washington, DC 20036

Optical Laboratories Association
P.O. Box 2000
Merrifield, VA 22116

Printing Industries of America,
Inc.
1730 North Lynn Street
Arlington, VA 22209

Scientific Apparatus Makers
Association
1101 16th Street, N.W.
Washington, DC 20036

Society of the Plastics Industry,
Inc.
1275 K Street, N.W.
Suite 400
Washington, DC 20005

Urban Land Institute
1090 Vermont Avenue
Washington, DC 20005

Paper Products

American Paper Institute
260 Madison Avenue
New York, NY 10016

National Paperbox and Packaging
Association
231 Kings Highway East
Haddonfield, NJ 08033

National Paper Trade Association, Inc.
111 Great Neck Road
Great Neck, NY 11021

Petroleum

Petroleum Equipment Institute
P.O. Box 2380
Tulsa, OK 74104

Petroleum Marketers Association
1120 Vermont Avenue
Suite 1130
Washington, DC 20005

Recreation

American Camping Association
5000 State Road, 67N
Martinsville, IN 46151

Bowling Proprietors Association of America
P.O. Box 5802
Arlington, TX 76011

National Sporting Goods Association
Lake Center Plaza Building
1699 Wall Street
Mont Prospect, IL 60056

Retail

Florists' Transworld Delivery Association/Interflora
29200 Northwestern Highway
Southfield, MI 48037

Menswear Retailers of America
2011 I Street, N.W.
Washington, DC 20006

National Appliance and Radio/TV Dealers Association
10 East 22d Street
Lombard, IL 60148

National Association of Music Merchants, Inc.
5140 Avenida Encinas
Carlsbad, CA 92008

National Farm and Power Equipment Dealers Association
10877 Watson Road
P.O. Box 8517
St. Louis, MO 63826

National Retail Hardware Association
770 North High School Road
Indianapolis, IN 46214

National Retail Merchants Association
100 West 31st Street
New York, NY 10001

National Shoe Retailers Association
9861 Broken Land Parkway
Columbia, MD 21046

National Tire Dealers and Retreaders Association
1250 I Street, N.W.
Suite 400
Washington, DC 20005

Shoe Service Institute of America
112 Calendar Court Mall
LaGrange, IL 60525

Wholesale and Distribution

National Association of Plastics Distributors
5001 College Boulevard
Suite 201
Leawood, KS 66211

National Association of Textile and Apparel Distributors
P.O. Box 1325
Melbourne, FL 32902

National Association of Tobacco
  Distributors
1199 North Fairfax Street
Suite 701
Alexandria, VA 22314

National Wholesale Druggists'
  Association
105 Oronoco Street
P.O. Box 238
Alexandria, VA 22313

National Wholesale Hardware
  Association
1900 Arch Street
Philadelphia, PA 19103

North American Heating and
  Air-Conditioning Wholesalers
  Association
1389 Dublin Road
P.O. Box 16790
Columbus, OH 43216

Glossary

Accounts Payable: Amount owed to creditors for goods and services rendered on an open account.

Accounts Receivable: Amount owed to a business for goods or services bought on an open account.

Accounts Receivable Financing: Short-term financing that uses accounts receivable as collateral for advances of capital.

Acid-Test Ratio: Financial ratio used to measure a company's liquidity. The formula for calculating the acid-test ratio is

$$\frac{\text{Cash + marketable securities + accounts receivables}}{\text{Current liabilities}} = \text{acid-test ratio}$$

Also called "quick ratio" or "quick-asset ratio."

Aging of Accounts Receivable: Classifying accounts receivable by due date. Also referred to as "aging schedule." Often used to interpret the quality of a business's accounts receivable.

Aging Schedule: The process of reducing debt by making equal payments with the goal of paying the debt off by maturity.

Alien Corporation: *See* Corporation.

Annual Percentage Rate (APR): A simple yearly interest charge on the outstanding principal of a loan.

Appraisal Fee: A charge for assessing the value of an asset.

Appreciation: Increase in an asset's value.

APR: *See* Annual Percentage Rate.

Asset: Anything of commercial or exchange value owned by a business or individual.

Asset Earning Power: A financial ratio used to get a sense of the earning power of a company's assets. Looks at operating profit in relation to total assets. The formula used to calculate asset earning power is as follows:

$$\frac{\text{Operating profit}}{\text{Total assets}} = \text{asset earning power}$$

See also Operating Profit.

Average Collection Period: A financial ratio used to calculate the number of days sales are tied up in accounts receivable. The calculations are made using information from a business's balance sheet and profit and loss (or income) statement. To calculate the average sales per day, first use the following formula:

$$\frac{\text{Net sales}}{\text{Days in accounting period}} = \text{average sales per day}$$

Next, calculate the average collection period (how long sales are tied up in receivables) by using this formula:

$$\frac{\text{Receivables}}{\text{Average sales per day}} = \text{average collection period}$$

Bad Debts: Uncollectible accounts receivable that are ultimately written off the books.

Balance Sheet: A financial statement showing a business's assets, liabilities, and the business owner's equity at a given time. It is usually prepared at the end of the month. The assets minus the liabilities show the net worth of the business. The balance sheet and the income statement together make up the company's financial statements.

Bankruptcy: A business's or a person's inability to pay debts owed. Involuntary bankruptcy occurs when creditors petition the courts to have a debtor judged insolvent. Voluntary bankruptcy occurs when the business or the individual petitions the courts to be deemed insolvent. In the latter case, the debtor most often seeks protection under bankruptcy laws.

Bond: An interest-bearing debt certificate, usually issued by a government or corporation, listing a due date by which the issuer guarantees repayment of the investment plus an agreed-upon interest.

Budget: A written estimate of revenue and expenses for a specified period of time.

Capital: The amount left on the balance sheet after a business's liabilities are subtracted from all its assets. Also referred to as "owner's equity." In a borrowing situation, capital is typically reflected by the net worth of the borrower. *See also* Equity.

Cash Discount: A discount for paying a bill within a specified period of time. Also called "trade credit." There are three parts to a cash discount: (1) the percentage discount being offered, (2) the time frame for which the discount is offered, and (3) the date after which the bill becomes overdue. *See also* Forward Dating; Trade Credit.

Cash Flow: An amount calculated by subtracting disbursements from cash receipts during a specified time period. Used to indicate a business's ability to pay outstanding debts during that time period.

Character Loan: An unsecured loan usually made for personal needs, not for business needs.

Charge-Offs: *See* Bad Debts.

Collateral: Assets pledged by a borrower to secure a loan.

Commercial Bank: A federal or state-chartered institution that accepts deposits, makes short-term business loans, and provides a broad variety of banking services.

Commercial Credit Company: *See* Commercial Finance Company.

Commercial Finance Company: A company that makes loans to businesses. Traditionally, commercial finance companies have charged higher interest rates than banks. In the past they would often charge 3 to 4 percentage points higher than bank rates, but in recent years the spread has narrowed quite a bit. These companies make only secured loans to businesses. While commercial finance companies make the same variety of secured loans as commercial bankers, accounts receivable lending is the staple of the industry. Also called "commercial credit company."

Commercial Loan: Any of a variety of loans made to a business, generally used for the financing needs of running that business.

Compensating Balance: A balance held by a business that is used to support a borrowing arrangement the business has with the lending institution.

Co-Owner: *See* Partnership.

Corporation: A business entity, chartered by a state or the federal government, which exists as a body separate from its owners. Usually a business will file for incorporation in the state in which it does business.

If it does business in a state other than that in which it is based, it is considered a foreign corporation. (Corporations from another country doing business in this country are called "alien corporations.") The main advantages of a corporation are that it limits your liability and that it gives you the ability to attract outside capital by selling shares.

Cosigner: Someone who signs a promissory note in addition to the borrower, giving the lender more assurance that the loan will be repaid.

Credit Card: A card, usually plastic, that a customer can present to a merchant in lieu of cash, check, or other forms of payment. Users are offered credit cards in much the same way that a person or business would be offered a revolving line of credit. A credit limit is established, an APR is set, and the customer pays interest each month on the outstanding balances.

Creditor: A person or institution that is owed money or something else of value.

Credit Union: A financial institution offering, to members only, an array of financial services similar to those offered by banks. Credit unions often pay slightly higher interest rates on deposits and offer loans at slightly lower interest rates than do banks. Credit union membership is based on some common bond among its members.

Current Assets: Things owned by a business—such as accounts receivable, inventory, and cash—that are converted into cash, usually within 1 year.

Current Liabilities: Debts owed by a business that will likely be paid off within 1 year.

Current Ratio: Financial ratio used to measure whether or not a company has enough current assets to pay off its current debts, plus a little extra to handle any emergencies that might arise. Calculated by dividing current assets by current liabilities. A general rule of thumb is that a good current ratio is 2 to 1, but this can vary, depending on the type of business and the company's assets and liabilities. Companies that have little inventory and accounts receivable that are easily collectible can have a lower current ratio than companies with less steady cash flow.

Default: Failure to make a principal or interest payment on a bond or promissory note when it is due.

Depreciation: The amortization of a fixed asset (e.g., equipment or buildings) to reflect its decline in value over its lifetime.

Equipment Loan: A loan for which equipment is used as security (collateral).

Equity: The monetary value of a business that is greater than liens or claims against it. Also called "owner's equity." The term "equity" also refers to shareholders' ownership interest in a corporation.

Factoring: The buying of an account receivable, usually on a discounted basis for cash, by a financing source. Collecting this receivable becomes the financing source's responsibility. The amount of the account receivable is taken off the original owner's books when the factoring arrangement is made.

Finance Charges: Costs, including interest, on a loan to a borrower.

Financial Statement: A business income (profit and loss) statement and balance sheet.

Fixed Assets: Buildings, land and improvements, equipment and fixtures, and other long-term assets that will not be converted into cash within the next year.

Fixed-Asset Loan: A loan used to finance purchase of large items, such as buildings, equipment, and improvement to existing structures. Fixed assets are used as collateral on the loans. The term of the loan is usually for more than 1 year.

Fixed Costs: Costs that remain constant in a business operation and that are not dependent on the business's sales volume. Executive salaries, rent, and insurance are examples.

Fixed Interest Rate: An interest rate that stays the same throughout a loan.

Floating-Rate Note: A debt instrument that has a variable interest rate.

Floor Financing: A form of financing that is typically used by businesses that sell large-size goods that they need to have on hand to show customers. In floor financing, a commercial finance company advances the money to the business, which buys the inventory and holds a lien on the items purchased. The commercial finance company maintains ownership of the goods and charges a monthly interest payment based on the business's outstanding debt to the finance company. When the business sells the product, it pays the commercial finance company. The business then usually has the option of buying more goods through the commercial finance company, financed in a similar fashion. Sometimes referred to as "wholesale sales financing." *See also* Commercial Finance Company.

Foreign Corporation: *See* Corporation.

Forward Dating: A form of trade credit that combines a cash discount with seasonal discount pricing. The buyer buys and is delivered goods during the off season, but doesn't have to pay for them until the season begins. *See also* Cash Discount; Trade Credit.

Franchise: A license to sell the products or services of a franchisor (a dealer or manufacturer), using that franchisor's name.

Gross Margin: *See* Gross Profit.

Gross Profit: Net sales minus costs of goods sold. Also called "gross margin."

Guarantee: *See* Guaranty.

Guarantor: A person obligated to pay off a loan in the event of default by the borrower.

Guaranty: A contract or agreement in which the guarantor agrees to ensure that a second party fulfills his or her obligation to a creditor.

Home Equity Line of Credit: *See* Home Equity Loan.

Home Equity Loan: A loan that allows the borrower to tap into the equity of his or home. Typically, the bank appraises the home to determine its value, then subtracts whatever outstanding mortgage debt exists on the house to find out how much equity has been built up. Most banks have a limit on how large an equity line they will allow. Unless the borrower opts for a fixed rate, most home equity loans work like a revolving line of credit. Sometimes referred to as "home equity line of credit."

Income Statement: A business's profit and loss statement for a specific time period. It is calculated by subtracting expenses from sales. The income statement and the balance sheet together make up the business's financial statement. *See also* Balance Sheet.

Industrial Time-Sales Financing: A financing arrangement in which a seller sells the merchandise on a credit basis to a buyer, and then sells the debt to a commercial finance company. The buyer pays the debt to the commercial finance company, which charges interest to the buyer. This type of financing is often used by businesses to buy equipment and fixtures.

Installment Loans: A loan for which payments are usually made on a monthly basis and which usually makes provisions for refinancing.

Intangible Assets: Imperceptible assets, such as goodwill, trademarks, or patents, that have value to a business.

Intermediate-Term Loan: *See* Term Loan.

Inventory: Goods that a business holds in stock for future sales.

Inventory Loan: A loan for which inventory is used as collateral.

Inventory Turnover: A financial ratio that tells how many times inventory has been turned over (i.e., sold and restocked) during a particular accounting period. To calculate inventory turnover, divide the cost of goods sold by the average inventory, as follows:

$$\frac{\text{Cost of goods sold}}{\text{Average inventory}} = \text{inventory turnover}$$

Investment Turnover: A financial ratio calculated by dividing net sales by total assets. It measures annual net sales in proportion to the total investment in the company—how much sales a company has for each dollar that has been invested in the company's assets. The following formula is used to calculate investment turnover.

$$\frac{\text{Net sales}}{\text{Total assets}} = \text{investment turnover}$$

Leasing: A method of financing whereby a company can rent equipment, machinery, fixtures, or buildings by paying a set amount to a leasing company that holds title to goods. Frequently, the leaseholder maintains ownership of the goods being leased, but in many circumstances you can lease goods with an option to buy.

Leverage: Essentially, borrowing money to be able to acquire assets.

Liabilities: A business's or an individual's debt obligations.

Lien: The legal right to take possession of and sell a property if a debt is defaulted on by the borrower.

Line of Credit: Financing set up between a bank and a business to provide the business with a recurring source of loans up to an agreed-upon amount. Lines of credit are usually unsecured and are in force for an agreed-upon amount of time, usually a year.

Liquid Assets: Cash or other assets that can be converted into cash, usually within a year.

Liquidity: The ability to convert assets into cash without suffering a loss.

Long-Term Loan: *See* Term Loan.

Maturity: The date on which a note, bond, line of credit, loan, or other obligation becomes due and payable.

Mezzanine Financing: A venture capital term used to describe financing that is made just before a company goes public.

Mortgage: An obligation that pledges property as collateral for a loan.

Net Earnings: *See* Net Income.

Net Income: Revenues minus expenses during a specific time period. Also called "net earnings," "net profit," or "net loss."

Net Loss: *See* Net Income.

Net Profit: *See* Net Income.

Net Profit on Sales: A financial ratio based on the amount of money coming into a business and how much is spent to conduct the business. The following formula is used to calculate net profit on sales:

$$\frac{\text{Net profit}}{\text{Net sales}} = \text{net profit on sales}$$

This ratio is used by a business to get an idea of where it stands in relation to other similar businesses, or historically in relation to its own past record. It can also be used on individual products or product lines to see how much profit separate products are making.

Net Sales: Sales minus returns and discounts during a specific time period.

Net Worth: Total assets minus total liabilities. Also called "equity" or "owner's equity." *See also* Equity.

Note: An instrument that is the legal evidence of a debt. The borrower signs the note promising to pay a specified sum of money on a specific day to a specific lender. Also called "promissory note."

Obligation: Debt.

Operating Profit: Earnings before interest and taxes are deducted.

Outstanding Balance: *See* Principal.

Owner's Equity: *See* Equity.

Owner's Return on Equity: A financial ratio used to show how much return the owner has received on the investment in the business. To make the calculation, the following formula is used:

$$\frac{\text{Net profit}}{\text{Total owner's equity}} = \text{owner's return on equity}$$

Another ratio makes the same calculation by substituting *tangible net worth*—owner's equity minus intangible assets (e.g., goodwill, patents, trademarks, licenses, software programs, and copyrights)—for owner's equity. Obviously the two figures will be the same if there are no intangible assets.

Partnership: A legal setup in which two or more people operate a business as co-owners. Partners are taxed individually. The business itself is not taxed.

Personal Financial Statement: A statement itemizing an individual's assets, liabilities, and net worth on a specific date.

Personal Guaranty: An individual's pledge of assets as collateral to ensure payment of a loan by a business.

Policy Loans: The cash surrender value in a life insurance policy that can be borrowed against.

Prepayment Penalty: A penalty for paying off a loan early.

Prime Rate: The rate charged by banks to their strongest borrowers.

Principal: The outstanding amount due on a loan. Sometimes called "outstanding balance."

Private Placement: Sale of investments to a limited number of investors.

Pro Forma: A phrase describing financial statements that are based on hypothetical information.

Profit and Loss Statement: *See* Income Statement.

Promissory Note: *See* Note.

Public Company: A company that offers stock for trading (buying and selling) by the public.

Quick Ratio: *See* Acid-Test Ratio.

Return on Investment (ROI): A ratio determined by dividing profit by investment, as follows:

$$\frac{\text{Profit}}{\text{Investment}} = \text{return on investment}$$

To calculate return on investment, a business owner must first decide which figures from the financial statements will be used to represent profit and investment. Profit could be a variety of items, among them net operating profit, net profit before taxes, and net profit after taxes. Investment could be total assets used in the company, or it could be just equity. Once the small business owner decides which figures to use to calculate ROI, the same figures should be used from one accounting period to the next, so that accurate comparisons can be made.

ROI is useful for comparing company performance within industries, as well as for comparing product lines within a company. It allows investors and other financing sources to see how well their investment is performing in a company.

ROI: *See* Return on Investment.

Rule of 78s: A way of calculating interest on a loan, on a sum-of-the-years-digits basis, that companies may use to figure out monthly payments. The name "rule of 78s" is based on the sum of the numbers between 1 and 12 (which adds up to 78). When the rule of 78s is used, the total interest for the whole year is calculated; the borrower pays $^{12}/_{78}$ of the loan the first month, $^{11}/_{78}$ the second, $^{10}/_{78}$ the third, and so on. As a result, the borrower can end up paying most of the year's interest in the first month.

Second Mortgage: A mortgage placed on a property that already has a first mortgage held on it by the borrower. *See also* Mortgage.

Secured Loan: A loan for which borrowers must pledge assets as collateral. *See also* Unsecured Loan.

Short-Term Loan: *See* Term Loan.

SIC: *See* Standard Industrial Classification.

Simple Commercial Loan: Usually a short-term loan offered for a term of 30 to 180 days. This type of loan is paid off out of cash flow and may be used for a variety of short-term needs, including inventory or seasonal needs.

Sole Proprietorship: A business owned and operated by one individual. The sole proprietor reports income and expenses on schedule C of the IRS personal income tax return. The net income (gross income minus expenses) of the proprietorship is added to any other earnings and taxed at the taxpayer's personal rate. The sole proprietor must also pay self-employment tax on all schedule C income. This tax is designed to cover Social Security payments.

Standard Industrial Classification (SIC): A system, designed by the federal government, that categorizes industries by numbers. Used by marketing professionals and others to identify various industry segments.

Tangible Asset: A physical asset that can be seen, such as land or equipment.

Tangible Net Worth: Total tangible assets minus total liabilities. *See also* Owner's Return on Equity.

Term Loan: A loan for a specified time period. Term loans can be classified as short-term loans, typically with 30- to 180-day maturities; intermediate-term loans, typically with 3- to 5-year maturities; or long-term loans, typically with 5-year or longer maturities.

Trade Credit: Credit offered when suppliers of goods or services don't require immediate payment, but instead give credit terms for the payment due. *See also* Cash Discount; Forward Dating.

Unsecured Loan: A loan for which a borrower is not required to put up any collateral. Banks will usually require that the borrower present a personal guaranty for the loan. Some common types of unsecured loans are simple commercial loans, installment loans, character loans, and lines of credit. *See also* Character Loan; Installment Loan; Line of Credit; Secured Loan; Simple Commercial Loan.

Usury: An excessive or illegal rate of interest, usually determined by state regulations.

Venture Capital Companies: Companies that raise private funds to invest in businesses with high growth potential. Venture capital firms can structure financing for businesses in which they invest as equity, convertible securities, loans, or hybrid securities.

Wholesale Sales Financing: *See* Floor Financing.

Working Capital: Money available for short-term business needs. Calculated by subtracting current liabilities from current assets. *See* Current Ratio.

Working Capital Ratio: *See* Current Ratio.

Bibliography

Bard, Ray, and Sheila Henderson: *Own Your Own Franchise*. Reading, Mass.: Addison Wesley, 1987.

Bel Air, Roger: *How to Borrow Money from a Banker: A Business Owner's Guide*. New York: AMACOM, 1988.

Bennett, Steven J.: *Playing Hardball with Soft Skills*. New York: Bantam, 1986.

Bittel, Lester: *The McGraw-Hill 36-Hour Management Course*. New York: McGraw-Hill, 1989.

Blanding, Bruce J.: *Introduction to Records Keeping*. Washington: Small Business Administration, 1986.

Breen, George, and A. B. Blankenship: *Do-It-Yourself Marketing Research*. New York: McGraw-Hill, 1989.

Brownlie, William D., with Jeffrey L. Seglin: *The Life Insurance Buyer's Guide*. New York: McGraw-Hill, 1989.

Cohen, William: *The Entrepreneur and Small Business Financial Problem Solver*. New York: John Wiley, 1990.

Colletti, Deborah L., Marjolijn van der Velde, and Jeffrey L. Seglin: *Small Business Banking: A Guide to Marketing and Profits*. Rolling Meadows, Ill.: Bank Administration Institute, 1987.

Directory of Federal and State Business Assistance, 1988–1989: A Guide for New and Growing Companies. Virginia: U.S. National Technical Information Service, 1989.

Dixon, Robert L.: *The McGraw-Hill 36-Hour Accounting Course*. New York: McGraw-Hill, 1972.

Downes, John, and Jordan Elliot Goodman: *Dictionary of Finance and Investment Terms*. Woodbury, N.Y.: Barron's, 1985.

Franchise Opportunities. New York: Sterling Publishing, 1988.

Fritz, Roger: *Nobody Gets Rich Working for Somebody Else: An Entrepreneur's Guide*. New York: Dodd, Mead, 1987.

Gary, Loren: *Commercial Loan Forms Handbook*. Rolling Meadows, Ill.: Bank Administration Institute and Andover Parris Publishing Group, 1989.

Goldstein, Arnold S.: *How to Buy a Great Business with No Cash Down*. New York: John Wiley, 1989.

———: *Starting on a Shoestring: Building a Business without a Bankroll*. New York: John Wiley, 1984.

Gumpert, David E., and Jeffry A. Timmons: *The Encyclopedia of Small Business Resources*. New York: Harper & Row, 1982.

Handbook for Small Business: A Survey of Small Business Programs of the Federal Government. Washington: U.S. Government Printing Office, 1984.

Hayes, Rick Stephan: *Business Loans: A Guide to Money Sources and How to Approach Them Successfully.* Boston: CBI Publishing, 1980.

—— and John Cotton Howell: *How to Finance Your Small Business with Government Money: SBA and Other Loans.* New York: John Wiley, 1983.

J. K. Lasser Institute: *How to Run a Small Business.* New York: McGraw-Hill, 1989.

Jones, Constance: *The 220 Best Franchises to Buy.* New York: Bantam, 1987.

Kuriloff, Arthur H., and John M. Hemphill, Jr.: *Starting and Managing the Small Business.* New York: McGraw-Hill, 1988.

Lynn, Gary S.: *From Concept to Market.* New York: John Wiley, 1989.

Merrill, Ronald E., and Henry D. Sedgwick: *The New Venture Handbook.* New York: AMACOM, 1987.

O'Hara, Patrick D.: *SBA Loans: A Step-By-Step Guide.* New York: John Wiley, 1989.

Peterson, C. D.: *How to Leave Your Job and Buy a Business of Your Own.* New York: McGraw-Hill, 1988.

Pratt, Stanley E., and Jane K. Morris (eds.): *Pratt's Guide to Venture Capital Sources,* 13th ed. Needham, Mass.: Venture Economics, 1989.

Rubin, Richard, and Philip Goldberg: *The Small Business Guide to Borrowing Money.* New York: McGraw-Hill, 1980.

Sanzo, Richard: *Ratio Analysis for Small Business.* Washington: Small Business Administration, 1977.

SBA Office of Advocacy: *The State of Small Business: A Report of the President.* Washington: U.S. Government Printing Office, 1989.

Seglin, Jeffrey L.: *The AMA Handbook of Business Letters.* New York: AMACOM, 1989.

——:*Bank Administration Institute Dictionary of Banking.* Rolling Meadows, Ill.: Bank Administration Institute/Andover Parris Publishing Group, 1989.

——: *The McGraw-Hill 36-Hour Marketing Course.* New York: McGraw-Hill, 1990.

Siropolis, Nicholas C.: *Small Business Management: A Guide to Entrepreneurship.* Boston: Houghton Mifflin, 1986.

The States and Small Business: A Directory of Programs and Activities, 1989. Washington: Small Business Administration, 1989.

Steinhoff, Dan, and John F. Burgess: *Small Business Management Fundamentals.* New York: McGraw-Hill, 1986.

Storey, M. John: *Starting Your Own Business: No Money Down.* New York: John Wiley, 1987.

U.S. Bureau of the Census: *Statistical Abstract of the United States: 1989,* 109th ed. Washington: U.S. Government Printing Office, 1988.

A Venture Capital Primer for Small Businesses. Washington: Small Business Administration.

Zwick, Jack: *A Handbook of Small Business Finance.* Washington: Small Business Administration, 1987.

Index

Page numbers in italic indicate figures; page numbers followed by t indicate tabular material.